FRENCH QUEER CINEMA

FRENCH QUEER CINEMA

Nick Rees-Roberts

EDINBURGH UNIVERSITY PRESS

© Nick Rees-Roberts, 2008

Edinburgh University Press Ltd
22 George Square, Edinburgh

Typeset in 10/12.5 pt Sabon
by Servis Filmsetting Ltd, Stockport, Cheshire,
and printed and bound in Great Britain by
Biddles Ltd, King's Lynn, Norfolk

A CIP record for this book is available from the British Library

ISBN 978 0 7486 3418 7 (hardback)

CONTENTS

Acknowledgements   vii

Introduction   1
    French   2
    Queer   4
    Cinema   6

1 *Beur* Masculinity and Queer Fantasy   13
    Black/Blanc/Beur   15
    Postcolonial Pornography   19
    The *Beur* Faces of French Queer Cinema   24
    Queering Migrations   38

2 Down and Out: Immigrant Poverty and Queer Sexuality   43
    Fantasy France   45
    Reality France   48
    Threesomes   53

3 *Mauvais Genres*: Transgender and Gay Identity   67
    Shoot and Run   67
    Get Therapy   71
    Transgender Screens   74
    From Transgender to AIDS   79

4 Queer Sexuality, AIDS and Loss   89
    Families and Form   90
    Queer Families   94
    AIDS Film   100
    The Demy Revival   109
    Not-about-AIDS Film   112
    Witnessing AIDS   117

5 The Emergence of Queer DIY Video   129
       Post-Porn   133
       Lesbian Porn   138
       Pop Porn   142
       Concluding Remarks and Emerging Trends   143

   Bibliography   151
   Index   159

ACKNOWLEDGEMENTS

I should like to thank the following friends and colleagues for assistance, dialogue, encouragement and feedback, plus invitations to speak and write on French queer cinema and Anglo-American queer theory in Britain, France and the US: Andrew Asibong, Marie-Hélène Bourcier, Maxime Cervulle, Derek Duncan, Florian Grandena, Hélène Hazera, Cristina Johnston, Didier Lestrade, Eric Macé, Bill Marshall, Dimitris Papanikolaou, Denis M. Provencher, Jean-Paul Rocchi, Lawrence R. Schehr, and Alan Sinfield, with whom it all started at the University of Sussex in 2000. I should also like to thank my new colleagues in both the French department and the School of Modern Languages at the University of Bristol, for their support in the book's final stages. Thanks also to my 2007–8 undergraduate students on the 'Gender and Sexuality in Contemporary French Film' unit for critical dialogue and fresh insights into these films during the book's final stages.

Parts of Chapters 1, 2 and 3 were published in earlier versions in *Contemporary French Civilization, Studies in French Cinema* and the *International Journal of Cultural Studies*. I am grateful to the editors of those journals for granting me permission to use some of that material here.

I am also personally grateful to family and friends for support, particularly to Silvano Mendes for the necessary encouragement and love to finish the book.

INTRODUCTION

French Queer Cinema documents forms of contemporary queer representation through coverage of auteur film, pornography and DIY digital video. Whilst there is important scholarship emerging on queer citizenship, identities and sexualities in France (McCaffrey 2005; Provencher 2007), this is the first study of the cultural formation and critical reception of contemporary queer-authored and queer-themed film and video. *French Queer Cinema* mixes ideological textual analysis with attention to the aesthetic codes and the socio-political context of a wide range of films from the late 1990s onwards. *French Queer Cinema* also aims to cut across genres by mixing auteur cinema with both small-scale local pornography and community-based activist video. The corpus includes recent queer-themed films by Patrice Chéreau (*Ceux qui m'aiment prendront le train* and *Son frère*), Olivier Ducastel and Jacques Martineau (including *Jeanne et le garçon formidable* and *Drôle de Félix*), Christophe Honoré (*Dix-sept fois Cécile Cassard* and *Ma mère*), Sébastien Lifshitz (*Les Corps ouverts* and *Wild Side*), Gaël Morel (*Le Clan*), Jacques Nolot (*La Chatte à deux têtes* and *Avant que j'oublie*), François Ozon (including *Les Amants criminels* and *Le Temps qui reste*) and André Téchiné (*Les Temps qui changent* and *Les Témoins*). The scope for queer representation is extended by post-colonial pornography, which shows *beur* men (French citizens of 'Maghrebi' origin) redefining queer masculinities. The final chapter charts the emergence of a radical, DIY digital video culture, combining queer theory, transgender activism and lesbian pornography.

Gay (male) identity is said to have entered an era of hyper-visibility (Pratt 2002).[1] In the arena of cultural representation, two primetime TV fictions, both directed by Christian Faure, are indicative of the current climate of increased gay assimilation – *Un amour à taire* (2005) documented the history of oppression through the deportation of homosexuals during the Nazi occupation; and *Juste une question d'amour* (2000), a contemporary coming-out narrative, showed gay male love as both natural and acceptable (Brigitte Rollet has provided a complete overview of homosexual representation on contemporary French television: Rollet 2007). Such 'positive images' of mainstream integration – images of conventional, straight-acting, young, white, middle-class gay boys who never indulge in anything vaguely sexual at all – mask the social hierarchies hard-wired in to LGBT (lesbian/gay/bisexual/transgender) identities, notably racial difference, gender inequality, class status and economic privilege (Sinfield 2004). The methodological basis for the present coverage of existing and emerging forms of queer cinema locates a number of 'faultline' issues. Alan Sinfield has defined 'faultline stories' as 'the ones that require most assiduous and continuous reworking; they address the awkward, unresolved issues, the ones on which the conditions of plausibility are in dispute' (Sinfield 1992: 47). This book's political reading of French cinema locates the following areas of contest: first, the emergence of post-integration ethnic identities, and their implications for same-sex, cross-race relations; second, the uneasy positioning of transgender within LGBT identity politics; and third, gay male sexualities, love and loss in the current HIV/AIDS conjuncture.

FRENCH

The contextual start is France in the late 1990s, an era of great socio-political change for lesbian, gay, bisexual and transgender communities. Medical break-throughs in second-generation HIV antiretroviral treatment drugs caused a profound shift in both political activism and sexual practice. The introduction of highly active antiretroviral therapy (HAART) from 1996 led to renewed hope for HIV-positive people. The post-1996 conjuncture has subsequently seen a 'relapse' of unsafe sexual practices among many gay men, a situation that has led to a current escalation of HIV-conversion rates and the trend of drug-fuelled unsafe sex as a lifestyle choice in urban gay subcultures by the early 2000s (Lestrade 2004). Outside AIDS activism, the state's recognition of existing lesbian and gay relationships, through the civil partnership agreement open to same-sex, as well as to heterosexual, couples (the PaCS – *pacte civil de solidarité*, passed in November 1999), illustrated faultlines in the dominant ideology of the French Republic as alien to minority discourse.[2] The years following the PaCS have been marked by the increased institutionalisation of a predominantly white, middle-class gay male identity. The continuing rise of this 'homonormative' formation (Cervulle 2008) is documented through calls for the implementation of same-sex marriage, the 'equal rights' package that currently dominates the LGBT political agenda (Michallat 2006). In their introduction to a special issue of *Radical History* on queer futures and homonormativity, Kevin P. Murphy, Jason Ruiz and David Serlin situate 'the configuration of homonormativity in current circulation' as 'part of a broader turn toward political economy in contemporary queer academic and activist work' (Murphy, Ruiz and Serlin 2008: 1). They draw on Lisa Duggan's definition of 'the new homonormativity' as 'a politics that does not contest dominant heteronormative assumptions and institutions but upholds and sustains them' (Duggan, quoted in Murphy, Ruiz and Serlin 2008: 1).

Enda McCaffrey has provided a comprehensive account of the earlier debates that had 'outed' institutional homophobia around the same-sex civil partnership law in the late 1990s. McCaffrey's retrospective account of the theoretical and political disputes surrounding the PaCS shows the extent to which the heterosexual norm was under attack. The intellectual establishment – notably academics such as anthropologist Irène Théry (Théry 1998) and philosopher Sylviane Agacinski (Agacinski 1998) – argued the familiar case for the need for biological and psychosexual difference to uphold the so-called 'symbolic order' (McCaffrey 2005: 45–74). In light of the heterosexual fundamentalism enacted in the institutional violence of both the academic and parliamentary confrontations, McCaffrey concludes that 'debates on sexual orientation, parity and the PaCS [brought] to the surface anomalies, inconsistencies and contradictions in the concept of universal equality, itself the cornerstone of citizenship in France' (McCaffrey 2005: 4). McCaffrey makes reference to sociologist Eric Fassin's view (Borrillo, Fassin and Iacub 1999; Fassin 2005) that the same-sex partnership legislation had wider implications on the state of the French Republic, 'the rehabilitation of homosexuality as a catalyst for reflection on the state of the republic' (McCaffrey 2005: 7). Cristina Johnston likewise argues that minority sexual discourses highlight 'discrepancies between republicanism in its "inherited" form, and a renewed, renegotiated form that would be more appropriate as an expression of the values of contemporary France' (Johnston 2008: 93). Johnston surmises that the 'debates on 1990s family structures, filiation, and what it is to be French, demonstrate that republicanism, as it is traditionally expressed, is not yet able to account for the difference which makes up the contemporary republic' (Johnston 2008: 93).

An earlier debate surrounding the release of Cyril Collard's film *Les Nuits fauves* in 1992 had already shown the threat posed to traditional republicanism by minority politics. Despite its explicit sex scenes and bisexual (in all but name), HIV-positive protagonist, *Les Nuits fauves* was taken as an example of the French rejection of Anglo-Saxon identity politics. Influential AIDS critic Simon Watney, writing in *Sight and Sound* in 1993, dismissed the film as evidence of the perceived fatalism and despair in the face of AIDS: 'For it illustrates with some insight the psychological workings of a culture which is so profoundly homophobic that the very idea of a *collective* social or cultural response to AIDS on the part of homosexuals is all but unthinkable.'[3] Like the activists of Act Up Paris, Watney devoted the first half of his article to an attack on the French state for its criminal passivity on AIDS – abstract citizenship stopped abruptly short of acknowledging sexual dissidence. In his autobiographical account of the formation and subsequent activity of Act Up Paris, Didier Lestrade recounts how the group's minority politics have been consistently opposed to the dominant take on AIDS, which suited the literary vision of AIDS as symptomatic of an unconscious death-wish, the vision of artists, such as Collard and novelist Hervé Guibert, who, Lestrade avers, were in political denial (Lestrade 2000). Dominant ideology all too readily assimilates the model of dissidence espoused by Collard's protagonist, whose unmarked sexual identity is untainted by his 'deviant' sex life. Chantal Nadeau has made the more general case for male bisexuality as hetero-normative in recent French cinema (Nadeau 2000). Other cinematic representations of bisexuality include Ilan Duran Cohen's *La Confusion des genres* (2000), which uses male bisexuality to challenge fixed identity categories.

Lestrade echoes Watney's point about *Les Nuits fauves*. In place of the perceived humanist individualism and prescribed martyrdom of early AIDS representation, Anglo-American critics were scrupulously analysing the cultural signification of the epidemic and its relevance to political actuality. Lestrade views the failure to transpose such analysis to the French context as an ideological delay (Lestrade 2000: 308). In an article comparing the boundaries of gay identity in different cultural contexts, Bill Marshall has criticised the cultural imperialism of such an argument, for its tendency to position Anglo-American analysis of AIDS as a master-narrative, artificially tacked onto unreceptive locations. Marshall takes up the challenge of *Les Nuits fauves* for its particular articulation of local sexual identities in the struggle to define French national culture (Marshall 2000: 84–95).

As McCaffrey documents at length, the US-style radical activism of Act Up Paris, set up in 1989, has been the most influential model for a broad queer, community-based activism in contemporary France, launched against a republican state that refused to acknowledge the mere existence of minorities at risk (McCaffrey 1995: 101–33). Commenting on the growing opposition between gay consumption and activism in relation to France, Murray Pratt suspects that, apart from campaign groups like Act Up confronting homophobia in the context of AIDS, radical political action is now largely overshadowed by the global conquest of consumer gay identity. Pratt worries that gay is deployed 'by the web generation as a marketing category with increasingly looser ties to any actual referent in lived sexuality' (Pratt 2002: 179). As critic Philip Derbyshire has commented, the current climate of uncertain hope since the introduction of advanced antiretroviral medication, and eager anticipation of the efficacy of new treatments, have led to a growing collective denial of the recent gay past, notably in the vulgarisation of a culture of sexual risk among many metropolitan gay men. Derbyshire urges us to put historical context, the *experience* of sexual communities, to the forefront of cultural commentary, 'for if the epidemic has any single lesson it is that sex is historical through and through, even in the recesses of fantasy' (Derbyshire 2001: 26).

QUEER

The queer in *French Queer Cinema* is to be read in two ways. First, queer is convenient shorthand for lesbian, gay, bisexual and transgender identities. Second, the queer (or rather Queer) in *French Queer Cinema* is to be read as an attempt to translate the Anglo-American mode of political and academic critique to a contemporary French cultural setting. Queer is said to have expanded identity politics beyond the confines of gay affirmation and social integration. Queer, according to its wide-reaching social brief (Warner 1993), aims to investigate interlocking areas of contest within LGBT subcultures, exclusions based on racial and ethnic differences, class prejudice, transgender dissent, and non-normative sexual practices. Queer critique, in short, attempts to undermine all normative or 'straight' representations of gender and sexuality, hetero or homo (for accounts of the origins and development of queer theory and politics, see Jagose 1997; Hall 2003). Whilst the film production covered in this book focuses primarily on gay male sexuality (due to the lack of 'out' lesbian filmmakers and of lesbian self-representation), the films in question do not promote a straightforward, affirmative vision of gay male subcultures. In fact, films such as Sébastien Lifshitz's *Wild Side* adapt some of the tenets of Anglo-American queer theory (de Lauretis 1991) – notably the intersection of race, ethnicity, nationality and transgender dissent with forms of same-sexuality – to the French context, by pointing to the sexual margins and the national boundaries of an increasingly institutionalised, whitewashed gay culture. The principal use of 'queer' throughout this book is intended to avoid a celebratory (white, middle-class) 'gay pride' rendition of French cinema, one that would necessarily exclude the primary areas of cultural contestation around race, ethnicity, migration, transgender and AIDS. *French Queer Cinema* is particularly influenced by recent materialist debates within Anglo-American queer studies, notably the attention to political economy and migration (Eng, Halberstam and Muñoz 2005),[4] and the importance of hierarchies of race, class and socio-economic status in queer interpersonal relations (Sinfield 2004). These vectors of power underpin the book's textual analysis, and the wider contextual account of political and institutional change in contemporary France.

The first four chapters not only develop accounts of the socio-political context of contemporary France, but also build on the wide-reaching social perspective adopted by contemporary queer critique, tackling issues of migration, nationality, citizenship and post-integration, in tandem with transgender politics, sex work, AIDS activism and queer sexualities. There is no attempt, however, to squash an imperialist, US master-narrative onto French representations of same-sex practices, a criticism of queer theory's imperialist bent made forcefully by Lawrence R. Schehr (Schehr 2005: 10–11). Rather, the aim is to take account of local instances of sexual dissidence within their specific national formation. The thematic trajectory of the first four chapters begins with the emergence of gay *beur* identities and subculture, moving onto the social margins of immigration, sex work and transgender, then onto the emergence of transgender politics, and gay male sexuality and loss in the time of AIDS. Chapter 5 incorporates local examples of queer theory (Bourcier 2001, 2005a; Preciado 2000, 2003) as they relate to the emerging DIY digital video culture and to an oppositional queer/lesbian/trans subculture, both contesting the dominant visibility and conservative ideologies of mainstream LGBT politics.

CINEMA

Marie-Hélène Bourcier's distinction between 'active' and 'passive' visibility provides the starting point for a working definition of queer film in the French context (Bourcier 1998: 15–16). 'Passive visibility' is shorthand for images of sexual dissidence produced from outside LGBT subcultures – Bourcier means films made by straight-identified directors such as Josiane Balasko's commercial success *Gazon Maudit* (1995), for example. This classification is not unproblematic, since popular commercial comedies, such as Gabriel Aghion's *Pédale douce* (1996) and *Pédale dure* (2004) for example, might be included under active visibility, but, as Darren Waldron argues, they also repeat the standard tropes of the straight 'temporary transvestite narrative' (Waldron 2006).[5] Waldron, however, dismisses an essentialist definition of queer authorship that would tie films narrowly to the sexual identities of their directors, arguing that the challenge of popular comedies such as *Pédale douce* is that they combine modes of both active and passive visibility. Conversely, cases of passive visibility based on authorship can also make important contributions to contemporary queer sexual imagery. Claire Denis's work reveals a thematic interest in cross-race gay sexuality – *J'ai pas sommeil* (1994) – and an artistic interest in male homoeroticism – *Beau Travail* (2000). Her queer-inflected imagery troubles not only racial and sexual hierarchies, but also the visual pleasure taken in male beauty itself. Arguing that *Beau Travail* queers the orthodox Freudian division of female envy and male fetishism, Sarah Cooper points to the film's ethical engagement with issues of spectator pleasure, showing how it 'asks us to address what is at stake in such visual gratification' (Cooper 2001: 174).

Despite the obvious restrictions of limiting a definition of queer cinema to the sexual identities of individual filmmakers,[6] Bourcier's use of 'active visibility' is none the less useful in accounting for both institutionalised forms of representation in the context of French cinema, such as auteur film production, and more politicised forms of representation outside mainstream cinema, such as pornography and DIY video. Queer, as it is currently understood in French translation, is resumed as 'political self-representation' ('autoreprésentatif et politique'): 'a mode of visual expression that interferes with filmic modes of representation in general' ('un mode de représentation visuelle qui interfère avec les modes de représentation filmique en général') (Bourcier 1998: 15). Such a distinction between a niche market of gay cinema and a local, politicised queer cinema transposes debates within Anglo-American film studies and production around the move from the so-called 'positive imagery' and identity politics of gay cinema to the influence of AIDS activism and post-modern queer theory on the early 1990s independent 'New Queer Cinema' (Harry Benshoff and Sean Griffin, and Jackie Stacey and Sarah Street have provided comprehensive accounts of the definitional history of queer cinema: Benshoff and Griffin 2004: 1–15; Stacey and Street 2007: 1–18). However, as Stacey and Street document, there is also academic resistance to a simplistic separation of gay from queer cinema; they explain that 'some scholars have suggested that far from being set against the terms lesbian and gay, queer should be articulated through a proximity to them' (Stacey and Street 2007: 2). *French Queer Cinema* adopts such a position by attempting to mediate between coverage of queer-themed work by gay-identified filmmakers and the politicised output of more marginal queer artists and activists.

Bill Marshall's entry on 'gay cinema' in the *Encyclopedia of Contemporary French Culture* (Hughes and Reader 1998: 262–3) provides the historical background to gay-authored and gay-themed film production preceding the contemporary framework of this book. Marshall documents the importance of homosexual artists such as Jean Cocteau, whose homoerotic imagery was embedded in heterosexual narratives; and Jean Genet, whose groundbreaking exercise in queer voyeurism, *Un chant d'amour* (1950), wittily described by Serge Daney as 'the story of three holes' ('l'histoire de trois trous') (Giles 1993: 5),[7] blended high-literary aestheticism with pornographic images of masturbation. Marshall also mentions the popular films of closeted directors such as Marcel Carné, to which one might add those of Jacques Demy, whose 1960s genre of musical fantasy is a current influence on the films of Christophe Honoré and on the collaborative films of Olivier Ducastel and Jacques Martineau. Marshall also includes the experimental and political films made after gay liberation in the 1970s by Lionel Soukaz, together with examples drawn from auteur cinema from the 1980s and 1990s, which explicitly focused on gay male sexuality. Marshall argues that following the 'socialist government's reforms and the consumerist appropriation of much gay culture in the 1980s . . . it became less clear what a "gay cinema" might be' (Marshall 1998: 262). Alain Brassart has documented mainstream media reaction to Patrice Chéreau's disturbing vision of gay passion and promiscuity, *L'Homme blessé* (1983), the explicit sexual theme of which was judged severely by the press (Brassart 2007: 135–46). In his historical schema of French gay cinema, Florian Grandena also cites *L'Homme blessé* as part of the 'pre-gay' lineage deriving from Genet, with its attachment to underground, nocturnal cruising culture. Grandena goes on to describe Collard's *Les Nuits fauves* as emblematic of the emergence of a defiant same-sex desire in the early 1990s, followed by Ducastel and Martineau's *Drôle de Félix* (2000), a 'post-gay' celebration of same-sex public visibility (Grandena 2008).[8]

A necessary addition to Grandena's schema of gay visibility would be the work of André Téchiné, 'whose consistent output since the 1970s depicts in "relaxed" and empathetic fashion the complex social and historical interactions that go to make up his straight and gay characters' (Marshall 1998: 263). Marshall's subsequent, comprehensive coverage of Téchiné's generous and modest form of gay cinema (Marshall 2007) highlights *Les Roseaux sauvages* (1994) as important in the recent French history of gay self-representation. Though not overtly gay-affirmative, it offers 'a more open view of sexualities, manifested in the camera's plural gaze' according to Emma Wilson's analysis of the film as a form of personal history (Wilson 1999: 36). Wilson's reading of post-1950s French cinema in terms of 'personal histories' plays on the double meaning of the French *histoire*: history and story, to explore 'life stories and love stories (looking at the autobiographical thread which runs through much modern French cinema), yet also public history (looking at films which represent trauma and response to historical events)' (Wilson 1999: 11). This revised account of authorship and discourses of auteurism in French cinema is important for how it juxtaposes textual interpersonal relations and contextual autobiographical inspiration, alongside attention to public events in a socio-political framework, an approach shared by *French Queer Cinema*'s combination of intimate and public 'histories' (the sexual enveloped within the social) in gay-authored and queer-themed films.

The conclusion to Marshall's historical sketch of French gay cinema blames both the institutional dominance of auteurism and the persistence of sexism in the French film industry for the absence of a distinctive lesbian cinema, a label disputed by Lucille Cairns, who accepts the necessity for terminological shorthand, but who complains that 'to anthropomorphise a cultural artefact by ascribing it a human and nationalised sexual identity is patently absurd' (Cairns 2006: 2). One rare, recent example of a lesbian-themed, lesbian-authored independent film is Valérie Minetto's *Oublier Cheyenne* (2004), which stages a materialist stand-off between a penniless journalist (Mila Dekker), who renounces urban living for a self-sustained existence in the countryside, and her bisexual lover (Aurélia Petit), a pragmatic teacher, who attempts to salvage their relationship despite the pair's ideological differences. Cairns analyses the history of representations of lesbian desire in French and francophone cinemas, in male and female-authored films, including filmmakers whose output is covered here, notably Téchiné (*Les Voleurs*, 1995) and François Ozon (*Regarde la mer*, 1997; *Huit Femmes*, 2001; *Swimming Pool*, 2002). Her readings of Ozon's 'lesbians' point to the persistent hetero-centric framework governing images of female same-sexuality – a manoeuvre also adopted by Honoré in both *Ma mère* (2004) and *Les Chansons d'amour* (2007) – according to which the momentary 'lesboerotic dalliance' between lesbian icon Catherine Deneuve and Fanny Ardant in *Huit femmes* is predictably 'liquidated and disavowed' (Cairns 2006: 96), in line with the hetero-centric conventions of the film's generic origins in boulevard theatre, according to which the two women are shown to be squabbling over a man. French critics such as Alain Brassart and Noël Burch have gone further than Cairns's measured critique of hetero-centricity by calling Ozon and Honoré – together with nearly all the other gay filmmakers covered in this book – misogynist (Brassart 2007: 195–211; Burch 2007: 151–7), a reductive, though not necessarily incorrect, claim that stalls all possible further lines of inquiry into the complex and contradictory political effects of representation (Dyer 1993: 1–2).

Of the contemporary filmmakers covered in *French Queer Cinema*, Ozon is the best known on the international independent film circuit. Andrew Asibong's book on Ozon's career up to *Angel* (2007) looks in detail at the filmmaker's early output (Asibong 2008),[9] including his series of short films that twist models of gender conformity and sexual propriety – *Victor* (1993), *La Petite mort* (1994), *Une robe d'été* (1996), *Regarde la mer* (1997); and the three feature films of his early period – *Sitcom* (1998), *Les Amants criminels* (1999) and *Gouttes d'eau sur pierres brûlantes* (2000), which, as Asibong observes, playfully develop a post-modern interpretation of genres such as melodrama and fantasy, and which include nods to the queer filth of John Waters, the trashy camp of Pedro Almodóvar and the melodramatic mode of Rainer Werner Fassbinder. *Gouttes d'eau sur pierres brûlantes* is both an adaptation of an early play by Fassbinder and a larger pastiche of his cinema (Handyside 2007). Richard Dyer has defined pastiche as 'a kind of imitation that you are meant to know is an imitation' (Dyer 2007: 1), which suits both Ozon's knowing irony and his expressive admiration for the original. *Gouttes d'eau sur pierres brûlantes* is also emblematic of Ozon's series of anti-naturalist fantasy spaces, described by Asibong as 'hybrid and sometimes unashamedly tacky,' fantasy representations of 'real life soaked in a heady perfume of bad romantic fiction, musical melodrama and perhaps a little light pornography' (Asibong 2008: 6). Whilst Asibong champions Ozon's queering of bourgeois, heterosexual family norms, particularly in his close readings of *Victor* and *Sitcom*, he avoids reducing Ozon's entire oeuvre to the filmmaker's sexual identity or to a conventional 'gay cinema' marketing label.

Conversely, Max Cavitch adapts psychoanalytical theories of mourning to *La Petite mort*, whilst expressing surprise that Ozon's output has been excluded from Anglo-American criticism and theories of queer cinema; this is an anomaly, in Cavitch's view, given that Ozon's output 'formally, as well as thematically, displaces, mocks or otherwise defamiliarizes the conventions of erotic narrative' (Cavitch 2007: 324). Whilst acknowledging that Ozon's earlier output has been explicitly marketed in the US as LGBT festival material, Asibong concludes that Ozon is less interested in a straightforward transcription of identity politics to narrative cinema, than in a 'more thoroughly generalised blurring of the very contours of desire' (Asibong 2008: 12). In light of the recent trend of sexual extremism in French cinema, Asibong situates Ozon as part of the larger French literary heritage of sexual transgression, a tradition that undermines normative heterosexuality and that also formed the basis for Honoré's visual adaptation of Georges Bataille's novel *Ma mère*, a recent critical turn in French queer cinema analysed in Chapter 4.

Asibong argues that both the human cruelty and the formal artifice of Fassbinder's cinema is transposed to remarkable effect in Ozon's *Gouttes d'eau sur pierres brûlantes*. Leopold, an established businessman (Bernard Giraudeau), perverts an innocent teenage boy Franz (Malik Zidi), together with the boy's pert ex-girlfriend (Ludivine Sagnier), in order to train them both as malleable sex toys, just as he had previously done with Vera (Anna Thomson), whom he callously rejected following her sex change operation. Whilst, as Asibong observes, Ozon ditches Fassbinder's more strident socio-political critique in favour of theatrical fantasy, the French gay press read the film's model of male same-sex relations as providing an implicit commentary on the concurrent debates surrounding the PaCS, at the time of the film's release in March 2000. Critic Didier Roth-Bettoni quoted Ozon as humourously labelling it the first 'anti-PaCS film' ('le premier film anti-PaCS').[10] Indeed, the sado-masochistic parlour games, in which Franz dresses up as a submissive houseboy in kitsch *lederhosen*, the framing of his emprisonment borrowed from Fassbinder's trademark geometric mise-en-scène, show the lengths to which Ozon went to counter the bland imagery of sexual affirmation, represented in TV narratives such as *Juste une question d'amour*, transmitted two months earlier in January 2000.

The most striking aspect of Ozon's dissonant fantasy couple, in contrast to the homely boys of gay realism, is the age disparity between the two men, a hierarchy supported by Leopold's economic and cultural superiority, and by Franz's feminised, sexual submission. This conflation of socio-sexual hierarchies of age, gender and class was later transposed to the less theatrical, but nevertheless anti-realist, mode of *5 × 2* (2004), which deconstructed a heterosexual relationship in reverse, from divorce through meltdown, childbirth and marriage to holiday romance. Critic Jean Douchet was particularly impressed by Ozon's inverted structure, which denaturalises the linear chronology and cultural archetypes of heterosexual coupling and kinship.[11] The meltdown scene also contains a parallel image of a gay couple, a device used to illustrate the relative freedoms and limitations of sexual relations lived outside monogamy. Unlike the emotional prison of Ozon's earlier man/boy couple, this gay relationship is depicted as relatively harmonious, though the older partner is shown to bear, rather than to condone, his cuter boyfriend's infidelities. The one vector of power absent from the present discussion of Ozon's gay men is race, described by Sinfield in his materialist taxonomies of same-sex relations as 'the most sensitive, threatening, and exciting hierarchy' (Sinfield 2004: 186).

> Historically, even benevolent relations between white people and people of color have characteristically involved condescension and stereotyping. It is still hard to think of intimate relations between black and white men without invoking a heritage of dominance and submission. (Sinfield 2004: 160)

The following chapter addresses questions of racial and ethnic difference in contemporary gay cinematic production, which includes Ozon's problematic objectification of actor Salim Kechiouche, the *beur* 'pin-up' of French queer cinema, a painted photograph of whom is reproduced on the cover of this book. This superficial framing of Kechiouche is not intentionally meant to reproduce the same manoeuvre I criticise in relation to Ozon's *Les Amants criminels*, but rather to situate the troubling gaze of white gay filmmakers and artists as one of the central critical inquiries of this book.

NOTES

1. 'Hypervisibility/Hypervisibilité' was the title of a bilingual conference on French and Francophone screen representations of homosexuality, organised by Florian Grandena at Concordia University, Canada, in 2006. In terms of media representations, in 2000–1 alone, alongside coverage of horrific hate crimes (Brigitte Vital-Durand, '«J'étais écœuré de voir ce type inconnu, à moitié à poil»: Les accusés du meurtre d'un gay se défendent maladroitement,' *Libération*, 14 November 2001, p. 22), there was attention to gay integration through the civil partnership law – *pacte civil de solidarité* (Blandine Grosjean, 'Deux ans après son adoption: Le Pacs dans les mœurs,' *Libération*, 14 November 2001, p. 18), to apparent social unity with heterosexuals and an integration of queer into urban trend (Blandine Grosjean, 'Un nouveau pacte,' *Libération*, 24–5 June 2000, *Gay Pride 2000*, p. 2) and to the continuing success of gay business culture (Loïc Prigent and Daniel Garcia, 'Quand les gays réveillent le Vieux-Paris,' *Le Nouvel Observateur*, Paris-Ile-de-France section, 8–14 February 2001, pp. 4–5; Renaud Revel and Agnès Verdier, 'Le pouvoir gay,' *L'Express*, no. 2607, 21–7 June 2001, pp. 84–94).
2. The dominant strand of republican thought dates back to the foundational 1789 Declaration of the Rights of Man and of the Citizen (*Déclaration des droits de l'homme et du citoyen*), according to which citizenship is embodied in an abstract individual who is born free, politically accountable to and represented by a secular, egalitarian state, which is supported by a weak civil society.
3. Simon Watney, 'The French Connection,' *Sight and Sound*, 3:6, 1993, pp. 24–5. In contrast to Watney's political analysis of the film, the magazine's official review praised the aesthetic values of clashing styles, the frenzy of the leading characters, the emotional realism and deft symbolism. See Amanda Lipman, 'Les Nuits fauves (Savage Nights),' *Sight and Sound*, 3:6, 1993, p. 62.
4. Whilst the first wave of queer theory was embedded within the post-structuralist philosophical and literary tradition (Butler 1990; Sedgwick 1990), it was in fact a more hybrid formation, also containing a strand on political economy and social theory that remained subordinate to the predominance of cultural theory (Warner 1993). A later volume of the journal *Social Text* posited queer as a broad critique of nationality, race, gender, and class, as well as sexuality (Harper, McClintock, Muñoz and Rosen 1997). The third queer volume of *Social Text* in 2005, entitled 'What's Queer about Queer Studies Now?' (Eng, Halberstam and Muñoz 2005), attempted to revive a flagging agenda, by reassessing the political utility of queer in light of the emergence of 'queer liberalism', the mainstream market incorporation of gay and lesbian identities as mass-mediated consumer lifestyles. The editors update queer theory's brief to assess what queer studies might contribute to questions of citizenship, empire, globalisation and immigration, alongside the earlier intersection of race, gender and sexuality.
5. Aghion is also a vocal opponent of the gay cinema/filmmaker label, immodestly claiming homosexuality as one of his assets, whilst rejecting the category of 'gay filmmaker' as restrictive: Hugo Deschamps, 'Ainsi soient-ils,' *Première*, April 2004, pp. 76–81.
6. In his article on screen images of queerness, Hugo Deschamps provides a reductive definition of queer authorship in French cinema (in relation to filmmakers Morel, Honoré, Lifshitz, Ozon, Giusti, Ducastel and Martineau), even quoting one source who quips that 'one can almost guess what they do in bed from watching their films' ('on pourrait presque deviner ce qu'ils font au lit en regardant leurs films'): Hugo Deschamps, 'Ainsi soient-ils,' *Première*, April 2004, pp. 76–81.
7. Daney's piece, 'Blind desire' ('Désir aveugle'), reprinted in the French translation of Jane Giles's *The Cinema of Jean Genet* (1991), was originally published in *Cahiers du cinéma* in 1976, and describes how the film's regime of pleasure in spectatorship

('scopophilia') works through the central focus on the eye itself, 'a sort of story of the eye' (Giles 1993: 5) ('une sorte d'histoire de l'oeil').

8. Cristina Johnston has also provided an outline of representations of homosexuality in 1990s mainstream French cinema (Johnston 2002), which provides extensive coverage of the socio-political backdrop to popular films such as *Gazon Maudit* (Balasko, 1995), *Ma Vie en rose* (Berliner, 1997), *Belle Maman* (Aghion, 1999) and *Le Derrière* (Lemercier, 1999).

9. Thank you to Andrew Asibong for kindly allowing me to see his pre-published manuscript.

10. Didier Roth-Bettoni, 'Cinéma: L'enfer du couple selon Ozon', *Illico*, 16 March 2000, pp. 6–8.

11. Jean Douchet, 'Dix sur dix', *Cahiers du cinéma*, no. 602, June 2005, p. 67.

1. *BEUR* MASCULINITY AND QUEER FANTASY

The first performer in the second DVD of Citébeur's postcolonial porn series *Wesh Cousin* (Studio Presse, 2003) bursts through the door of a disaffected warehouse located somewhere outside Paris and points a fake plastic gun at the camera, playfully encouraging us to come watch him masturbate before he goes off to work. The preceding voice-over has introduced the urban consumer to the supposedly sexy underworld of poor, peripheral housing estates, supported elsewhere by the Citébeur iconography containing every possible indicator of urban, lower-class masculinity – the canine logo, mural tags, street-wear, sports gear, bling, fake guns, kick-boxing apparatus, you name it. This opening scene acts as an ironic initiation for the presumably voyeuristic viewer to the fantasy world of hot available ghetto-boys. The jerky hand-held DV camera follows the performer up the stairs, positioning itself below him as he shows off his slim hairy torso and licks his weapon. This is all quite self-consciously amusing and seeks to break with the humourless wooden acting spliced into traditional porn. We watch him relieve himself before masturbating to a climax that visually directs spectator pleasure, by placing the camera above him on the stairs, slightly to the left of his head. This mobile 'money-shot' is either inviting the viewer to identify across potential class and ethnic lines, or else is not solely intended for the mainstream gay market at all, but to give young, lower-class *beur* men the raunchy images they might desire for and of themselves. A later sequence picks up on inter-racial fantasy, this time between Arab and black boys by blending in other markers of social power – class and gender. This scene is between a straight-acting, well-built *beur* man and a younger-looking, trim black boy, decked out in a chic ensemble, suggesting a combination of upward-mobility and effeminacy (predictably stifled by the manly verbal exchange). The sex however turns out to be more egalitarian (fellatio and mutual masturbation) and does not quite deliver on the potentially charged disparity of race, gender and class established between the performers at the outset.

I am drawing attention to these sequences not just to make the obvious point that porn imagery neatly packages a complex array of explosive dynamics into a sexy commodity, but as a means of introducing the ideological lines of the argument of this chapter. In their introduction to *Post-Colonial Cultures in France* (Hargreaves and McKinney 1997), Alec G. Hargreaves and Mark McKinney examine the historical conditions for the neo-colonial gaze in French popular culture. The self-definitional use of *beur* from the 1980s onwards was an attempt by the North African Maghrebi youth of the *banlieues* (the deprived suburbs surrounding the major French conurbations) to seize representational power. The original radicalism of *beur* was later diluted when it entered the mainstream vernacular. Whilst *beur* and *rebeu* ('backslang' in which the syllables are reversed, deriving from *Arabe*) are used more neutrally to represent second and third-generation Arabs of North-African origin (less classificatory than *maghrébin*), the term *racaille* (which has evolved historically from riff-raff to louts or scum) is a term of abuse. At its most, the Citébeur video production might be seen as a political attempt to twist the insult to symbolise a degree of lower-class sexual pride across ethnic lines, incorporating young *beur*, black, mixed-race and white men. This independent porn certainly shows how the *racaille* myth has been erotically incorporated into queer production and aims to undermine the continued racial homogeneity of dominant middle-class gay culture, whose hasty rush to the altar serves to exclude those who cannot (or will not) buy into the ideology.

Alongside this empowering imagery that uses commercial stimulation to re-define *beur* male subjectivities is the erotic gaze of white gay men, who tend to see black and Arab men as convenient receptacles for their own postcolonial angst, frustrated machismo and white shame. Following an overview of *beur* representation in French queer cinema, including the acting career of Salim Kechiouche, I take a look at two early films by Sébastien Lifshitz to refute the notion that sexual objectification would form some kind of inevitable structure to male cross-race relations, for Lifshitz's films both offer alternative templates for *beur* sexual subjectivity. I begin at the centre to set the institutional scene for contemporary postcolonial politics, before moving back to the margins to pull together the threads of debate within queer milieu on racism, cross-race relations, and class disparity. In the subsequent extended readings of queer porn video and art cinema, I slant my argument heavily towards gender imbalance. The erotic attraction of the *'racaille'* image for white, middle-class men is bound up in a strategic branding of lower-class masculinity; on the other side of the equation, the disavowal of femininity is particularly strong for *beur* men for cultural and religious reasons, making everyday effeminacy often impossible to live openly. In short, the danger of venerating the masculine on both sides is the consequential exclusion of male femininity.

BLACK/BLANC/BEUR

The year 1998 witnessed the branding of a harmonious version of ethnic and racial integration in France. The World Cup soccer victory on home soil was notable for the ensuing media promotion of the multi-ethnic team members as postcolonial role models. The euphoric critical reception of the team told of black and *beur* children proudly singing the *Marseillaise*, calls of 'Zidane for President!' and scenes of jubilation along the *Champs-Elysées*, invaded by a million citizens – more than at the Liberation. A photo of star player Zinedine Zidane, projected onto the *Arc de Triomphe*, singled him out as the face of 'successful' integration, a celebrity profile commercially exploited by his subsequent endorsement of a wide range of brands from the luxury (Dior) to the low-cost (Leader Price). Thomas Deltombe and Mathieu Rigouste argue that the celebration of stars such as Zidane (the subject of Douglas Gordon and Philippe Parreno's portrait *Zidane: un portrait du 21e siècle* (2006), the footballer taken as the symbol of his epoch) or celebrities such as comedian Jamel Debbouze (the instigator of the *Jamel Comedy Club*, a multicultural comedy talent search launched in 2006), not only reinforces received assumptions about success in sport and entertainment, but is part of a larger media strategy designed to single out supposedly successful cases of integration (the 'friend' – Zidane is not in actual fact Arab but Berber) from the mass of young, socially-deprived, Muslim Arab men who are stigmatised as socially marginal and potentially dangerous – the figure of the inassimilable Arab 'enemy' within (Deltombe and Rigouste 2005). By contrast, in 1998 *Le Nouvel Observateur* wondered whether the World Cup victory had allowed the French to make their old republican dream of fraternity come true.[1] The magazine does not advocate anything vaguely egalitarian such as the regularisation of all 'undocumented' immigrants – there was much public debate at this time over Prime Minister Jospin's unfulfilled electoral promise to abrogate the successive right-wing immigration laws (*les lois Pasqua/Debré*). The victory is taken as evidence of the healthy state of French republicanism, specifically grounded in Ernest Renan's nineteenth-century understanding of the nation as not exclusively based on origin, but rather on a collective project, a shared destiny (Renan [1882] 2007).[2]

The electoral power of Jean-Marie Le Pen's far-right *Front National* party was notably obscured by the media frenzy on multicultural football. In the first round of the April 2002 presidential elections, Le Pen eliminated socialist candidate Lionel Jospin and all the other left and far-left candidates, including Christiane Taubira, France's first black woman candidate. This victory was partially put down to centre-right candidate Chirac's vulgarisation of Le Pen's obsession with social instability – 'l'insécurité' being the political buzzword of the time. In between the two rounds of voting, celebrities, among them Zidane, urged the nation to boycott the extremist candidate Le Pen in favour of Chirac, whose subsequent presidency was mired in sleaze allegations. Act Up Paris later argued that, in light of Nicolas Sarkozy's hard-line social policies as Minister for the

Interior, Le Pen effectively won the 2002 elections by forcing far-right ideology onto the mainstream political agenda, thus making xenophobia and racism politically acceptable. A satirical poster campaign in late 2005 featured a photo of Sarkozy with the slogan 'Vote Le Pen'. Act Up's point is to be understood polemically because it overlooks a more balanced account of existing ideological tensions and fractures on the right, between Sarkozy's opportunistic gestures to the far right and Chirac's concurrent, more consensual centre-right politics.

France has for long expected all immigrants (and the second and third generations) to integrate republican values, to discard ethnic particularity for neutral secularism, without receiving any form of solidarity in return. Algerian intellectual Abdelmalek Sayad explained the process of integration as 'determined retroactively, depending on whether it has succeeded or failed' (Sayad 1999: 307), an idealistic process originally aimed at taking the immigrant from the position of radical otherness to one of totalised identity. The state accordingly produces identity as 'the identical' in order to foreclose difference. In a collection of critical essays seeking to redefine the French Republic, asking whether its vocation is indeed still relevant to the contemporary political conjuncture, Gino Raymond examines the proliferation of late twentieth-century works, notably Régis Debray's pedagogical edition *La République expliquée à ma fille* (Debray 1998), 'aimed at reasserting the centrality of the Republic, and the exercise of the civic values it represents, as the means of successfully confronting some of the more testing challenges to the cohesion of French society' (Raymond 2006: 6). Raymond traces the history of the republican ideal emerging from the 1789 revolution:

> The constitutional foundations for the Republic that were finally laid by the Assembly with the vote that was passed in 1875 would give France a political regime that would elevate the aspirations of the Declaration of the Rights of Man and the Citizen; inalienable and individual rights, served by accountable government, held together by an impartial justice that embodies the sovereignty of the people, operating in a public space where the individual defined himself by assuming the right and responsibility to act, all contained within a polity that would be the Republic one and indivisible. (Raymond 2006: 5)

Raymond's account provides a theoretical framework to understand the retreat of the republican paradigm, an ideological decline that is in fact generating new formations, 'a platform for a new politics' (Raymond 2006: 6). He locates the early twenty-first-century conflicts around citizenship, focusing particularly on the rights of Muslim women to display signs of religious belonging in state institutions, as part of the wider erosion of abstract universalism, a crisis of modernity with particular resonance for France, where identities based on faith or ethnicity are seen to contravene any accepted or plausible definition of national citizenship.

Achille Mbembe has likewise attacked the republican blind spot on 'race' asking why in a time of globalisation through financial markets, cultural flux and mass migration France has stubbornly refused to accept its new reality, and to embark on necessary postcolonial critical thinking (Mbembe 2005). The opening up of the republican tradition to this new reality of plural identities is further complicated by interaction with non-normative sexualities. I wish now to point to some queer faultlines disrupting dominant universalism, marking a transition from the mere visibility of ethnic minorities (the widespread media coverage of the 1998 World Cup team) to a highly contested politics of representation. From the evidence I now gather of accusations of racial 'othering' within queer culture in France and anxieties around issues of inter-racial intimacy, I deduce that the republican model is also being radically modified by an emerging postcolonial struggle around the practices of sexual dissidence.

Fouad Zéraoui, president of Kelma, a Paris-based not-for-profit organisation for gay *beur* visibility, explains the aim of Kelma's *Black Blanc Beur* (BBB) events (raï, funk and hip-hop parties) as a conscious rejection of gay identity stereotypically fixed as white.[3] Around the time of the launch of Kelma, Nidam Abdi, writing in *Libération*, expressed the discomfort many men felt when faced with the latent racism present in certain gay milieu, quoting various troubled voices constantly confronted either by rejection or else exotic fascination.[4] Others felt trapped as convenient objects of a collective gay desire that maintains Arabs as inferior. The creation of separate gay space along ethnic lines is promoted as the means of dismantling the hegemonic racism and (perceived) body fascism of white gay subculture, marking the ideological cleavage between the white, middle-class, relatively institutionalised world of the Marais (the commercial gay village in central Paris) and the young *beurs* and blacks negotiating the closet in a climate of almost endemic homophobia in the estates in and around Paris.

The BBB events at Pigalle certainly point to a significant degree of autonomy from the gay mainstream, conventional representations of which never show gay *beur* men collectively. Until recently, no HIV prevention campaign in France has been explicitly targeted at people of colour; when they are represented in HIV prevention, they are invariably alone, alongside other white men or in mixed-race (more often than not straight) couples. Put schematically, in terms of representation, gay identity and *beur* and black subjectivities are bound to mutual exclusion in order to protect both the racial homogeneity of white, middle-class gay identity, and the dominant masculinity of heterosexual men of colour. I realise that any *beur*/black generalisation is sociologically tenuous. The hierarchy that puts people of Maghrebi origin at the bottom of the social heap must logically impact on sexual fantasy, making *beur* men often wearier of white erotic interest than black men. *Beur* men are clearly beginning to demand that their sexuality be acknowledged and respected in close proximity to their culture of origin; to some extent the initial difficulty in terms of collective militant action stems from the social disempowerment of their parents, disenfranchised by the state. The weight of Islamic condemnation of homosexuality clearly contributes to a greater sense of sexual guilt and self-oppression than for white gay men, simply because religion plays a more fundamental role in Maghrebi culture. Some gay Muslims try to modify their beliefs to fit round their sexual identities; others reject Islam as homophobic and incompatible with same-sex metropolitan life.[5]

Going on coverage of cross-race relations by the gay press, the complexities of lived sexual relations are bundled up into two concurrent models: the first seeks to promote equality between partners to exorcise the lingering colonial fantasy of Arab masculinity (the hypersexual, exclusively virile, active *beur*); the second works through some of the unresolved conflicts raised by positive imagery such as the erotic impact of age, gender and class on racial and ethnic difference. According to an article in gay magazine *Têtu* published in 1996,[6] oppressive white fantasy structures are to blame for a widespread reluctance to accept gay as multi-ethnic and the refusal to afford gay *beur* or black men any degree of visibility: the fantasy space allotted to gays of colour by white men is inversely proportional to their actual degree of social recognition. One strand of this criticism is idealist, rather than materialist: white men tend to segment their desire for non-white men, passing over the individual for the popular Arab or black fantasy package from the troubled histories of colonialism, seeking to pin otherness uniquely to the sexual. Rachid O., a Moroccan novelist living in Paris, writes in this vein: there is attention to inter-racial desire, but it is most often wrapped up in romanticised notions of individual couples (Rachid O. 2003). This hinges on the question of bypassing histories of oppression to clean up popular fantasy. It does not necessarily follow that to achieve racial equality, we must also necessarily forget questions of hierarchy in sexual relations, particularly in fantasy. The crucial issue is to ascertain whether it is possible for white people to acknowledge (or even promote) the sexiness of racial and ethnic difference without retaining the imperialist baggage.

The *beur* men interviewed for the *Têtu* article express their anger at the pain caused by the near systematic racism in their sexual relations with white men; one man views the Marais (of the late 1990s) as racially segregated – white gay men who hit on *beur* men are said to be hypocritically racist. Another interviewee claims absolute equality as a necessity, never engaging in bestial relationships that would trap him as an object of white fantasy. However, whilst this model attempts to correct forms of explicit or latent racial prejudice, it has the disadvantage of fitting all sexual relations into a neat model that bypasses the historical formation of fantasy. This point comes from Alan Sinfield: ideology requires (what are regarded as) egalitarian couples, much like the heterosexual norm that privileges the sexual over any other difference. Hierarchical couples of course occur, but often with an attempt at disavowal (Sinfield 2004).

In a later article in *Têtu* investigating gay *beur* men in a climate of internationally sanctioned racism against Arabs following the '9/11' terrorist attacks on the US, the interviewees express a greater degree of ambivalence as to their sexual relations with white men.[7] They tend to agree that white partners often view them uniquely as temporary or one-off lovers, criticising those who go to the BBB or Citébeur events to pick up *beur* men; they are, however, keen to differentiate between popular fantasies and particular individuals, whose strong attraction towards *beur* men does not involve crude objectification, or who are reluctant to admit to the lure of racial difference.

POSTCOLONIAL PORNOGRAPHY

The recent porn produced on digital video by the local studio Citébeur (an expanding community-business consisting of Internet sites and cheaply made porn) aims to queer the 'orientalism' that the *beur* men rail against in the *Têtu* interviews. The series *Wesh Cousin* can be read straight as an obsessive reproduction of the very racial stereotypes that position Arab men as virile, lower-class objects of white, middle-class fascination – the *racaille/banlieue* myth eroticised by gay culture. These videos are in fact more ambiguous than their brand imagery would suggest and seek to twist the *racaille* insult to symbolise a degree of lower-class sexual pride across ethnic lines, incorporating young *beur*, black, mixed-race and white men. Beyond the porn production, the online Citébeur business itself is a visible space for a more complex representation of *beur* masculinity than is catered for in mainstream gay subculture. One strand of the journalism on gay/*beur* identities concerns the need to combat the colonial cliché of sexual savagery and the postcolonial cliché of *banlieue* machismo. There is the suspicion from some quarters (particularly from effeminate men) that gay culture's perceived 'masculinist' bent is symptomatic of the longing to ape male heterosexuality.[8] Others, however, disagree with this vision of masculinity as an imposed burden: Stéphane Chibikh, founder of Citébeur, however promotes the commercialisation of the *racaille* trend. Chibikh is said to forge a new template for gay fantasy: boys who appear manly but not self-consciously so, boys both in the 'hood and out of the closet.[9] This is about perverting a brand of masculinity that dictates that sexual acts perceived as 'submissive' or 'feminine' are never admitted to. Received wisdom holds that in Maghrebi Arab culture, the active partner is rarely perceived as homosexual, rather as a hyper-virile man; the passive partner consequently loses his honour by being feminised. It is less the sexual object-choice that is at stake than the policing of masculinity, which in turn taps into uneven dominant gender relations privileging boys over girls.

The Citébeur performers parody all the trappings of lower-class masculinity (particularly sports such as kick-boxing – unlike affluent gym queens, these boys cannot pay through the nose for a fit body) and channel them into a package of sexual fantasies by developing their bodies as merchandise. The series does run the risk of promoting old-fashioned virility as a new enthusiasm, the danger, as in most gay porn, being the potential exclusion of effeminacy. This is referenced by the butch porn star François Sagat,[10] chiefly recognised by his scalp tattoo, who in one interview describes his adolescence as an average effeminate boy (hanging out with girls, rejected for the football team), explaining his constructed image of muscular expansion and body tattoos as a conscious rejection of the stigma of effeminacy.[11] Sagat is the first international porn star launched by the studio – he is white but often plays Arab or mixed-race parts in films for the Raging Stallion studio in the US, notably in their orientalist *Arabesque* (Ward, 2006). Sagat has since moved to rival studio Titan, starring in Brian Cam's action porn *Breathless* (2007).[12]

The Citébeur porn could be said to be realigning the coordinates without actually proposing new horizons for traditional gender hierarchy – it tends to play off *rebeu* (which automatically slides into *lascar* – sexually active, urban, virile) against *cefran* (sexually passive, white, middle-class), a move that could be said to bolster traditional gender roles. This is backed up by the accounts accompanying the interview in *Têtu* that document how this new generation is following dominant ideology by concentrating same-sex desire on the dis-avowal of male femininity.[13] Mainstream urban-trend guide *Technikart* also ran a piece on Chibikh in May 2004.[14] *Technikart* presented Chibikh as a single-handed cultural revolution, producing sociological porn with his digital camera, and apparently breaking with existing stereotypes of *beur* manliness. The last claim is debatable – some of the porn does gently parody contempo-rary hip-hop machismo, but it is hardly an all-out assault on virility; to be fair though, Chibikh is certainly doing his bit to promote the representation and acceptance of widespread same-sex practices among *cité*-boys. His technique is often more challenging than the content – the amateur home-video style allows Chibikh's camera to participate as an equal in the action rather than as the frame for a self-conscious mise-en-scène. The action is clearly staged, but by using real locations (deserted carparks and cellars) and by eschewing the inva-sive CCTV surveillance favoured by voyeuristic reality TV, Chibikh, as a dis-creet insider, establishes a real complicity between camera and performer.

The Citébeur porn is an emerging commercial enterprise having produced eight DVDs in the *Wesh Cousin* series to date, and two more recent *beur* spin-offs (*Ali et ses potes* and *Tarek et ses potes*). The website also points to Citébeur's brand extension with links to other related merchandise (called 'cousin' sites) including the *Bolatino* and *Matoss de blackoss* series, the more explicitly orientalist *Gay Arab Club*, and the innovative annual gay reality-porn production *Hotcast*, which sees a *black/blanc/beur* group of six perform-ers in stiff competition to become the new star of the gay porn industry. The original brand positioning for Citébeur sought to balance *beur* sexual self-representation with the commercial exigencies of mainstream gay consump-tion.[15] A cursory glance at the products themselves would seem to support the claim that the early DVDs uncritically reproduced *banlieue* clichés of male sav-agery – the enduring myth of 'le garçon arabe'. Nacira Guénif-Souilamas has examined the sexual politics of such representations of the 'Arab boy' (Guénif-Souilamas 2004, 2005, 2006). She argues that through a steady decomposition of gender relations between those at the margins of society (the *cité*), the Arab, black and white *cité*-boys are stuck in an archaic machismo, unable to engage with femininity apart from through scorn or violence, and are denied the gender flexibility so in vogue among metropolitan heterosexuals (Guénif-Souilamas 2004). The *beur* boy sketched by Guénif-Souilamas is noted for his excessive miming of virility, one that clashes with a more gender-neutral performance on the part of more socially privileged men. Guénif-Souilamas picks up on the underlying class formation in *cité* homophobia, in which male youths are condemned to a violent heterosexuality, a hatred of effeminacy, and an excessive miming of virility – a gender performance perceived as well past its sell-by date when placed alongside an increased intolerance of homophobic insults elsewhere (Guénif-Souilamas 2004: 75). Denied any form of metropolitan gender ambiguity, the figure of the socially deprived Arab boy – called elsewhere 'the impossible citizen' (Guénif-Souilamas 2006: 118) – is in this account shown to be as much a prisoner of his own body as of his social milieu and geographical surroundings. Whilst the author accepts the empirical evidence that only an actual minority of *cité*-boys conform to the pervasive negative stereotyping of their lives (seen as unable to express their feelings for fear of effeminacy, responsible for their own educational failure and tempted into delinquency or criminality due to a lack of future job prospects), she blames the local institutional infrastructure for measuring social achievement uniquely in terms of individual responsibility to get out of the *cité* and personal blame for failure to do so (Guénif-Souilamas 2004: 78).

Read without irony, the Citébeur pornography clearly plays up to the archetype of heterosexual violence described by Guénif-Souilamas, by showing performers described by the cover blurb as natural, virile and spontaneous street-guys, who sport hoods and carry guns. Many of the scenarios situated in squalid basements and various squats revolve around queer parodies of potentially violent situations – in volume two there is a fake hold-up, and in volume five two masked intruders ambush a white/*beur* couple. Whilst some of the sequences are actually quite soft-core, sometimes even sensual, including scenarios in which the partners seem to respect each other, much of the action is low-key S/M *sans le savoir*, including a good deal of playful abuse, the plastic guns slung around freely and the fetish for sportswear replacing leather. The penetration scenes in the early DVDs are at times lopsided and unevenly filmed, tending to focus more on the active partner's pleasure, accompanied by a passive manhole, though the Arab men are not always, but more often than not, leading. However, the later videos multiply every possible racial and sexual position to include the odd black, passive performer – *Matos de blackos* (2006) seeks to reverse the black active/white passive formula. But the white model in volume two who is blindfolded at gunpoint is predictably a cute blue-eyed boy, and class or age barriers are rarely transgressed: the white partners are still typically *local* boys. Some of the models may of course be older but are got up in street-gear, so age is hard to decipher.

It is important nonetheless to give an idea of the variety of plausible fantasy positions on offer in the *Wesh Cousin* series. Beyond the uniform brand imagery of urban virility, the series actually often twists the standard codes of masculinity to provide a mix of straightforward sex with some fun over-the-top parodies of *banlieue* clichés. Reading the sequences as straightforwardly sexist (the insult 'slut' is occasionally directed at the passive partners) would simply ignore the central role of fantasy and role-play in pornographic fiction. Clearly the utterance of the injurious term '*salope*' in common fantasies of submission within gay male sexual practice does not necessarily imply actual sympathy with sexist structures of oppression. Take *Caïd superstar* (the fourth DVD), for example, in which there is one conventional scene, shot outdoors to the sound of passing traffic, in which a straight-acting local white boy is fucked by a *beur*, then by a black boy; directly followed by the video's final, staged set piece, it is a camp take on a gang-bang fantasy, in which the humour arises from the class parody.

Three supposedly bad boys drive into a deserted carpark in their sleek BMW break with their abducted partner tied up in the boot. It is the over-attention to apparel that gives the game away: whilst the feminine, passive, middle-class boy is explicitly whitened by a tight T-shirt (kept on for its sex appeal), there is more than a hint of the 'bling-king' about the active trio with their flashy accessories and diamanté medallions. The parading of male fashion accessories gestures not only to a cultural translation of African-American 'gangster rap' culture to the local context of the Parisian *banlieue*, but also to the queer practices of drag performance that seek to lay bare the artificial construction of gender (Butler 1990). I agree with Maxime Cervulle (Cervulle 2007) that the carpark sequence is closer to a queer appropriation than to a straight rendition of *banlieue* virility. In hegemonic representations of masculinity influenced by African-American popular culture, the gender performance of both the boys and the girls is dependent on conspicuous consumption – the penchant for gold chains and diamonds. However in this parody version, it is only the active masculine trio that gets to dress up, whereas the more feminine passive boy is characterised by a more low-key gender performance. The effect of this opposition is that it inevitably tends to re-position the white gay subject (whom the studio presumably targets as its main consumer) at the 'natural' centre of the action, by associating middle-class whiteness with femininity and passivity. This revealing sequence effectively locates a blind spot in Citébeur's ambitious project to decentre gay subjectivity. After all, as is the case in much gay porn, it is the white passive performer who leads the action and orientates the spectator's gaze towards his own objects of desire – in this case towards his lower-class masculine partners.[16]

Critics might indeed argue that this porn dovetails neatly with the demands of the dominant white market, because all this talk of urban virility simply mimes one underlying colonial perception of Arab men as potential rough trade. But, whilst some gay *beur* men are keen to resist the dominant image of *racaille/lascar*, others evidently take serious pleasure in such identification and exploit the commercial interest in same-sex *racaille* identities. The Citébeur website and porn production act as necessary alternative spaces from which to challenge the somewhat parochial purview of much of the gay milieu. The point of Chibikh's cheap, independent porn is not only to cater to middle-class curiosity to sell the expensive DVDs, but to give some *cité*-boys the images they want, to reject the colonialist porn of the sort made by Jean-Daniel Cadinot, famous for his classic fetish film *Harem* (1984) and its controversial update *Hammam* (2004), and by Jean-Noël René Clair (the *Studio Beurs* series), who plays on the notion of 'auteur-porn' by developing a distinctive sub-genre of documentary-naturalism. His *Studio Beurs* series has been described as Arab fetish porn pushing the erotics of poverty to their limits. The overall perception from *Studio Beurs* is that the pornographer's technique is to lure poor, working-class Arab immigrants in off the streets of Marseille to perform for cash, a manoeuvre that makes much of the unease of the performers, who are persuaded to strip from their workmen's overalls as a kind of vicarious foreplay for the spectator.

René Clair is a prolific producer, expanding his niche in ethnic fetish porn to uncharted national markets, notably Eastern Europe. A political as opposed to a user-friendly reading would see René Clair's *Studio Beurs* series as old-school colonialist porn, a neatly packaged and updated colonial fantasy that bundles up ethnicity, masculinity and class. In relation to the series, Royce Mahawatte has described what the fetish porn genre teaches us about the lurid workings of the gay gaze. 'Are these men no more than a blank canvas for the inscription of white ethnic angst?' (Mahawatte 2004: 133). The raw simplicity and amateurishness of the scenes filmed in Marseille point to class (overriding ethnicity) as the principal turn-on; Mahawatte astutely draws our attention away from the fit models to their social shells:

> The clothes the models wear are cheap and comfortable – probably their own. There has been no attempt to dress these men up as anything else but working-class immigrants who have just walked into the studio off the street. In fact this is, clearly, the unique selling point of the film . . . The inference is that these are the kind of men who are socially dangerous, from a forbidden part of town and sexually masculine. They are part of an underclass – this association emphasises the men's foreignness and their sexual allure. (Mahawatte 2004: 132)

Mahawatte is right to argue that René Clair's is old-school colonial porn. But it is also technically proficient.[17] Although the solo scenes of *beur* men in his video *Bidasses: Blacks/Blancs/Beurs* make the ethnic voyeurism and class exploitation too apparent, the sequence between a blond passive performer and his black active partner is more nuanced. While the colonial ideology underpinning the video's marketing strategy would seek to coerce the white gay user to identify accordingly (desire for the butch black man), it is the sexy white man who leads proceedings. This move supports the widespread consumer perception of gay porn as seeking ideally to combine a passive performer, who is meant to have the required technical expertise, with an active performer, who merely has to be butch.

René Clair is particularly defensive about the apparent heterosexuality of his Arab models, wishing to divorce perverse acts from the threat of gay identity. Take it like a man, it won't make you gay, we are to infer. In one TV interview, he is anxious to promote his models' straight credentials, thus sweeping aside the possibility of Arab same-sexuality.[18] This is not just a matter of over-simplistic representation; it is a neatly packaged and updated commercial manipulation of colonial fantasy, in which difference and otherness, manliness and class are all bundled up together to sell and to control. Echoing Saïd's point in *Orientalism* that '[e]ach age and society re-creates its "Others"' (Saïd 1995: 332), Mahawatte concludes by remarking that '[t]he spectre of gay orientalism is still with us; it has simply changed its medium' (Mahawatte 2004: 135). I agree with Mahawatte that all this interest in masculinity by white and *beur* men alike sees class subsumed into ethnicity. Ultimately such myths of manliness are always over-blown: *beur* men see them either as an artificial strait-jacket, or as images to be excessively parodied or venerated. But the potential side-effect of such pornography is the over-determination of hegemonic masculinity, obscuring the more intricate web of social factors that potentially go to make erotic fantasy and sexual relations so exciting.

THE *BEUR* FACES OF FRENCH QUEER CINEMA

The spectre of gay orientalism is of course not limited to pornographic production; more culturally prestigious modes of representation such as art cinema simply wrap it up in challenging aesthetics or lofty speculation. In fact, it provides the ideological basis for a cluster of contemporary queer films that work interest in the bodies and subjectivities of *beur* men (with differing emphasis depending on the director) into their fields of vision. Carrie Tarr's comprehensive survey of *beur* and *banlieue* filmmaking in France (Tarr 2005) includes analyses of two films incorporating transgender dissent into the *beur* thematic landscape. The first is Liria Bégéja's melodrama *Change-moi ma vie* (2001), with Fanny Ardant as a failing actress supported by two of the most prominent *beur* actors in recent years – Roschdy Zem and Sami Bouajila, who improbably, as Tarr notes, play transgender sex workers out on the boulevards, a dubious ideological manoeuvre that predictably conflates prostitution and transgender with performance. Tarr also discusses Ahmed Bouchaala's *Origine contrôlée* (2001), which, she argues, encourages the targeted white audience to identify with the male protagonist to gain an insight into the lives of transsexuals and immigrants, a laudable, but hardly radical, strategy. The first film to deal with myths of *beur* masculinity and same-sex attraction in tandem in a contemporary setting was Gaël Morel's *A toute vitesse* (1996), a precursor that deftly positions the *beur* male character as the subject (rather than the object) of unrequited desire.

Olivier Ducastel and Jacques Martineau's gay road-movie *Drôle de Félix* (2000), which is covered in Chapter 4 with regard to its no-nonsense representation of HIV-positive identity, has rightly been admired for its attempt to juggle issues of cultural and sexual difference within the broader political landscape of far-right extremism. Joseph McGonagle commends the film's ability to structure its protagonist's plural identities (mixed-race *beur*, gay, HIV-positive, unemployed) as fluid, 'at times both aware and unaware of homosexuality as having a wider political meaning, constructed as "beur" and yet never confirmed as such' (McGonagle 2007: 31). The erasure of Félix's ethnic roots has however been criticised by Vinay Swamy who sees the film as a trade-off between ethnic identity and the re-configuration of alternative family structures:

> By privileging an all-white cast of characters as the face of Félix's family, the film problematically puts under erasure both the multi-ethnic origins of the protagonist, and the multicultural reality of contemporary France. In so doing, it subscribes, perhaps inadvertently, to the myth of the Republican ideal of seamless integration into a 'French' melting pot. (Swamy 2006: 62)

Whilst *Drôle de Félix* seeks to play around with identity categories, it tends to avoid putting them into play at once; it consequently avoids the complex question of how the formations of gay identity and seropositivity, kinship relations and ethnic origins can be articulated together. Whilst *Drôle de Félix* is not pushing a wholly republican agenda on minority politics, it tends to focus on the protagonist's sexual identity at the expense of a fuller exploration of his mixed-race ethnicity. When the issue of racism is tackled towards the last quarter of the film, Félix is given a clumsy tirade against *le Front national*, leaving us to assume that Ducastel and Martineau are meaning to address the politics of identity in the film's narrative resolution. This is confirmed by Martineau, who, at the time of the film's UK release, located the film's ideological point as 'the question of identity. Félix finds a lot of opportunities to redefine his whole identity, because he's gay, he's of Arabic origin, he's HIV-positive and so on. The trip was really a way to experiment with his whole identity.'[19] Ducastel, however, argues that 'none of these preoccupations is the subject of the film'[20] ('aucune de ces caractéristiques n'est le sujet du film'). This contradiction highlights how openly gay French filmmakers are more willing to promote a queer reading of their work to Anglo-American audiences than on home soil where identity politics are perceived as a critical liability to a film's promotion in spite of the existence of an expanding niche market for gay cinema.

Tarr also argues that *Drôle de Félix* successfully avoids an obsessive focus on its protagonist's body despite discreetly exhibiting Bouajila's beauty as the object of desire not purely for an admiring audience, but also for other characters such as the elderly lady (Patachou), whom he meets on the course of his journey.

> Such a plurality of desiring gazes at the body of a youth of Maghrebi descent is extremely unusual in French cinema. Although a desiring homosexual or homosocial gaze is to be found in films such as Gaël Morel's *A toute vitesse* (1996) and Jean-Pierre Sinapi's *Vivre me tue* (2003), the ethnic minority bodies which are the objects of desire in such narratives are often subsequently contained or destroyed. In this case, however, Félix is not just the object of the gaze, but also an active, optimistic, desiring subject in his own right. (Tarr 2005: 149–50)

This insight into Ducastel and Martineau's approach to filming *beur*/mixed-race masculinity points to the care taken to avoid the pitfalls of the Arab fetish film that would rigidly contain or violently destroy the *beur* male body. Philippe Valois's *Un parfum nommé Saïd* (2003) traps the Arab body through the tourist's visual framing of Morocco. A fictive documentary filmmaker Gérard is passionate about a beautiful younger man Saïd, quaintly perceived as an oriental mirage, who happens by perfect coincidence to be drawn to the older, less physically appealing Western tourist. The age difference is the key vector as Valois's tourist traces the precedent for passionate affairs with younger, masculine, married men back to Jean Genet. Another example of Arab fetish film would be Philippe Barassat's short film, *Mon copain Rachid* (1998), part of a collection of Barassat's short stylised films released as *Folle de Rachid en transit sur mars* (2001), which recounts a young boy's fascination with his older friend's penis. The early sequences reduce both characters to their physicality to comic effect, contrasting Rachid's emerging manliness with Eric's scrawny whiteness. The film's ideological strands are ambivalent, however; whiteness is certainly attacked by excessive parody and Arab culture fantasised as a joyous antidote, but the dominant representation of the virile *beur* boy, with connotations of the sexually voracious, is nevertheless reinforced. The *beur* male is still inevitably reduced to his body.

Gay culture's insistent promotion of the *beur* male body is channelled through erotic and artistic imagery that effectively exploits ethnic and racial difference as a profitable means of varying its bland iconography of white physical perfection. For instance, from 2002 onwards *Têtu* magazine has consistently promoted white, muscular and hairless torsos on its cover, sticking to the dominant imagery derived from US/north-west European gay male identity. The co-opting of *beur* male bodies for mainstream gay consumption in fashion photography, for example, seeks to draw attention to their 'essential' difference from the intended white consumer (for example, by emphasising darker skin tone and perceived 'ethnic' physical features) while adapting the context to comply with the existing visual codes of white gay culture. The ethnicity of the model may be dissimilar to that of the targeted audience but his image will inevitably be re-packaged to appear less alienating (unlike the commercial strategy used in 'ethnic' porn in which the visible signs of class or racial difference are an instrumental selling-point).

A photo-spread of actor Salim Kechiouche for *Têtu* in February 2006, shot by Youssef Nabil and styled by Romain Vallois, aimed to promote not only a range of clothing that mixed luxury labels (Gilles Rosier, Jean-Paul Gaultier and Prada) with high-street (American Apparel) and sports labels (Nike), but also the media profile of an actor whose career had taken off in the 1990s with roles in films by gay directors, including Gaël Morel's *A toute vitesse* (1996) and François Ozon's *Les Amants criminels* (1999), followed by Robert Salis's *Grande école* (2003) and Morel's *Le Clan* (2003). Gay culture's contextual promotion of Kechiouche predictably regards the actor's fit body as his leading asset – unlike Michel Giliberti's sensual oil paintings of Kechiouche that emphasise his musculature,[21] all but one of Youssef Nabil's six photos 'feminise' the model to some degree either by figuring him in submissive poses or vulnerable positions, or by dressing him in flamboyant attire from labels with a clear gay creative (Gaultier) or consumer (American Apparel) appeal. The image accompanying the interview with the actor dispenses with clothing altogether by showing off his trim, naked torso, cutting the image off at the midriff. Another shot self-consciously juxtaposes various gender signs through clashing sartorial styles – it shows Kechiouche sitting cross-legged and smiling seductively at the camera; the effeminate top-half of the frame, which includes a frilly dress-shirt and a made-up face, contrasts with a virile lower-half of dark hairy legs in revealing sports shorts. The one more traditionally masculine image works markers of foreign national and working-class origins into the frame by showing the model stern-faced, sitting open-legged, and wearing Nike sportswear, including a sleeveless T-shirt in the colours of the Moroccan flag with the country's name emphatically printed across the *beur* man's chest. This is clearly part of the brand's wily commercial strategy to recuperate patriotic imagery, the arrogant imperialism of which is all the more striking considering the model is of Algerian and not Moroccan origin.

Kechiouche is one of the two prominent *beur* faces of French queer cinema (alongside Yasmine Belmadi), particularly following his role as the object of psychotic desire in Ozon's *Les Amants criminels* which brought him to the attention of other filmmakers. He has since worked on queer projects that have cashed in on regressive archetypes of Arab masculinity, playing disturbed gigolos – playing Pasolini's murderer Guiseppe Pelosi in Michel Azama's biographical stage play *Vie et Mort de Pier Paolo Pasolini* (filmed by Cyril Legann and Antoine Soltys in 2004), and acting alongside gay icon Amanda Lear in Bastien Schweitzer's short film *Gigolo* (2004). The publicity still by artists Pierre et Gilles for *Vie et Mort de Pier Paolo Pasolini* pictured a semi-naked Kechiouche as the incarcerated Pelosi, handcuffed and kneeling submissively.

Kechiouche has also taken roles that have cast him against type, playing the vulnerable, spurned lover in *Grande école* for example, a film promoted as an exploration of the bisexual plurality of desire. The publicity included a titillating image of the naked intertwined bodies of the five principal actors shot from behind and lighted so as to erase the visible signs of ethnic difference between Kechiouche and the other actors. *Grande école* is set in a prestigious university, in which the prevailing sex/gender system is upheld by white middle-class hegemony. A schematic economic divide between the select elite and the non-white labourers is disrupted by a male student's desire for a manual worker played by Kechiouche. Paul (Grégori Baquet) is embarrassed by the social shame of falling for a labourer, an anxiety echoed by a Freudian flashback, in which his father reprimands his son for playing with the workers. Kechiouche's character Mécir plays the role of the '*beur de service*' for director Robert Salis and screenwriter Jean-Marie Besset (from whose stage play the film was adapted), who use him as proof of their liberal credentials. The populist anti-elitist message is that Mécir's own school is the street, as valid an education as the posh institution. Mécir also feels used by the protagonist, who comes out to his colleagues but cannot reconcile the social barrier in their relationship. The two men only connect when they escape from their social prison to a hotel on the coast, where they are free to make love. The scene is filmed as an overwrought homage to Cocteau, in which the use of multiple mirrors only magnifies the naked embarrassment of the two heterosexual actors who struggle to perform together.

Kechiouche's first acting role was as Jamel in Morel's teen movie *A toute vitesse*, influenced by the American tradition of fast cars and sexy motorbikes, transposed to the *banlieues* of Lyon. Kechiouche's body is exposed to a captive audience to show them the scars of a racist attack, a political stunt instigated by the protagonist Quentin (Pascal Cervo), who is fast becoming a successful writer and who wants to use his local celebrity to contest far-right extremism. Although Kechiouche's body is not primarily intended for voyeuristic consumption in this sequence, Jamel uses the opportunity to smile at a keen girl on the front row, and his brother is later angry at Quentin's manipulation of the episode, using Jamel as an object paraded in front of the local community. However, Morel's film works hard to reject the restrictions of *beur* objectification by including a shot of Jamel secretly writing in a deserted cellar (writing perceived as a secret escape route from the *banlieue*) and a more sustained narrative strand on unrequited love, focusing on Samir (Meziane Bardadi), an Algerian character who is in love with Quentin.

The evocation in *A toute vitesse* of a turbulent male youth expressed through poetic naturalism – an American theme in a French package – matured into the post-adolescent male angst of Morel's third film, *Le Clan* (2004), co-written by Christophe Honoré, described by Morel on the DVD edition as a 'homophile' rather than an explicitly gay or queer film. *Le Clan* opens with a dynamic shot of the athletic Kechiouche running along a country lane pursued by a group of youths on motorbikes. *Le Clan* marked the end of a cycle of films on teen masculinity – his later star vehicle *Après lui* (2007), also co-written by Honoré, with Catherine Deneuve transgressing sexual taboos of age difference as a grieving mother obsessed by her son's best friend, marked a more 'feminine' orientation to Morel's filmmaking. His directorial career began with the short film *La Vie à rebours* (1994), which established his provincial landscape of male fraternal bonding and violence in a rural working-class milieu, and which was dedicated to André Téchiné, who had cast him as the sexually confused teenager in *Les Roseaux sauvages* (1994). Morel waited six years after *A toute vitesse* before releasing *Les Chemins de l'oued* (2002), a narrative of cultural self-discovery focusing on an errant *beur* boy (Nicolas Cazalé) exiled from Paris and on the run in Algeria.

The relentless pace of the narrative of the first section of *Le Clan* is also emblematic of Morel's insistence on male characters in perpetual movement. The film is divided into three equal sections in distinct genres (teen movie, social realism and lyrical melodrama) focusing in turn on one of the three mixed-race brothers from a *banlieue* near Annecy: Christophe (Stéphane Rideau), who strives to rebuild his career after being freed from prison; Marc (Nicolas Cazalé) whose aggressive melancholy leaves him paralysed from a self-inflicted car accident; and the youngest brother Olivier (Thomas Dumerchez), who is struggling to come to terms with their mother's death and his own homosexual desire, and who falls in love with the brothers' friend Hicham (Kechiouche), who is considered throughout as a non-blood brother, but is ultimately rejected by Olivier from their fraternal intimacy.

The final section of *Le Clan* makes the underlying sexual tension between Hicham and Olivier explicit. The sentimentalism of the final section, which indulges in reassuring melodramatic clichés of doomed love, an emotional relief after the dour social realism of the middle part, is reliant on the contrapuntal editing of images of the lovers' ephemeral happiness – including a luminous sun-bleached shot of Dumerchez and Kechiouche riding a moped around Annecy lake – with Hicham's poignant commentary on their failed relationship. In a voice-over letter addressed to his former lover, Hicham recounts his new life in Paris, where he has discovered that *beur* men are hot commodities on the gay market. The humanist ideology upholding *Le Clan* seeks to showcase Hicham's kindness (through the loving attention he gives to the brothers early on) and vulnerability (through the loss he feels for Olivier by the end), a manoeuvre designed to balance the aggressive machismo of Marc with this softer, more humane face of *beur* masculinity.

This contrast also works to direct spectator sympathy towards the gay couple earlier on by separating out Olivier and Hicham from the other members of their male entourage, whose gender identities are formed through a combination of narcissistic mirroring and self-conscious preening. During a group visit to a sex worker, who takes a stand against the men's aggressiveness and shame, Hicham asks her to turn over and display her male genitalia – the other men will only engage in queer acts if the sex worker is in drag with her male genitals obscured. Body shaving is used as a leitmotif for the men's volatile, insecure masculinity with shots of Marc being shaved surrounded by his mates and then later shaving his pubic hair in private. Morel hints at the proximity between a heterosexual performance of masculinity – the film's 'homosocial' mode[22] – and a queer desire for the male body, by mirroring the homoerotic sequences of male bonding with one of the two lovers, in which Hicham shaves Olivier's ass as foreplay to passionate sex.

Critics of the film were particularly harsh towards Morel's explicit eroticisation of the actors' bodies, a dubious critical bias when one considers that the same reviewers tend not to protest when male heterosexual directors linger on the female form. Actor Nicolas Cazalé was perceived as the main focus of Morel's directorial desire, caught between a standard virility and a 'ridiculous femininity' (comprising of body shaving and excessive affection for his pet dog) according to *Cahiers du cinéma*.[23] Group sex notwithstanding, sport is shown to be the primary social outlet for masculine prowess, establishing a contrast between the tough boys' physical training – the results of which are displayed for one another in a sequence shot by the lake in which Morel's camera insistently pans across their fit bodies – and Hicham's practice of the Afro-Brazilian martial art/game *capoeira*, which mixes martial art with fluid movement akin to dance, suggested as a sign of the character's own more fluid queer identity. (The title chosen for the US release of *Le Clan* was *Three Dancing Slaves* in reference to *capoeira*'s roots as a black Brazilian slave dance.)

The film's most enigmatic shot of the three brothers naked, their bodies suggestively intertwined, silently observed by their father, not only highlights Morel's erotic interest in the male form, but also acknowledges voyeurism as one of the film's most consistent and problematic concerns. Morel's directorial bent was criticised in homophobic fashion by the reviewer of *Le Figaro*, who wishfully thought that *Le Clan* could be viewed as the story of a family, were it not 'first and foremost the story of a director who allows his own tendencies for male bodies to interfere' ('*Le Clan* pourrait être l'histoire d'une famille, si ce n'était avant tout l'histoire d'un réalisateur qui se laisse aller à son penchant pour les corps masculins'). Morel is cavalierly dismissed as a director who is 'visibly obsessed by beautiful young men' ('visiblement obsédé par les éphèbes').[24] Morel has always been open about his directorial desire. In an early report on the shooting of *A toute vitesse* in 1995 in *Cahiers du cinéma*, Morel exposed his artistic grounding within the French cinematic tradition of poetic naturalism (including the importance of social milieu and spontaneous non-acting) and his own directorial desire for the marginal populations he chooses to film.[25]

There is, however, a difference between admiration and the occasional touches of voyeurism in *Le Clan* – an objectification that goes beyond the obvious technical imperative of a camera to focus on an object. Morel acknowledges his strategy as a gay director is to eroticise male bodies, but he declines to acknowledge the ethical complications involved in the gaze of a white director. This contradiction is particularly apparent in the interviews accompanying the DVD release of *Les Chemins de l'oued*, which includes the casting of actor Kheireddine Defdaf. The scene includes a fair amount of seduction as the experienced director asks the nervous actor about any previous film experience, the camera shooting him head-on, zooming in and out to inspect his face. On balance, though, it is fair to say that Morel goes to some lengths to shoot *beur* male subjectivity in complex and varied guises (particularly in his refusal to comply with Kechiouche's established image) and whilst he consciously eroticises male bodies, he avoids focusing solely on *beur* men.

Morel's ambivalent approach to *beur* masculinity is not one shared by Ozon, whose critical stance is one of apparent postcolonial unawareness. As Alain Brassart explains (Brassart 2007: 200), Ozon's fantasy film *Les Amants criminels* reworks the fairy-tale genre historically associated with queer directors such as Cocteau (*L'Eternel retour*, 1943, and *La Belle et la bête*, 1946) and Demy (*Peau d'âne*, 1970). It also updates the genre by mixing in hybrid elements from the crime thriller and by taking the male body as the primary source of pleasure – Kechiouche is filmed as an object to be desired and devoured, figuratively by the camera and literally by the criminal lovers. Luc (Jérémie Renier) is persuaded by Alice (Natacha Régnier) to kill their classmate Saïd (Kechiouche) because she claims that he had filmed his friends raping her and is now blackmailing her for a date. Following the murder, the lovers flee to a forest, where they dispose of Saïd's body before being captured and tortured by an ogre (Miki Manojlovic). The police finally hunt them down and shoot Alice dead. It is the couple's macabre fantasies (the film's final shot acknowledges Luc's own desire for the ogre) that frame Ozon's images of Kechiouche. The *beur* boy is here denied any sense of subjectivity, existing purely as a figure of the lovers' distorted imaginations. As Andrew Asibong has argued in relation to the ethical trajectory of Ozon's early filmmaking, it is 'the fetishized and dehumanized body of a person, Saïd – a feared, hated, eroticized object of study that needs to be endlessly watched, described and mastered – that serves as the conduit for the transgressive desires of the protagonists' (Asibong 2005: 211).

The film was originally structured in a straightforward linear chronology that was then edited into a final cut using flashbacks as a means of explaining the lovers' criminal motivation and perverse fantasies. The film was hailed as a flop on its release in 1999,[26] a disappointment that led Ozon to cut the use of flashbacks down to a minimum for its later DVD release in 2001, a re-structuring aimed at simplifying the chronology. The original montage inserts the flashbacks into the narrative as subjective fantasies of Saïd, allowing the spectator fuller insight into the lovers' disturbed psyches. The original cut also presents Saïd as a crude colonialist cliché of the 'Arab boy' – he is shown preening in front of a mirror in front of his friend Karim (Yasmine Belmadi) while preparing for his date with Alice, fantasising over sexual possibilities, with both characters reproducing the sexist language assumed to suit the *racaille* stereotype. However, the use of cross-cutting between the criminal lovers and the *beur* boys is effective at suggesting the homoeroticism beneath their performance of macho bravado – Saïd is shown re-enacting the seduction of Alice by assuming her place and stroking Karim's torso, the brief suggestion of male desire broken by their return to their properly homosocial friendship based on a shared rejection of an abject queerness. A more ambitious edit would have kept the ambiguous possibility of ensuing action between the two boys by cutting the scene before the inclusion of the final heterosexual imperative.

Elsewhere, the film uses flashback fantasy as a devise to move the fairy tale off the straight and narrow. The revised montage actually dilutes the queer undercurrent to the heterosexual coupling, an element present in the original cut through the pair's reversed gender roles – Alice shows proof of her mastery of Luc by blindfolding him, then photographing him naked, threatening to expose his sexual submission to his male peers. He subsequently assists her by making up her face in the mirror in a sequence that indicates the couple failing to comply with the logic of heterosexuality founded on the normative distribution of gender attributes. That Luc and Alice do not form the picture of a 'normal' couple is enhanced by the subsequent fairy-tale mode of the forest sequences suggesting an incestuous Hansel and Gretel motif, and by the felicitous casting of two actors with virtually homophonic names (a minimal pair), a virtual sameness acted out through their characters' reflection in the mirror. The magical sequence in which the tripartite mirror is theatrically opened out to reveal Régnier's reflection dominating the frame's foreground positions Renier's naked torso in the background, with Luc subjugated as Alice's handmaiden, dressing her for murder. The couple's heterosexuality is suggested to be psychically troubled and potentially queer – the sequence finishes with Luc giving Alice a platonic peck on the cheek as they complicity admire one another in the mirror. Saïd's traditionally virile performance of masculinity is also undercut by its traditionally 'feminine' positioning as the focus of the couple's shared lust. The *beur* man exists here only as an empty receptacle for the fantasies of others.

The revised montage of the film opens with the scene in which Alice reads a poem by Rimbaud in front of the class, projecting its theme of demise onto Saïd, whose neck she has been sketching. The prolonged close-up of Kechiouche turning around to acknowledge her seductive reading establishes his character as the object of her predatory lust. Alice is one in a line of threatening female characters who end up getting pretty much what they deserve, hence the charges of misogyny against Ozon (Brassart 2007; Burch 2007). The publicity for the film draws attention to Alice's aggressiveness through a still of Régnier wearing Saïd's boxing gloves. Luc, in contrast, is not shown actively to desire her at all unless provoked – the self-consciously ironic parody of heterosexual lovemaking towards the end, in which the lovers, having escaped the ogre's clutches, celebrate their freedom at one with nature and serenaded by uplifting orchestral music, effectively renders heterosexual desire highly artificial and intentionally hard to take. The irony derives from the camera's close-up insistence on Renier's active backside during the love-making; the same backside that was penetrated by the ogre a few minutes earlier.

Luc's gaze is more willingly directed at Saïd in the flashback sequences in the original and in the early sequences in the revised montage. An establishing shot of Luc entering the potentially homoerotic space of the male toilets is followed by one of him observing Saïd and Karim compare notes on style at the urinals; male bonding is shown to be a possible sublimation of queerness, as Karim takes a look while Saïd urinates. Luc observes them cautiously from a distance as they goad him about his virginity in front of Alice, who has burst in, replacing Luc as the scene's voyeur. The painted photograph of Kechiouche in character by artists Pierre et Gilles (*Saïd*, 1999) humorously points to the queer desire in all-male space by having Kechiouche pose next to a urinal, thereby including a sly reference to gay cruising. Pierre et Gilles's image more problematically focuses on the model's skin as part of his prized beauty. The artists chose to elaborate on the deadly shower scene in *Les Amants criminels*, with a shot of Kechiouche looking over his shoulder, frowning at the intrusive photographer, with drops of water running down his naked back, the actor's dark skin and hair made to gleam in contrast to his spotlighted face. The image is indeed ambivalent: while it showcases Kechiouche's beauty, it also points to the *beur* male body as the object for gay visual consumption par excellence. In that respect, the expression of resentment on Kechiouche's face is all too revealing. Taken out of the immediate context of Ozon's film, Pierre et Gilles's image of Kechiouche is simply beautiful; read in the context of a film that gives him very little to do except to be desired and consumed by everyone else (including the director), the image is indeed problematic, since it could be said to reproduce the colonialist logic whereby the *beur* man would essentially be trapped as a victim of his own physicality.

Luc's subsequent observation of Saïd boxing is the first indication of his desire for *beur* masculinity, as his gaze scans the room before settling on Saïd in action. The editing works to display Luc's reaction to Saïd's body as the camera cuts from a subjective shot of the boxing ring to a reverse shot moving dramatically back into the frame and emphasised by a musical crescendo to capture the actor's prolonged expression of arousal before Luc dutifully slopes off into the locker room to steal Saïd's knife in preparation for the killing. The gory climax to these scenes of voyeurism includes a prolonged shot of Alice pleasurably observing Saïd shower, Kechiouche even turning around to display his naked body to the camera. Luc passively watches Saïd scramble over Alice's body, waiting until she turns Saïd over to enable Luc to stab him. Ozon's ruse is to parody the psychological codes of the horror genre by pointing to the closet as the home of psychotic drives – a knowing nod to Hitchcock's famous shower scene and his grossly homophobic portrayal of the killer in *Psycho* (1960). By foregrounding Luc's deviant desire, Ozon denies a straight reading of the killing of Saïd, pointing instead to Luc's feelings of shame and self-disgust, leading him to kill the wrong object, stifling his queerness through a homicidal projection onto the Arab body.

The hint of queerness about Luc is further suggested through the editing of the flashbacks in both the original and revised versions including a sequence inserted before he eats Saïd's flesh, in which he is shown to cry at the sight of Alice and Saïd kissing, an ambiguous reaction that could easily register jealousy of either of the two characters. The shower scene is not unproblematic since it replaces the sadistic pleasure (one that is vicariously imposed on the audience) of stabbing the helpless blonde woman in the traditional horror genre with the similar defiling of the helpless *beur* man in this post-modern tribute. Ozon's slow-motion editing of the killing for the final cut (changed to accelerated editing for the director's cut) certainly works to distance the actual effect of the slaughter, and the subsequent imagery of cleansing the characters' bodies of Saïd's blood might easily symbolise their complacent evacuation of guilt. Yet the cumulative effect of the repeated thrusts of the knife, Alice's sexual voice-over expressing her racially motivated lust for Saïd's skin, her later masturbatory fantasy of the ogre seducing then strangling Saïd, and the images of his dismembered body, invite the spectator to indulge in the film's vicious pleasure. They also evoke the history of violence done to Arab bodies examined by Sidi Mohammed Barkat in *Le Corps d'exception: Les artifices du pouvoir colonial et la destruction de la vie* (Barkat 2005), where he describes the reduction of the colonised to their dehumanised and organic bodies, a reduction to organic matter rendered literal by the fictive slaughter of Saïd.

In light of the second half of the film, it could of course be argued that this ideological reading of *Les Amants criminels* misses the ironic point (Ozon's celebrated mode), for the ogre digs up the corpse and sadistically spoon-feeds Saïd's decomposed body to his 'slave' Luc, a sinister, but cheeky, take on erotic deviance in which the body Luc desires is literally served up to him on a plate. Asibong argues, however, that criticism of Ozon's ironic superficiality obscures any analysis of the filmmaker's more ethical project: 'Through this vector of fantastical metamorphosis, Ozon's films confront us with the possibility of actually becoming the "foreign body" we always thought of as somebody – or something – else, and through which we have hitherto channelled our unchecked desires' (Asibong 2005: 206). Asibong's analysis of Saïd as the 'fetishized' object shows how Luc is substituted by the ogre as the object, 'like Saïd, he can be ceaselessy watched; like Saïd, he can be ruthlessly penetrated; like Saïd, he can be cheerfully eaten' (Asibong 2005: 214). In relation to Ozon's subsequent film *Gouttes d'eau sur pierres brûlantes* (2000), the ironic distance of camp is likewise seen by Fiona Handyside to be part of Ozon's re-working of the genre of melodrama through the declared lineage to Fassbinder and Sirk (Handyside 2007). I would argue in the context of *Les Amants criminels* that his fantasy aesthetic works here as a defence mechanism against possible criticisms of the retrograde imagery of *beur* masculinity, in much the same way that the pastel pastiche of *Huit femmes* (2001) works overtime to neutralise a complacent manipulation of its female characters. Handyside argues that Ozon's generic play clearly aims to move away from the French realist tradition of engagement with political and social issues (*Les Amants criminels* is certainly not making a specific point about *beur* men in French society). It may also be said to deflect criticism of the regressive ideologies contained within the rubric of a post-modern parody of the generic codes of cinema. *Les Amants criminels* is complemented by imagery from artists Pierre et Gilles, who are celebrated for their consistent gender-bending, their saturated colours and their post-modern re-spinning of myths. Another of their stylised images of Kechiouche as the defunct Saïd, entitled *Le Renard* (*The Fox*, 1999), shows the actor's glistening body placed in an open grave in a highly artificial moonlighted forest, accompanied by an image of the criminal lovers in a similarly fake setting, Régnier's blood-stained dress edged out of the frame by the cheeky focus on Renier's naked buttocks.

Pierre et Gilles's original publicity shot for Sébastien Lifshitz's first full-length feature *Presque Rien* (2000) also showed the full-frontal nudity of the film's principal actors (Jérémie Elkaïm and Stéphane Rideau), and was coyly cut off at the midriff for the film's official release. The image nevertheless focused on the boys' white bodies as the product's selling point. *Presque Rien*, a narrative of sexual discovery, holiday romance and subsequent loss, returned to the pre-occupations of Lifshitz's early shorter films about *beur* same-sexuality, but focused instead on white teenagers. One surprising sex scene between the two boys disturbed conventional gender assumptions by showing the more feminine of the boys (Elkaïm) take his more masculine partner (Rideau) in the sand dunes, breaking the conventional pattern of sliding femininity into passivity. Unlike this exploration of adolescent discovery, Lifshitz's two earlier medium-length features, both co-written with Stéphane Bouquet – *Les Corps ouverts* (1998) and *Les Terres froides* (1999) – offer more articulate and engaged readings of inter-racial relations, both navigating the traps of the dominant fetishisation of the *beur* male body in queer film. *Les Corps ouverts* was first presented at Cannes in 1998 and won the Jean Vigo prize for short film. The Franco-German channel Arte commissioned *Les Terres froides* for its political series 'Left/Right' in 1999. Lifshitz began his career with a documentary portrait of his mentor, Claire Denis (*Claire Denis la vagabonde*, 1995). Unlike Denis's poetic stylisation, Lifshitz's domain is more traditional narrative realism. Both Lifshitz's earlier films focus on the social predicament of young Arab men: in *Les Corps ouverts*, Rémi is a teenager caught between his duty and love for his ailing father and the discovery of his desire for men; and in *Les Terres froides*, Djamel, a young man who arrives in Grenoble in order to track down his father (a wealthy factory owner who promptly rejects him), decides ultimately to seduce his half-brother as the means of entry into the world of the white bourgeoisie. The title is a pointed reference to contemporary France as inhospitable. Djamel's treatment at the hands of the French bourgeoisie is set in Grenoble in mid-winter, the camera lingering on the frozen landscape.

The same actor (Yasmine Belmadi) plays both Rémi and Djamel. The camera actively seduces Belmadi who, as the uncertain teenager Rémi, aches to surrender to passivity. Conversely, in *Les Terres froides*, Lifshitz positions the spectator as Belmadi's object through identification with Laurent, the bourgeois son. The first shots of Rémi illustrate the two parallel thematic strands of ethnicity and sexuality. The opening shot is of Rémi on a bridge overlooking the Seine in central Paris, singing in Arabic to himself; this is followed by a scene with Rémi in bed observing a spider creep across his naked torso – the camera is initially focused on the spider climbing up his arm, then slowly pans out to reveal the rest of his open, upper body.

Lifshitz's most notable artistic technique is to splice up the film's chronology, enabling the spectator to jump from Rémi's scenes with a female lover to the central seduction scene and subsequent relationship scenes with a film director Marc (Pierre-Loup Rajot), who films Rémi on the casting couch. The interview scene first shows Marc question Rémi on his life, school and film preferences; as in the later part of the scene (a reading of Marc's film script), Rémi lets go, surrendering to Marc, who, assuming Lifshitz's position opposite Rémi, places a spotlight on his actor and films the interview from a side angle. In a later argument with Marc, Rémi admits to having spent the afternoon cruising in a sex-shop, abandoning himself to a male partner. (This is actually expressed by a deceptively passive construction, 'Je me suis laissé faire', literally 'I let myself be persuaded'.) The sex-shop encounter is with Lifshitz himself, who briefly slips in front of the camera to play Rémi's trick, enacting the director/actor seduction on screen.

Clearly part of Lifshitz's design was to sweep aside the image of the macho *beur* male. Working against the grain of fixed archetypes involves digging around for other images of *beur* men than the predictable drug dealers or rappers dominant in French cinema since Mathieu Kassovitz's celebrated dissection of urban ghetto life *La Haine* (1995). Crucial to the concerns of same-sex relations, the premise of Lifshitz's project is to chip away at dominant colonial stereotypes. Lifshitz captures the crucial point of passivity in the brief sex scene: he pictures Rémi taken by Marc face down on the bed, his expression of painful or ecstatic surrender shot in close-up. This same position is reversed in the later film in which Djamel enacts a revenge fuck on the white bourgeoisie.

Whilst Rémi is the sexually confused teenager, submissive to his director and charming to his female lover, Djamel in *Les Terres Froides* is the opposite, initially presented as sexually assertive. The opening scene shows him being fellated by a girlfriend. His arrival as an employee at his father's factory sees him charming a hostile female colleague; he eyes up girls in a restaurant and is shown masturbating to pornography. This of course is part of Lifshitz's device to change tack halfway following the father's racist rejection of Djamel, devoting the rest of the narrative to his seduction of Laurent. An element of the intrigue of the first half revolves around class envy and Djamel's obsession with the factory owner. He observes the palatial family house, spying on the son through binoculars, and surveys Laurent and a male lover ice-skating. This last instance reveals Lifshitz's interest in playing around with the camera to mobilise the sexual positioning of his performers: this is the moment Djamel realises that Laurent is gay. Djamel is filmed watching Laurent and his lover skate past, the lover in question again played by Lifshitz himself. The camera shoots Djamel's careful surveillance of the lovers panning round the ice rink, imagining them from Djamel's viewpoint. This is cut by a spotlighted shot of the two lovers kissing passionately, in what could quite realistically be a dark corner near the rink, or more symbolically Djamel's own fantasy scenario – the crucial moment of truth revealing (to us as much as to him) his subsequent sexual orientation. Director and actor have swapped positions: Belmadi, who has slipped behind the camera, is now spying on Lifshitz. We are ultimately envisioning same-sex passion from the position of the *beur* subject, no longer the fantasy object.

Djamel's plan is to pursue the son to get to the father. He stalks Laurent in a gay bar. Our gaze is directed solely at Djamel through a lingering shot of him actively desiring Laurent. Their subsequent date allows Djamel to achieve his goal of penetrating the father's household. It is unclear as to whether the seduction is calculated – his desire for Laurent is shown to be perfectly natural and adolescent. This involves shots of the two men joshing around in the snow, rather like the homosocial bonding of teenage boys, or brothers even. Between the two rounds of the 2002 presidential elections that saw the largest anti-fascist demonstrations ever in France, *Têtu* magazine asked filmmakers, artists and fashion designers to contribute images expressing their anger towards the rise of fascism. Lifshitz's image, entitled 'Brothers', consisted of two side-shot close-ups of himself and Belmadi, head to head, eyes closed in contemplation, surrounding a symbolic centrepiece of their joined hands.[27]

Alternative family structures form part of Lifshitz's thematic landscape. In *Les Terres froides*, Djamel's desire for Laurent is not only a projection of his desire for revenge on the unreceptive father, but a form of desire for the whole white middle-class culture that excludes him. His confession of lust for Laurent is highly symbolic, for it provides the means to enter the white bourgeoisie, the family he has been obsessively observing from the outside. The actual scene of sexual penetration resembles Marc penetrating Rémi in *Les Corps ouverts*: Djamel violently fucks Laurent, the camera focused on the facial expression of pain or exhilaration of the receptive partner.

Lifshitz slips ideology into the brothers' seduction scene. At one point, Laurent expresses his admiration for the resilience of young black and *beur* men, a different take on the issue of white fetishism. In this instance, the fascination is perceived as positive, an erotic mix of envy, admiration and idealisation. Djamel brings Laurent down to earth by referring to relations who have let themselves go to drugs or alcohol, but Laurent insists on black and Arab pride in being fit (physically and sexually) – the familiar truism of men as tough as nails – as an asset, a strategy for survival in a hostile society. This queer projection of *beur* and black masculinity attempts to avoid crude cliché by wrapping up physical attraction in positive values, notably pride and strength. Lifshitz shares Laurent's outlook on gay fantasy. He comments:

A lot of gay men have fantasies of Arab and black men. We see them as symbols of masculinity or a type of virility. They are obsessed by power and are forever shaping their bodies. Even powerless, the immigrant youth is magnificent. They take ultimate pride in their bodies, even if they often feel socially worthless. Gay men recognize that in black and Arab men.

(Chez beaucoup d'homos, il y a un fantasme des Beurs et des Blacks. On les voit comme des symboles de la masculinité ou d'une certaine virilité. Ils sont obsédés par la puissance et cultivent sans cesse leur corps. Même désoeuvrée, la jeunesse immigrée est magnifique. Leur corps, c'est leur dernière fierté, même s'ils ont souvent le sentiment de n'être rien dans la société. Les gays, eux, reconnaissent ça chez les Blacks ou les Beurs.)[28]

The drawback to this point of view is its tendency to slide *beur* and black men automatically into the masculine position, excluding ordinary effeminacy. However, Lifshitz's model of attraction and fascination for the Arab world does more than merely acknowledge erotic interest; he allows us to envisage some kinds of queer desire less as crude objectification, and more as possible forms of cultural contact across ethnic and racial lines.

QUEERING MIGRATION

The next step is to chart the overlapping intricacies of ethnicity and sexuality beyond white/*beur* couplings. Rémi Lange's *Tarik el hob* (2001) avoids the fantasies and involvement of white men altogether (apart from the director's own frame), preferring to explore *beur* sexual self-discovery outside of contact with the traditional structures of gay subculture. Lange's protagonist Karim (Karim Tarek) discovers his sexual desires for other men as bound up in his own Maghrebi cultural history and postcolonial milieu. As Denis Provencher remarks, Lange's film shows that 'any semblance of full expression of both sexual and ethnic identities must break away from the confines of [the] republican-based system [. . .] toward an alternative model that does not erase queer French and North-African references to difference' (Provencher 2008: 58–9). The film's first sequence works as a metaphor for the character's lack of sexual fixity. It shows Karim precariously balancing on a ledge outside a window much to the consternation of his girlfriend (Sihem Benamoune). Karim is a student of sociology working on a term paper on the Maghreb – the initial preoccupations of which are resumed as virginity, male anxiety, sex before marriage and the clash between tradition and modern life. Notwithstanding the obvious reference to Genet on the background-reading list, it gradually becomes apparent that Karim's interests are turning towards homosexuality, a television report on which is interwoven into a scene of concentrated study. Lange's technique is to alternate between the narrative of self-discovery and a cultural awakening to the history of Maghrebi and Egyptian same-sex practices. Karim's ethnographic project allows Lange to impose a grainy reality (shot entirely on digital video) and to insert interviews with author Abdellah Taïa, who recounts the institution of same-sex marriage as a long-standing tradition near the Libyan border with Egypt until the mid-twentieth century. This provides a long view on recent French debates on the PaCS and same-sex marriage, and calls into question the arrogant assumption that relatively local Euro-American formations should be exported to other settings as part of a project of cultural enlightenment.

Karim finds willing interviewees through the gay press who mistake his scholarship for the casting couch, but he is better served by immigrant organisations such as l'ARDHIS that provide social provision and legal counsel to queer 'undocumented' immigrants. Karim's developing relationship with another interviewee Farid (Riyad Echahi) enables him to acknowledge the possibility of an interest in homosexuality beyond the strictly academic. Lange works hard to avoid any cheap voyeuristic thrills by dispensing with devices used to position the spectator as 'naturally' white – the absence of any white actors eliminates a straightforward racial identification, and the casting of a physically unremarkable non-actor (Karim Tarek), whose own imperfect body is filmed without effect, blanks out gay culture's commercial and aesthetic demands for the *beur* pin-up. Without de-sexualising his characters, Lange shows their attraction to be less body-obsessed than is the case in standard gay representation, and more attuned to their shared cultural roots – the last section takes place in Marrakech, where Farid's ploy is to reconcile Karim's sexuality with his origins, setting an ultimatum whereby they should marry for Karim to be able to accept his desire as rooted in a specifically Egyptian and Maghrebi same-sex tradition (though they also pay homage to Genet's grave). Farid's novelist friend, Farid Tali, expresses doubts as to the scientific relevance of Karim's initially neutral observation of Arab homosexuality, throwing open the debate on directorial legitimacy in visual representation, a political debate about how *beur* men are both empowered (they are given interesting acting roles) and disempowered (the roles sometimes reinforce existing archetypes) by queer cinema, an existing tension exploited, as we have seen, by other directors such as Ozon or Morel. The session with a casting agency in *Tarik el hob* incorporates issues of objectification into the frame by filming Karim (Tarek), beautified by make-up and lights, though adorned less by Lange's camera than by the reaction shots of Farid. *Tarik el hob* shows the emotional commitment between *beur* and Maghrebi men themselves, a move that decentres gay visual production by ousting whiteness from the field of vision altogether, thereby managing to avoid any trace of directorial voyeurism or ethnographic condescension in the process.

The subplot in André Téchiné's *Les Temps qui changent* (2004) also situates a relationship outside the concerns of metropolitan gay culture in the wider context of social inequalities between France and the Maghreb. This thematic mix of sexuality and migration returns to the preoccupations of Téchiné's earlier *Loin* (2001), which had seen Gaël Morel and Stéphane Rideau reunited seven years after the filmmaker's landmark *Les Roseaux sauvages* (1994), and which had briefly featured the cultural history of gay artistic attachment to the Maghreb (through the peripheral figure of an American expatriate poet closely resembling Paul Bowles) within the larger scheme of East/West socio-economic disparity. The mixed-race character Sami (Malik Zidi) in *Les Temps qui changent* comes to Tangiers with Nadia (Lubna Azabal), to whom he is passionately but not sexually engaged, to visit his parents (Catherine Deneuve and Gilbert Melki) and to pay secret visits to his lover Bilal (Nadem Rachati). Sami's desire for Bilal is shown to be hindered not only by the character's own romantic notion of inaccessibility (his paternal feelings for Nadia's son are ultimately perceived to be incompatible with his desire for men) but also by the practical question of economic inequality – Bilal claims to have been unable to settle in Paris for fear of dependency on Sami. The two characters' desires are couched respectively in postcolonial pride and guilt – Bilal, who demands respect, accuses Sami of adopting the tendency of enlightened Europeans to apologise constantly. His explanation of Sami's emotional dislocation is rooted in his lover's bi-national origins (half French, half Moroccan) and his own more local understanding of homosexuality as a mix of the genders (half man, half woman).

Writing in *Têtu*, Yann Gonzalez criticised the film's apparent idle repetition of clichés of Arab masculinity and its failure to deliver a positive image of gay male relations by comparing heterosexual reconciliation – the main plotline foregrounds the efforts made by Antoine (Gérard Depardieu) to reunite with Cécile (Deneuve) – with homosexual impossibility, shown through a relationship mired by cultural misunderstanding and mutual distrust.[29] *Têtu*'s desire for positive images misses Téchiné's more challenging point, which is less concerned with a sexual comparison between the couples than with the presence of national and economic divisions in the gay relationship that are absent in the heterosexual one, more preoccupied as it is with the possibilities of enduring love between its ageing stars.

Les Temps qui changent sees the balance of power in gay relations shift from ethnicity and class (shown elsewhere in this chapter to be the primary vectors of power in gay representations of *beur* male sexuality) to nationality and migration. Bilal even dismisses his 'confused' lover for an apparent attempt to insert their relationship into the European tradition of sexual tourism, whereby the wealthier visitor would seek to take home an Arab boy as a commodity souvenir. This suspicion of imperialist intent is more blatantly formulated as the actual merchandising of the Arab body in Cadinot's porn 'classic' *Harem* (1984), the final scene of which showed the tourist attempting to persuade his reticent partner to leave Morocco; this scenario is later modified in an altered geo-political landscape by the sequel *Hammam* (2004), in which, in the context of post-9/11 phobia of an Islamic invasion of the West, the arrogant tourist has to fend off one 'salesman', who is keen to accompany him back to France by explaining the immigration policies of Fortress Europe (only then to haggle for his goods as if to re-assert his economic superiority). Cadinot actively promotes the underlying ideology of European sexual imperialism subtly criticised by Téchiné, though Sami is depicted more as an unwilling victim than a conscious perpetrator of the French/Maghrebi cultural divide. The images of groups of clandestine sub-Saharan African refugees attempting to cross to Europe from the in-between zone of Tangiers again develops the geo-political preoccupations that had been more thoroughly explored in *Loin*. Their oblique inclusion in *Les Temps qui changent*, alongside the gay cross-cultural subplot, signals the emergence of a critical engagement with the contemporary politics of migration in gay cinema, one which challenges the climate of increased national security and hostility towards so-called 'illegal' immigration.

NOTES

1. Olivier Péretié, 'Nous nous sommes tant aimés . . .', *Le Nouvel Observateur*, no. 1758, 16–22 July 1998, pp. 30–6.
2. Jacques Julliard, 'L'Homme vertical', *Le Nouvel Observateur*, no. 1758, 16–22 July 1998, p. 35.
3. Curtis Newtown, 'Les beurs gays: les mille et un ennuis', *Factory*, 15 June–15 July 2001, p. 23.
4. Nidam Abdi, 'Les Beurs Gays s'affichent. L'association Kelma se bat contre l'isolement et le racisme', *Libération*, 17 March 1997, p. 16.
5. Sabah Rahmani, 'Beurs homos: briser la loi du silence', *Têtu*, April, 2004, pp. 98–102.
6. Luc Arbona, 'United colors of têtu: Blacks, Blancs, Beurs', *Têtu*, December 1996, pp. 25–32.
7. Yannick Barbe and Thomas Doustaly, 'Ali, Salah, Mustapha et les autres . . .', *Têtu*, December 2001, pp. 70–4.
8. Fouad Zéraoui quoted in Daniel Garcia, 'L'avant-garde soluble dans le Marais?', *Le Nouvel Observateur*, Paris Ile-de-France section, 28 February–6 March 2002, pp. 14–16.
9. Patrick Thévenin, 'citébeur: caillerattitude', *Têtu*, April 2002, p. 78.
10. Sagat is marketed on www.francoissagat.com (accessed 15 August 2007).
11. Jean-Marc Lalanne, 'La Saga de François', *Les Inrocktuptibles*, nos 557–9, August 2006, pp. 50–3.
12. Jean-Marc Lalanne, 'Breathless de Brian Cam', *Les Inrockuptibles*, nos 609–11, July/August 2007, p. 101.
13. Patrick Thévenin, 'citébeur: caillerattitude', *Têtu*, April 2002, p. 78.
14. Patrick Thévenin, 'Bites, Blancs, Beurs', *Technikart*, May 2004, pp. 50–3.
15. Chibikh situates the product on the gay porn market and responds to *Têtu*'s early reservations about the 'racaille' trend in Louis Maury, 'Cantique de la racaille', *Têtu*, July–August 2003, p. 36.
16. Thank you to Maxime Cervulle for kindly allowing me to reproduce our collaborative work on this sequence here.
17. Didier Lestrade picks up on JNRC's personal style and technical proficiency in his interview with the director, 'JNRC Mateur-né', *Têtu*, May 2006, pp. 142–8.
18. *La Nuit du Cyclone*, Canal Plus, 22 January 1999.
19. Jacques Martineau quoted in Chris Gallant, 'French Fancies', *Gay Times*, November 2000, p. 19.
20. Olivier Ducastel quoted from a pre-publicity television interview with Martineau and Ducastel, *Nulle Part Ailleurs*, Canal Plus, 19 April 2000.

21. A selection of digital reproductions of Giliberti's paintings can be found on www.salimkechiouche.com (accessed 20 November 2007), a self-promotional profile of the actor that includes images and personal commentary.
22. Eve Sedgwick uses the word 'homosocial' as a term used to describe the 'affective or social force' structuring all-male relations. 'To draw the "homosocial" back into the orbit of "desire," of the potentially erotic, then, is to hypothesize the potential unbrokenness of a continuum between homosocial and homosexual – a continuum whose visibility, for men, in our society, is radically disrupted' (Sedgwick 1985: 1–2).
23. *Cahiers du cinéma*, no. 591, June 2004, p. 40.
24. 'Monotone,' *Le Figaro*, 16 June 2004.
25. Stéphane Malandrin, 'La vie cinématographique de Gaël Morel', *Cahiers du cinéma*, no. 488, February 1995, p. 20.
26. See the negative reviews in both the *Cahiers du cinéma* (no. 538, September 1999, p. 75) and *Positif* (no. 463, September 1999, p. 48).
27. See *Têtu*, June 2002, p. 83.
28. Laurent Rogoulet, ' "Aller plus loin dans la représentation du sexe" – Sébastien Lifshitz détaille son rapport au désir et au cul', *Libération*, 24 June 1998, p. 35.
29. Yann Gonzalez, 'Téchiné en mode "repeat" ', *Têtu*, January 2005, p. 18.

2. DOWN AND OUT: IMMIGRANT POVERTY AND QUEER SEXUALITY

Amid the World Cup football frenzy in June 2006, *Libération* titled its Lesbian and Gay Pride edition 'Mariage et adoption: Les gays près du but' ('Marriage and Adoption: Gays close to their goal'). Beyond the cartoon iconography of twinned figurine grooms and meringue brides, *Libération* heralded a recent shift in political attitudes to LGBT civil rights. In the run-up to the presidential elections of 2007, gay marriage and adoption were being pulled towards the centre of political debate. Following the example of socialist prime minister José Luis Rodríguez Zapatero's progressive example in Spain, the French socialists finally quietened dissent (from future candidate Ségolène Royal) to inscribe a same-sex marriage proposal into their official electoral programme. Even the resistant members of the ruling UMP (*Union pour un mouvement populaire*) party, it was reported, were being coerced into pragmatism, interior minister Nicolas Sarkozy cited as no longer seeing same-sex family configurations as remotely contestable. This was discounted two months later when Sarkozy admitted to a re-think and announced his clear opposition to gay marriage and adoption for the usual reason of upholding the heterosexual family.[1] Sarkozy was fighting an assumed presidential nomination on two fronts: he had to rally the regressive members of the UMP, traditionally hostile to LGBT rights, to avoid losing votes to the far right, whilst maintaining credibility as a 'modern' potential president in the eyes of floating voters. It is noteworthy that Sarkozy's hastily publicised concession to LGBT organisations remained within the strict confines of middle-class propriety, notably fiscal equality above all else.

> I've thought long and hard about it and I'm opposed to both same-sex marriage and adoption. That's clear and precise. On the other hand I'm deeply hostile to any form of discrimination against homosexuals, which is why I'm in favour of financial equality. There needs to be a system that will guarantee fiscal equality between heterosexual and homosexual couples for inheritance and property.

(J'y ai beaucoup réfléchi et j'y suis opposé tout comme à l'adoption d'enfants par des couples homosexuels. C'est clair et c'est précis. En revanche, je suis profondément hostile à toute forme de discrimination. Les homosexuels ne doivent pas en subir. C'est pourquoi je suis partisan de l'égalité sur le plan financier. Il faut donc créer un système qui, sur le plan fiscal, patrimonial et successoral, garantisse l'égalité entre un couple hétérosexuel et un couple homosexuel.)[2]

Put bluntly, allowing homosexuals to marry, adopt and arrange their intimate lives according to the middle-class prerogatives of state recognition, property, inheritance, tax breaks and kinship through coupling might no longer be thought of as troubling as it would keep the lid on other forms of queer disturbance. As Interior Minister, Sarkozy's real *bêtes noires* were poor immigrants, and his crusade, in which all roads invariably led back to immigration, was essentially motivated by xenophobic antagonism (Sarkozy 2006). In contrast to the apparent march of gay socio-economic inclusion, the back page of the same 2006 gay pride *Libération* profiles Malika and Karima Boucherka, mother and daughter, both undocumented Algerians, threatened with imminent expulsion under Sarkozy's circular of 13 June 2006 questioning the validity of a child's right to a stable education in influencing her (and her family's) immigration status.[3] The accompanying photo of the two women serves to support the piece's melodramatic title, the pained gaze of the mother directed to the camera, with her daughter's obscured face sheltering on her shoulder. I begin with these media snapshots of political debate in France to call into question this polarised opposition of queer sexuality and immigrant poverty. I wish here to contest an unequal balance of social power that would give the front page to gay assimilation and the back page to precarious immigration. What is happening in between?

Following Le Pen's appearance in the second round of the April 2002 presidential elections – an event left undigested until the 2007 elections in which he was eliminated in the first round – something like an epochal change occurred at an institutional level with the subsequent formation of the right-wing UMP government. This climate of intensified moral and social authoritarianism was largely instigated by Sarkozy, perhaps the most ubiquitous politician of our time, the son of a Hungarian immigrant, whose continuing hard-line policy on immigration has airbrushed the far-right extremism of Le Pen into a package of reforms (including the 2006 law on so-called selective immigration) pleasing to much middle-class France. Sarkozy's ability to make the move from Interior Minister to President in April 2007 was helped by his populist discourse on the need for economic change through neo-liberalism and his knack of reducing and polarising political debate to re-ignite underlying social tensions (of class and race). It is his contrived simplicity and forthright rhetoric that gave him the edge over Royal in the pre-election televised debate. Despite loathing from the left, Sarkozy's previous popularity as Interior Minister had been bolstered by a poll for the *Figaro* in June 2006, which had showed that a majority continued to consider the right more effective than the left at tackling delinquency and insecurity.[4] In this chapter I want in parallel to take up the argument familiar to recent Anglo-American queer criticism that excessive attention to the gay marriage and kinship package is dragging queer critique away from crucial issues of social inequality, potentially securing dominant white gay men in a narcissistic critical ghetto in which personal sympathies, sexual relations and political alliances across lines of class and race are disappearing.[5] In comes economic middle-class inclusion; out goes social exclusion, pushing the interlocking dynamics of immigration, race, AIDS and transgender dissent to the margins of critical debate.

This chapter assesses the sexual component of the authoritarian conjuncture in France and its effect on cinematic visions of poverty, marginality and immigration. The mainstream hit comedy *Chouchou* (2003) ended on a celebratory dream of ethnic integration, a fantasy France that, by the time it was screened, seemed far from actuality. Starting with this harmonious image of a multiethnic France, and then taking a detour via reality France, I move on to two art films that weave poverty and sexuality into their social fabric. Amal Bedjaoui's *Un fils* (2003) and Sébastien Lifshitz's *Wild Side* (2004) both take up the social and sexual dynamics of this current retreat into conservatism, the economic residue of which was expelled onto the streets in the *banlieue* riots of 2005, and in the student demonstrations against the cack-handed first-employment contract of 2006. Against this political backdrop, Bedjaoui and Lifshitz both point to precarious material lives and increased emotional anxiety for those they figure as excluded from neo-liberal hegemony – migrants, sex workers and transgender communities.

FANTASY FRANCE

Both the inclusive social language and ethnic landscape of the hit comedy *Chouchou* (Allouache, 2003) go some way to accounting for its phenomenal box-office success, together with massive publicity from Canal Plus, and the celebrity coverage of its star and writer Gad Elmaleh. The film grossed over one million entries in its opening week in March 2003, only the second French film ever to do so.[6] Moroccan-born comic Elmaleh already had a youthful fan base following his ironically titled stand-up sketch show *The Normal Life* (*La Vie normale*, 2000) in which the Algerian transgender character Chouchou was conceived. Elmaleh had also acted in Merzak Allouache's *Salut cousin!* (1996), an earnest take on urban immigrant poverty; alongside another funny man Antoine de Caunes in the Jewish comedy of sexual mores in which a gay character gets straightened out, *L'Homme est une femme comme les autres* (Zilbermann, 1998); and in the sequel to the grossly stereotypical marriage of Sephardim Jewry with flashy business, *La Vérité si je mens!* (Gilou, 2001). Elmaleh's original sketch was more sharply political than the subsequent film version (containing references to religious fundamentalism, the Algerian civil war and French colonisation) and less fairy-tale glossy (Chouchou was initially not a psychotherapist's assistant but a sex worker based at the run-down Place de Clichy in north Paris). Beyond the upbeat imagery of ethnic harmony and sexual emancipation, and despite its flimsy plot, approximate direction and shaky camerawork, Chouchou the film, as the title indicates, is very much Elmaleh's main event. Much of the North-African Magrehbi humour derives from his smart word play, in which language is corrupted by puns and malapropism. The camp badinage is largely untranslatable – l'épée de Damoclès becomes le pied de Damoclès, for example. Elmaleh's wit, timing and charisma give the 'general public' some proximity to transgender (however overblown), rather than grabbing laughs at its expense in the vein of La Cage aux folles (Molinaro, 1978).

The film's first shot of a ferry docking in Marseille, followed by a subsequent train arriving in Paris, exposes its thematic interest in boundary crossing. Chouchou sneaks into France landing somewhere in the Parisian suburbs, outlandishly disguised as a Chilean refugee anachronistically fleeing the Pinochet dictatorship, poncho and all. The Catholic Church is figured as a tolerant haven, its doors flung open to an illegal immigrant with an undisclosed wish to crossdress. Homophobic insults are nowhere to be heard in this idyll of integration. The gentle parody of Christian good works includes the intuitive Père Léon (Claude Brasseur), assisted by the bulimic convert and former junkie Frère Jean (Roschdy Zem), whose work for social regeneration includes an unlikely local youth choir – cue images of tough youths devoutly singing Il est né le divin enfant. Since the couch has usurped the social function of the confessional, so Chouchou goes to work for the enlightened psychotherapist Dr Milovavitch (Catherine Frot) who encourages him to cross-dress as her personal assistant (assistante particulière in Elmaleh's neat slip). Chouchou comes out to the compassionate specialist, the film thus appropriately referencing inversion theory and slipping transgender into same-sexuality. Gay transvestism, if indeed this is how the film seeks to explain Chouchou's gender identity, is explained in the terms of coming out, as if the character's gender identity were subordinate to his/her sexuality, and not vice versa. Elmaleh effectively updates sexology by tracing not so much a female soul in a male body, as much as transgender identity as part of gay sexuality. The film adds to the popular conflation of transgender and same-sex desire rather than attempting to refine non-normative patterns within the sex/gender system. Chouchou reads up enough on the history of neurosis to counsel one patient, a psychotic cop, that his weapon obsession is a symptom of latent homosexual urges, a plot device to introduce an element of tension, as the irate cop chases after Chouchou, who manages to escape through a carwash (allowing for Elmaleh's parody of shampoo ads), before ending up at the Place de Clichy, a home to a flourishing North-African trans-subculture.

The remainder of the film contrasts the idealised suburbs with two other sociological milieus, the low with the high – the gay/trans nightlife of the flashy

Apocalypse club and the noble family of Stanislas de la Tour-Meaubourg – a hierarchical world away from Chouchou de la Place Clichy. Chouchou teams up with friend Djamila (Yacine Mesbah) and nephew Vanessa (Arié Elmaleh), a performer at the local drag club, thus allowing the film to establish a sense of supportive Maghrebi subculture – Chouchou consoles the homesick Djamila, and all three trade hot gossip together in the hammam. The retro gay aesthetic of the festive club scenes harks back to a drag scene of yesteryear, a nostalgic blend of gaudy waitresses, boys in tight tops and camp lip-synching to familiar divas. In an article on images of ethnicity in Allouache's *Salut Cousin* and *Chouchou*, Darren Waldron argues that the club scenes combine the film's two strands of cultural and sexual hybridity through

> an interesting permutation of camp codes that crosses the conventional divide between Western and Eastern gendered behaviour . . . The drag queen performers – including Chouchou – are of Maghrebi origins and mime to French hits of the 1980s . . . Yet, it could also be argued that these Maghrebis simply assume the mannerisms of the white female pop stars they impersonate rather than providing new renditions of their heroines' performances, thereby articulating less clearly an intercultural exchange between white Francophone culture and Algeria. (Waldron 2007: 44)

It is at the drag club that Chouchou falls – literally – for a liberated aristocrat, making room for a good old comedy of class errors, involving Chouchou's failed lady impersonation, Diana worship, sushi dropped down her cleavage and so forth. The meeting with the elevated in-laws is a nod to the climax of *La Cage aux folles* in which bourgeois propriety is momentarily hoodwinked by female impersonation; but some thirty years on, the posh couple now seem to find gender-bending pretty much par for the course. Beneath the grating boulevard recuperation of gay transgender for the mainstream, *La Cage aux folles* was not only preoccupied with class climbing, but also with racial hierarchy in the guise of the effeminate black 'maid' Jacob, the representation of whom invoked racist clichés of black savagery – the fact that the character went without shoes for instance. When the birds migrated to Hollywood in the remake, *The Birdcage* (Nichols, 1996), the rich in-laws were Jewish and the 'maid' Latino, a revealing indicator of US social strata and their attendant anxieties. The 'maid' could clearly not be black.

Chouchou ends on the potentially uplifting dream of a multi-ethnic France, rather than adhering to the representation of a nation whitewashed by republicanism. The final tableau provides an alternative vision to the social and ethnic fracture exploited of late by demagogic politicians. Partially uplifting is perhaps more accurate because, from a queer perspective at least, the narrative resolution is limited, and given its mainstream brief, the outcome is compromised. The film's flirtation with more radical potential has finally to be dispelled, and national assimilation through marriage – however unorthodox – is invariably suggested as the natural course for an immigrant. The possibility of forms of relations that are not state-sanctioned is not part of the ideological agenda. Following the narrative climax that sees Chouchou's threatened expulsion from France dismissed, Père Léon wraps things up by preaching tolerance to the crowd assembled to witness the union of Algerian transgender and French nobility. Against the bleak realistic backdrop of the local tower blocks, the camera pans round as Stanislas the aristocrat runs across the field in time to a rock version of Mendelssohn's wedding march to greet the oncoming bride. Their embrace shows his blue suit complement her white dress and red wig, thereby producing a deviant cliché of standard republican imagery and parodying the notion of 'national cinema' the idea of cinema as a means of federating a national community (Hayward 2005 [1993]). The uplifting utopian moment is the slow pan shot of the united congregation – the lofty in-laws, the accepting priests, the progressive psychoanalyst, the camp divas and the local kids, all joyfully approving and cheering on the queer union.

REALITY FRANCE

Before moving on to visions of sexual exclusion that counterbalance the apparent social idyll of *Chouchou*, let me flesh out a brief history of the post-April 2002 political landscape of immigration and sexuality. A heated exchange published in July 2005 in *Libération* between Sarkozy and Julien Dray, at that time spokesman for the Socialist Party, established immigration as the key to Sarkozy's anticipated break with the indulgent 'end of reign' lassitude of President Chirac, widely perceived as partly responsible for the political quagmire of the Fifth Republic. Asked to comment on the terrorist attacks on London in July 2005, Sarkozy promoted zero tolerance as the policy for those who disrespect republican values (and as a means of deporting those of them who are not French).[7] The historical backdrop of terrorist attacks allowed him to slip agilely from Islamic extremism to prescribed quotas on 'illegal' immigration. The call for clarity – his detractors would call it dogmatism – on matters of migratory flux entailed fixing precise quantifiable objectives and rooting out the perceived procedural loopholes, cited examples of which are fake marriages, emergency medical treatment and family reunion. Sarkozy railed against overcrowded asylum centres, overloaded due to burdensome bureaucracy, the promised quick fix to which is a policy of immediate deportation. So by responding to calls for much-needed administrative reform, Sarkozy appeared progressive to floating middle-class voters on the backs of powerless immigrants. *Libération* was quick to pick him up on his concessions to the far right (flights chartered to deport undesirables, loss of French nationality for suspected terrorists), to which he feigned indignation by asking if any of his policy outlines were in fact anti-republican. Republicanism, disembowelled of its three central tenets of liberty, equality and fraternity, can therefore act as an empty receptacle for any old regressive ideology.

Dray's response (the cheeky strapline to which can be loosely translated as 'Sarkozy round two, all mouth no action')[8] countered Sarkozy's right-wing measures with the socialist package of pragmatic alternatives, promoting 'shared immigration' in contrast to the right's 'selective immigration'. Not seeming able to lead the ideological dance, the socialists proposed forcing France to accept its share of world poverty in the name of solidarity (in effect to accept its post-colonial duty) and to establish closer political ties with African states in order to alleviate the pressure on Italy and Spain which were being left to cope with the escalating 'boat people' crisis.[9] In turn, Sarkozy's response rebutted Dray's accusation that the immigration system had become a factory churning out undocumented immigrants by mentioning his closure of the Red Cross refugee camp at Sangatte in northern France in 2002, which had become, in Sarkozy's opinion, a symbol of the lax and chaotic socialist coalition (1997–2002). (The Red Cross site had initially been set up in September 1999 as a temporary humanitarian structure, but had housed more than 60,000 refugees attempting to seek asylum in the UK by the time it closed in December 2002.) In fact the botched partial regularisation of thousands of undocumented immigrants under the Reseda law of 11 May 1998 – *la loi dite Reseda (relative à l'entrée et au séjour des étrangers en France et au droit d'asile)* – is cited as the primary cause of the current incoherence. (This argument has been refuted by demographer Michèle Tribalat who, whilst favourably describing the concurrent tough-on-immigration policies of the Blair government in Britain as pragmatic border-management, also explains that long-term immigration has continued to increase since 1996 without any correlation to the policies of successive left or right-wing governments.)[10] Sarkozy promised to fight without respite against undocumented immigration (with shades of a xenophobic witch-hunt in the dogmatic language) and to allow France a filter-effect policy conducive to economic stability. The pernicious effect of his discourse is that it recuperates solidarity as a good excuse to pull up the EU drawbridge on the short-sighted pretext that France cannot supposedly cope with increased immigration, and that it is wrong to strip other countries of their human resources – that last point paradoxically inconsistent with Sarkozy's own acceptance of the brain-drain effect if it be of short-term economic benefit to France.

The updated legislation on so-called selective immigration passed by the National Assembly in May 2006 was indeed intended to bolster Sarkozy's 2007 presidential campaign. The bill (*CESEDA – le projet de loi réformant le code de l'entrée et du séjour des étrangers et du droit d'asile*) was passed by the National Assembly on 17 May 2006. It hinged on Sarkozy's reductive rhetorical ploy to ditch 'subjected immigration' (thus airbrushing far-right paranoia about foreign invasion) in favour of selective immigration, which regressively sees immigrants as tools for economic prosperity and expansion, as exploitable labour, potentially thrown out when worn out.[11] The law restricts the rights of family members to join relatives in France, and suppresses the automatic right for undocumented immigrants to gain residents' permits after ten years on French soil.

This law came in the wake of the widespread student-led revolt against the first employment contract (CPE – *Contrat première embauche*) from February to April 2006. The student unions ignored the international call for necessary reform to make the French job market more flexible. The CPE, they argued, legalised insecurity for a growing underclass of young workers – *précarité*, the buzzword for the nefarious effects of market exploitation. The anti-globalisation group Attac argued that fiddling with unemployment by creating flexible youth contracts, in which employers could fire employees at will for a two-year trial period, as well as underpay or not pay interns, was not proven to stimulate economic growth in the long term.[12] By early April 2006 and the embarrassing U-turn on prime minister De Villepin's pet project, Sarkozy could take advantage of the left's demonstration-fatigue and the prime minister's dismal public image to push through his crucial immigration reform. Sarkozy's evident opportunism aside, the imbalance of power evident in the overlap from the CPE to the immigration reform is a clear indicator that poor immigrant groups simply do not have the financial might or media influence of the union-backed middle-class youth to capture the public attention for long enough to threaten even a punch-drunk government.[13]

The upheaval of early 2006 (chimes of '*la France va mal*', indicative of overwhelming social discontent) had of course been prefigured by the *banlieue* riots of late 2005. A mid-December issue of *Métro* gave a bleak outlook for 2006,[14] 53 per cent of those polled declaring good health as their priority for the coming year, significantly higher than either quality of life or purchasing power. Unlike the students' subsequent concerns about adequate working conditions and remunerated training, the disaffected youth of the suburban estates had given up on integration, a concept exposed by the riots as an all-purpose cover for social (and by extension, ethnic) segregation.[15] It was Sarkozy's injurious language that was widely considered incendiary in the context of the riots. Adding fuel to the flames of the burning estates surrounding the major French cities, Sarkozy labeled the rebels louts, and threatened to have them wiped off the street with a high-pressure hose. Colin Falconer has provided an astute assessment of the complex web of underlying factors that sparked off the riots, seen as 'a conscious, if largely unorganized, response not only to years of neglect, but to repeated provocations by Sarkozy and other right-wing demagogues' (Falconer 2006: 2). Islam, he argues, is at the heart of the matter, despite Sarkozy's tactical flirtation with middle-class pro-business representatives of *Le Conseil français du culte musulman*, which in practice represents a small fraction of the four million French Muslims. Falconer sees alienation from capitalism as a major reason for the increased turn to religion, strengthened by reluctance on the part of socialists to engage with issues of ethnic exclusion, obsessed as so many of them are with maintaining abstract secularism as the benchmark of French national order. Falconer is right to criticise the Socialist Party's offshoots, *SOS Racisme* and *Ni Putes Ni Soumises* ('Neither whores nor submissives'), who grab media attention by blaming young Arab and black men for violence against women, thus ignoring in-built socio-economic factors. The immediate political effects of the 2005 insurrection included a three-month-long state of emergency (last used during the Algerian war), an extension of police powers to stop, search and arrest at will, which rode roughshod over civil liberties, and increased expulsion of clandestine immigrants.

Rewind now to the start of the UMP government in 2002, to round one of Sarkozy's domestic agenda in which sexuality acted as a smear screen for the real target of immigration. The civil rights of minorities were first on the minister's hit list.[16] Sarkozy had set up camp in the re-branded 'Ministry of Internal Affairs, Internal Security and Local Freedom', devoting his first public engagement to an anti-prostitution operation in Paris. Sex work organisations (notably *Cabiria, Grisélidis, Les Amis du bus des femmes*, and *Le PASTT – Prévention, Action, Santé, Travail pour les Transgenres*, an HIV-prevention, health and support group led by Brazilian transsexual doctor Camille Cabral) argued that the government's priority of national security entailed transforming areas of prostitution into military-patrolled zones, targets including the Bois de Boulogne and the exterior boulevards encircling Paris.[17] The crux of the policy was the visibility of street prostitution – it was not made illegal in itself, but closeted or else hunted down as a means of tightening up on immigration. Indeed, Sarkozy's white paper on internal security, put before the National Assembly in July 2002, proposed automatically expelling from France immigrant prostitutes caught inciting clients, thus denying them any right to enter into the usual immigration procedure.[18]

Sarkozy was perceived to be leading a public crusade against immigrant prostitutes,[19] and the socialist mayor of Paris, Bertrand Delanoë, supported him, arguing the so-called feminist case for the abolition of prostitution. While *Le Monde* announced Delanoë's socialist projects to alleviate the social exclusion of prostitutes in Paris (easier access to council housing and health-care, and a plan to open various council-funded, drop-in centres), his deputy mayor, Anne Hildalgo, was keen to maintain the dogmatic stance on male oppression, the logical consequence of which is to criminalise the clients.[20] Alongside Act Up, the PASTT organised a protest rally at night in the Bois de Boulogne (4 June 2002) to draw public attention to the climate of increased repression. Such a policy, it was argued, pushed sex workers into further precariousness, as well as endangering them, for, underground, they are at greater risk of violence and unable to gain sufficient access to targeted HIV-prevention.

The National Assembly passed Sarkozy's law on domestic security on 13 February 2003, after the first national prostitution protests in France in early November 2002.[21] This punitive package not only criminalised street prostitution, but also included harsh measures against travellers, 'aggressive' street beggars, people who congregate in stairways or in the entrances to high-rise flats, and those who commit acts of anti-republicanism such as destroying the national flag or booing the *Marseillaise*. 'We should not be afraid of condemnation, repression and punishment'[22] ('La sanction, la répression, la punition, il ne faut pas en avoir peur') was Sarkozy's pitch to convince the National Assembly of the necessity for such measures. However, according to a telephone survey published in *Elle* magazine, the French were reported to be largely hostile to such punitive measures and in favour of social protection.[23] Sarkozy defended the legal turn from abolitionism (the aim to eradicate prostitution without criminalising prostitutes) to 'prohibitionism' (prostitutes become outlaws) by claiming to protect the victims of exploitation; the only means of saving them from slavery, the legislation holds, is to penalise it. The most regressive part of the legislation involved a prison sentence of up to six months for 'passive soliciting', the precise definition of which is left to the arbitrary discretion of the police. Sarkozy's logic even saw the expulsion of immigrant sex workers twisted to their advantage, as part of their sexual emancipation.

> Who can explain the difference between passive soliciting, currently permitted, and active soliciting, which is illegal? From now on both will be punished because it's absurd to oppose the predicament of the prostitute with that of the pimp, who prospers because the prostitute is permitted to walk the streets. By penalising prostitution, we will put a stop to the exploitation of those poor women from Eastern Europe and Africa. In addition undocumented prostitutes (some 60 per cent of the total number) will be deported . . . This is the only way to free them from slavery.
> (Qui peut me dire la différence entre le racolage passif, autorisé aujourd'hui et le racolage actif qui, lui, est interdit? Désormais les deux seront punis, car il est absurde d'opposer la situation de la prostituée et celle du proxénète. Si le proxénète prospère c'est bien parce que la prostituée est autorisée sur les trottoirs. En pénalisant la prostitution, on empêche l'exploitation de toutes ces malheureuses venues de l'Est ou d'Afrique. Par ailleurs, les prostituées en situation irrégulière, qui représentent 60 pour cent des prostituées, seront reconduites dans leur pays . . . C'est la seule façon de les sortir de l'esclavage)[24]

Sarkozy effectively made public visibility, not morality or sexuality, the crucial concern. Sociologist Eric Fassin argued that the right had upped the ante by deliberately avoiding the now tired abolition/liberalisation dead-end. Whilst the different currents on the left were squabbling over which model to adopt (for the feminist-inspired abolitionists, it was Sweden, where the clients are criminalised; for liberals and radicals alike, it was Holland where the job is unionised and protected by the state), the right shifted the ground onto domestic security. Sex panics require convenient scapegoats, invariably those least able to fight back. In this vein, the insistence on the part of the UMP government on appearing to have the interests of 'la France d'en bas' (common French people) close to heart effectively meant discriminating against those really at the bottom of the social heap – immigrant prostitutes. Citing Sarkozy's original white paper on internal security which sought to attack illegal immigration through prostitution, Fassin described the process as:

> the identification of a sexual pathology with a specific milieu, weighed down with all possible wrongs and fantasies. As in the days of good old Victorianism, aren't we witnessing a worrying conflation of 'dangerous sexualities' and 'dangerous classes'?'
> (l'identification de la pathologie sexuelle à un milieu particulier, chargé de tous les maux, et de tous les fantasmes. N'assiste-t-on pas aujourd'hui, comme aux beaux jours du victorianisme, à une inquiétante assimilation entre 'sexualités dangereuses' et 'classes dangereuses'?)[25]

Threesomes

In surprisingly retro language for a centre-left publication ('Sexual insubordination against social alienation')[26] Le Monde's review of Sébastien Lifshitz's third feature film, Wild Side (2004), gave it radical attitude. Indeed fellow filmmaker Claude Miller admired the extent to which the film tackled sexual dissent in tandem with social exclusion.[27] In fact Lifshitz's brand of contestation owes as much to Lou Reed's Transformer album (1972) as to actual social transformation. There is plenty of hanging around and making up, but not many perfect days, for Lifshitz is not hung up on happiness, as Têtu magazine quipped.[28] He takes the sexually transgressive elements of Reed's Walk on the Wild Side (transgender, hustling and cruising), drops the drugs and adds immigration. Lifshitz does not exactly transpose the myth of the US underground alluded to in the film's title as a template for contemporary France. As Le Monde picks up, Lifshitz's more modest aesthetic is certainly less influenced by the flashy subjective provocation of pop film, of Morrissey and Warhol say, or even by post-modern European art film (Almodóvar's consistent 'trans-camp', for instance), but is closer in style to the home-grown bitterness of realist filmmakers like Maurice Pialat, or to the poetic structures of his early mentor Claire Denis. In parallel, Amal Bedjaoui's short film Un fils (2003, co-written by Isabelle Pichaud) supports Lifshitz's preoccupations by taking up similar motifs of transgender and hustling, but she gives more room to the ethnic context of her Arab protagonist whose fraught relationship with his father is established as the film's narrative backbone. Both films seek to contrast the precarious sexual and economic situations of their characters (the non-normative content) with more traditional interest in their biological and elected families, and in a narrative resolution of former identities and current relationships. I wish here to address not only the various ideological premises to these representations of queer lives, but also the experimental editing and hybrid aesthetic of Wild Side, whose mix of artistic cinematography and documentary naturalism, is gesturing, I argue, to the evolving brand of French queer cinema.

Lifshitz professes to a love of socially marginal characters whose affective lives are formed outside the habitual scheme of things and outside accepted fictional archetypes.[29] In theory, his trio of outsiders (illegal Russian immigrant, transgender sex worker and bisexual Arab hustler) would not look out of place as the objects of voyeuristic TV inquiry. But the aim here is to twist received wisdom on national and sexual dissidents, to flesh out their inner lives and interpersonal relationships, so as to depict them as social *subjects*. Yet in TV, radio and press coverage of the film Lifshitz tends to invoke (in order to revoke) the recurrent stereotypes of transsexual prostitution, Arab rough trade and illegal immigration, but then shies away from a more articulate account of the film's political fabric, trying to avoid the trap of didacticism by falling back on safer notions of individual suffering and loneliness. It might be argued that Lifshitz is more politically engaged than his humanist framework would suggest. He begins the process of blurring dominant visions – the 'gender cluedo' of the sort underpinning films like *The Crying Game* (Jordan, 1992) – right from the start with director of photography Agnès Godard's still frames of Stéphanie Michelini's naked body, thereby ousting the gender-normative expectation of matching anatomy with identity, in favour of the 'beauty, sui generis, of sexual indeterminacy'[30] to quote *Le Monde*. By robbing the audience of the trite shock-value of a later genital shot, Lifshitz is able to draw attention to the character's social milieu: she is next figured in the company of other trans people (largely from the PASTT) serenaded by Antony Hegarty (from the band Antony and the Johnsons). Hegarty addresses Michelini directly, asking her 'are you a boy or a girl?', thus ironically throwing the (assumed normative) spectator's question right back. The haunting song – 'I fell in love with a dead boy' – neatly sets the scene for the film's troubling interrogation of transition and loss. In Britain, *Wild Side* was criticised particularly for its perceived incoherence on transgender, for dwelling too much on Stéphanie's boyhood, thus putting 'the spectator in a problematic position, as we are being asked to make sense of Stéphanie with almost exclusive reference to her past, something she explicitly wants to avoid.'[31] Whilst *Libération* praised Michelini for the standard and determination of her acting,[32] *Sight and Sound* reviewed her as statuesque and lifeless, an unresolved enigma for spectator and director. In *The Other Side*, the 'making-of' documentary accompanying the DVD version, Lifshitz explains that he perceived her as a mystery, Godard's shots of her femininity being echoed by occasional flashes of her former masculinity.

Apart from one scene of light relief amid the ensuing gloom, involving Stéphanie and friends attempting a game of *pétanque*, and later shots of a nightclub, the vision of trans-subculture is not further developed outside of professional sex work. The scenes filmed in the Bois de Boulogne initially present the girls from afar, the camera lingering on bared breasts, with the distant framing shots behind passing traffic resembling the frontal (brutal) technique of documentary, before cautiously cutting to the accompanying (intimate) side shots of the girls' own social interaction without any clients in view, with Stéphanie amused by the high-jinks of her colleagues. The camera effectively jumps from the intrusive sidelines to the inclusive action. This is followed by the nitty-gritty of the job – performing fellatio on one client, being strenuously fucked by another, spied on by an elderly voyeur, cash changing hands, and so on. A later scene spliced into the narrative shows Stéphanie on one job where the roles are reversed as she fucks the client this time, giving an insight into plausible fantasies of transgender sexuality.

Djamel (Yasmine Belmadi) hustles at the Gare de l'Est, where gay cruising goes on in the dingy below-level toilets. He is presented as at-once sexually assertive and psychologically fragile. The shots of him roaming the station in the early-morning rush-hour (the camera lingering on prospective clients) are balanced by the sex scenes in which he takes control – fucking one middle-aged woman, then surprising her by asking for remuneration; and coercing a male trick into giving him a blow-job. These brief snapshots of his life encourage us to view Djamel as lost without the security of his absent lovers. Like his earlier films with Belmadi, Lifshitz is invoking the cliché of a predatory Arab male sexuality, only then to chip away at the archetype of dominant virility, to point to the vulnerability beneath the macho bravado. And unlike Gaël Morel whose camera virtually zooms in on his actors' fit bodies in *Le Clan* (2004), Lifshitz has Godard film Belmadi coldly (as opposed to erotically), naked in the bath holding his breath underwater – not to give the viewer a kick at the sight of his flesh, but rather to visualise a psychological point about the character's loneliness.

Overall, *Wild Side* is perhaps hesitant on sex work, not wishing to take the moralistic side in the concurrent prostitution debates (while clearly echoing them), but unsure of the exact point it is trying to make. Stéphanie the character, unlike many of her co-workers, would not have immigration restrictions on work and, like Michelini, could find employment elsewhere (though not all that easily in view of France's high unemployment rate). In short, given the film's sparse dialogue, it remains unclear whether we are to read sex work as an economic imposition, or as a personal choice – she could more unexpectedly have been shown to enjoy her job – '*Wild Side* never quite shakes off this sense of tired convention',[33] according to *Sight and Sound*. At any rate the film seeks simply to render sex work (like transgender) unremarkable or at least as mundane and potentially unfulfilling as many other forms of employment. After all, many jobs require bodily submission for work and pay that offer little in return. But the documentary *The Other Side* hints at a lurking middle-class unease with the film's subject matter – Elisabeth Méhu, the costume designer jumps for joy at locating an enormous, gaudy, dollar-sign accessory to be hung later on a girl in a nightclub scene. Méhu is shown photographing the half-naked extras, a rather crude parody of the worst excesses of fashion shoots. Erudite co-writer Stéphane Bouquet also comes out with some dubious references to grand theory (bodies as discourse, Deleuze on 'becoming animal' to describe prostitutes squatting in the woods and so forth) in an attempt to give some theoretical clout to prostitution. The fact that the social reality of transgender is not attended to adequately outside prostitution perhaps inadvertently cements the inevitable trans/prostitution equation by individualising the character's social predicament within the close-knit threesome as opposed to a larger network of supportive friends and like-minded associates. *Wild Side* makes nods to groups like the PASTT but is concerned less with developing the potential benefits of active participation within civil society than with the real and symbolic violence of the neo-liberal state (social exclusion put down to the disavowal of ethnic minorities, the rejection of foreigners, and the second-class rights allotted to transgender citizens). I am pointing here to the relative limitations of the film's political scope, for it is within a social milieu that people tend to gain awareness of the collective means to oppose an unjust economic status quo, rather than just seeking solace in an isolated if fulfilling and experimental relationship.

Lifshitz is certainly on firmer ground extending the relational possibilities of his central threesome, founded not only on mutual attraction but also on the characters' shared alienation from the stability of secure employment. *Wild Side* points accurately to the material structure of dissident sexuality. The three characters' design for living is presented as unremarkable and offers us an alternative vision of modern love outside the perceived constraints of the monogamous couple. Given the film's elliptical format, the history of their set-up is unknown, and Lifshitz prefers to visualise their attachments rather than fill in the biographical detail. The film resists the conventional trap of singling out one couple and adding a third party, by showing both the emotional commitment of all three and their separately declined couples. Beginning with a slow pan shot of the industrial view of north-east Paris at night, Djamel's assurance of love to Stéphanie (she asks him why he does not encourage her to get out of prostitution) is followed by the scene in which the three make love, with Godard's artistically blurred and rapidly cut series of close shots of their writhing bodies designed to deny the viewer potential voyeuristic pleasure (the curiosity about who does what in bed). The men's love for each other is also fleshed out mostly through non-verbal communication – they enjoy messing around with a football together, and attempt more intimate conversations despite the considerable linguistic hurdle, including Belmadi's comic pigeon English. (A scene that ended up on the cutting-room floor was of the two men taking a bath together.) A later image of the three tumbling down a grass slope in the Buttes Chaumont park is a conscious nod to *Jules et Jim* (Truffaut, 1962), and is followed by a shot of them peacefully walking together arm in arm (in arm). It is Lifshitz's aim to paint their triad as a natural, spontaneous form of being together, to sweep aside the psychological baggage of perversion, which may indeed frustrate the more curious spectator – 'the trio's chemistry is not always obvious'[34] was *Têtu* magazine's one gripe.

I would argue, however, that Lifshitz does attend to the intricacies of their mutual attraction but from the oblique viewpoint of the family and its fantasy substitutions. In a noticeably non-narrative-driven film, the skeletal plot revolves around Stéphanie's return to her childhood origins in poor, rural northern France to tend to her dying mother, thus enabling her to exorcise her boyhood ghosts. The final sequence is particularly striking in this respect, as she observes a father and son in the train back to Paris after her mother's death: she turns and walks away, resolutely shutting the door on her former self. Following the swish shots of the French countryside marking the transition back to Paris, the film's haunting coda is Godard's still sunlit tight shot of the three lovers asleep in the train, clasped together for comfort. Midway through the film is a sequence in which Mikhail watches harrowing images of the Chechen war, followed by his one strained attempt to contact his mother in Russia. Again it is left to Godard's visual craft to convey the character's unspoken anguish – the extreme close-ups of his pained inanimate face are immediately cut by a fast tracking shot of him running (escaping?) through a forest, and then juxtaposed with Djamel's own family situation, the editing allowing the characters' parallel stories to segue seamlessly into one another. The scene in which Djamel's brother rejects his offer of soiled cash functions to show his dislocation from a family to whom he is unable to articulate his life. Lifshitz also uses documentary photos of Belmadi's own childhood to frame Djamel's solitude; he is filmed earlier observing his mother and brother in the tower block opposite, a device to provide a snatch of the character's complexity without giving in to the detailed biographical necessity of the conventional fiction film.

Obvious from its title, the more straightforward narrative of Bedjaoui's *Un fils* is structured around an estranged father/son relationship. The ailing father (Hammou Graia), who is grieving the loss of his wife, rejects his son Selim's (Mohamed Hicham) offer of financial help to pay for a necessary operation (cash he has been putting aside from hustling) but is seemingly ignorant of his son's proclivities. Following Selim's fatal, accidental overdose (after being attacked by a group of homophobic thugs), the father is called on to identify his son's belongings, including the stash of unmanly clothes, forcing him to accept his son's former ghost life. Bedjaoui visualises the loss at the core of the narrative by picturing Selim's friend and work partner Louise (Isabelle Pichaud) locked rigid in the middle of the street, with no ready future, literally disorientated by her friend's death. The film's arresting opening presents the couple's working practice: a mirror image of Selim shows him washing his hands, post-sex we infer from the off-screen sighing, then the camera cuts to a more inclusive shot of Selim at the washbasin and a client fucking a half-clothed Louise in the bath. To come, the client fucks the girl whilst gazing at the boy. He then approaches the object of his desire, gently touching his arm, whilst Louise, the vehicle of male intercourse, stares emptily off frame, only turning enviously towards the men in the last seconds of the scene.

Max, the predatory married man the pair meet in a club, is figured as a potential father figure, played with irresistible allure by Aurélien Recoing, who in the space of a few recent films has carved out a varied niche in masculinities – from the perturbed impostor of *L'Emploi du temps* (Cantet, 2001) through the sexual predator of *L'Ennemi naturel* (Guillaume, 2004), to the brute killing machine of *13 (Tzameti)* (Babluani, 2005). Max and Selim's meeting is subjectively shot to underline Recoing's older animal magnetism opposite Hicham's youthful sexy femininity – the imposing Max nervously dances with Louise while staring at Selim, his submissive prey, seated nonchalantly, to be looked at. (Louise is predictably ousted from the subsequent action, her own sexual pleasure again left unarticulated.) This image of male passivity/femininity takes Lifshitz's project of dismantling hegemonic Arab masculinity one step further. Bedjaoui has her protagonist partially cross-dress or at least appear strikingly feminine when on the job – Hicham's face is made-up, his fit torso moulded by a tight diamante top – though Max later tells Selim that he actually prefers him in straight masculine attire.

Likewise, in *Wild Side* there is a sequence, directly preceding the climactic scene of voyeurism, in which parental substitution also glides into transgender and trans-generational fantasy. Djamel picks up an unappealing older man who declines to see him again (not wishing to pick up bad habits) and ungraciously turfs him out before his wife returns. The couple is shot in bed as the slim Belmadi reassuringly strokes the client's expansive hairy chest, before asking about his children. The next scene (out of chronological order – again the editing works to sequent thematic effect over narrative progress) complements this by having Djamel spy on Stéphanie's naked mother. The sequence then jumps to a (presumably past) role-play scenario in which Mikhail coerces Stéphanie into disguising herself as she was, as a boy (or as he imagines she was), dressing her in drag in an outsized workman's shirt and asking her to adopt a deeper voice. These strands of dissident fantasy are then woven together in *Wild Side*'s most striking set piece, a three-way that folds spectatorship into the action.

A man hits on Stéphanie in a club, the establishing shots of which are of her dancing among other sexy girls, including some over-insistent close-ups of the gaudy jewellery. The client suggests to her a more elaborate scenario than usual involving a supposedly anonymous stranger chosen at random to fuck her. Over an hour into the film's shifting tableaux, this final sequence is remarkable not only for Lifshitz's elaborate sexual mise-en-scène but for a sense of narrative intrigue. Stéphanie plays along with the client's fantasy but subverts the alienation he attempts to impose on her by cautiously choosing the unassuming Mikhail in the street as the 'stranger'. Given the spliced-up chronology, this scene could of course equally be read as their first chance meeting, both of them joined together out of compliance with the client's wishes (and to earn a quick buck). The sense of movement is achieved through Godard's extreme close-ups of Nikitine's (Mikhail's) eyes as he observes the cash transaction from the backseat of the car. The sex scene begins with the client instructing the pair to undress, the camera jumping from his cold surveillance to their hesitant movements. His mastery of the scenario runs to instructing Stéphanie how to suck Mikhail. In a scene in which voyeurism is the preoccupation, the viewer's interest is directed as much to the client's cold lust and subsequent self-disgust as it is to his rutting objects. It is Godard's camerawork that takes on such voyeurism without technically reproducing it as the scene's dominant mode. She blocks the possibility of the viewer occupying either the theatrical position outside the frame, or the distant keyhole position of the voyeur, for instead of subjective shots from his perspective, and without porn's persistent zooming in on body parts, Godard discreetly moves the camera closer to the lovers, to the accompanying space of the medium distance shot, enabling us to feel closer to them than to the client. He thereby ends up excluded from the scene's visual field (shamefully fleeing postorgasm), the camera ignoring him by moving in closer still to focus on the lovers' hands clasped together in reassurance. It is this gradual movement away from shots that showcase the client's lust to those that convey the lovers' intimacy that works to deny the viewer the quick fix of crude voyeurism.

This technique is not of course reserved for Lifshitz. Godard is celebrated particularly for her work as director of photography with Claire Denis, whose striking poetic structures (notably in *Nénette et Boni* (1996), *Beau Travail* (1999), *Trouble Every Day* (2001) and *Vendredi soir* (2002)) have singled her out in recent years from run-of-the-mill verbose realism. Martine Beugnet picks up Godard's practice throughout her collaboration with Denis:

> Godard's camera scrutinises bodies as well as inanimate objects, but eschews the voyeuristic mode: the use of the macro lens in love scenes or scenes of intimacy in particular denies the necessary distance for this kind of objectification . . . As the image hovers at the frontier between the figurative and the abstract, the gaze is less one of observation calling for identification or objectification than one of sensual closeness inviting empathy. (Beugnet 2004: 29–30)

Commenting on *Beau Travail*, Denis seems to support Godard's quaint vision of sensuality (as opposed to actual sex) as the key to stimulating fiction:

> Cinema cannot exist except through eroticism . . . Sex between characters doesn't interest me. What's important is the sexual charge that passes between the actors and the spectators . . . What interests me is often what precedes the sexual act – which, despite everything, has very few variations. One can't really film sex unless one pretends or one works with actors who specialise in it.[35]

Godard's first film as Denis's director of photography, *J'ai pas sommeil* (1993), clearly prefigured *Wild Side*'s interest in sexual and social marginality. Chris Darke explains the background:

> Denis' controversial 1993 film . . . was based on the notorious case of Thierry Paulin, a serial killer who murdered twenty-one elderly women in

Paris between 1984 and 1987. Denis' film is as much about the anonymity that the murderer, a prostitute, drug-dealer and drag artist played by non-professional Richard Courcet, was able to maintain within a fluid demi-monde of drifters and immigrants as it is about his crimes. While the social canvas of Denis' films has tended to depict uneasy micro-communities of underbelly-dwellers, her filmic style has increasingly moved away from a traditional French realism towards more elliptical, poetic and sensual structures.[36]

Lifshitz's patchwork of three plausible positions of marginality echoes Denis's decentred narrative and anti-psychology, described as a sort of cine-matic behaviourism by *Cahiers du cinéma*.[37] Her three protagonists are also outsiders – Daïga (Katherina Golubeva), a Lithuanian immigrant looking for a fresh start in the West; Camille (Richard Courcet), a black HIV-positive man, living precariously at a cheap hotel with his lover; and his brother Théo (Alex Descas) a dissatisfied odd-job man planning to leave his partner to return to Martinique. The attention Denis gives to queer zones (in the eighteenth arrond-issement of north Paris) is acknowledged as an oblique nod to Fassbinder, whose loose formal approach to filming desire tended to avoid overly pristine images.[38] The risky scene in which Courcet is filmed offering his body to the gaze of other men, lip-synching in drag in a basement club, whilst employing stylised lighting and décor (one shot of men framed behind bars hints at the arti-ficial interior underworld of Fassbinder's Genet adaptation, *Querelle* (1982)) is simply shot, Godard's hand-held camera precisely following Courcet's languid body movements amongst the crowd. Beugnet describes how this scene was edited into the overall sequence to emphasise 'the contradictions and the com-partmentalisation of urban existence'. Like Lifshitz after her, Denis is said to favour 'a continuous wandering. In the complex narrative structure of her films, time is rarely bound to plot. Not only does the editing favour elision, but it allows for the narrative to stray', creating

> a narrative space where a multitude of lives, of realities, and several time zones seem to collide or to overlap. Through editing, a multiplicity of con-nections are created without strict chronology and the necessities of explaining or justifying a scene: there are always potential exchanges of gazes, closeness between characters suggested through graphic cuts and apparent eye line match rather than dialogues or actions. (Beugnet 2004: 91, 25, 23)

Judith Mayne has argued that Courcet establishes a distance from standard drag representation by emphasising sexy femininity over elaborate camp, his male chest protruding from the tight dress. Mayne underscores the scene's sur-prising grace, in which the spectators of Camille's performance appear to be as much the camera's objects as the performer himself (Mayne 2005: 82–3).

Godard's knack of establishing proximity between spectator and spectacle in this instance fits well with Denis's aim to sweep aside moral and pathological assumptions about the serial killer. Indeed her feminisation of such a figure (starting with his feminine name) breaks with dominant US cinematic imagery of black underclass and animal savagery. As Yannick Lemaire remarks, instead of disfiguring Courcet through harsh lighting, Denis and Godard's technique is to eroticise his body through emphasis on its effeminate beauty.[39] The low-key murders aside, the scene in which he is threatening is paradoxically an intimate one in which his lover expresses a desire to leave. It is the respective positioning of their bodies that conveys the potential threat more than their verbal exchange. To ensure his lover's entrapment, Courcet's back is shot in medium close-up, as he looms large (standing) over his lover's obscured body (seated).[40]

It is this experience of Denis's sensual structures that Godard was able to bring to Lifshitz's project, which whilst gesturing towards the elaborate stylisation, elliptical editing and sparse dialogue of Denis, tries to keep one foot within the realist tradition of narrative and identification. The issue of how to visualise sex through technical framing is broached in the documentary *The Other Side*. Lifshitz and Godard in turn explain their difference of opinion over the original screenplay, the sexually explicit nature of which Godard found excessively crude. She comments defensively that real sex acts would have overstepped the mark, going beyond cinema into the realms of pornography. I understand her as not necessarily positioning herself against pornography per se (though she is surely protecting art from the taint of mass media), but simply not wishing to be the person directly responsible for filming it (in the company of non-professional porn actors to boot). Lifshitz effectively compromised to keep Godard on the project, toning down his initial wish for a raunchy local brand of New Queer Cinema. The original chronologically organised script saw the trio in a sexual spiral in Paris, broken in the last part by the temporary move to the north. Recourse to actual sex acts was conceived to show the practical dynamics of sex work and to infuse Godard's art with a certain documentary realism, hence the casting of Michelini and Nikitine, two unprofessional actors who drew on their own personal life experience of transgender identity and immigrant poverty.

Whereas Godard's framing works to organise the depiction of desire and sexuality, her attention to the contrasting lights of Paris and northern France contributes to Lifshitz's shifting tableaux of urban and rural poverty. The dense saturated colours of night (one memorable shot of Stéphanie sees the artificial red light reflected back on her face) oppose the harshness of the barren north. (Lemaire picks up on Godard's practice of not working in a blurred half-light, but rather in a stark contrast between light and shadow. In the following interview Godard explains that she sees framing and lighting as inseparable, that her ideas on how to light a scene depend on the actual choice of focal distance.)[41] The childhood flashbacks, whilst falling into the biographical expectations of conventional narrative (considerable attention is given to Stéphanie's boyhood), are luminously shot to counterbalance the bleak present, 'impossibly green fields give the images their remembered quality'.[42] Lifshitz conceived of the north as the scenic extension of the figure of the dying mother, hence the over-significant slideshow shots of rural desolation, abandoned habitation and industrial ruin, the omnipresent slagheaps a reminder of past economic activity. The formal beauty of these photographic clichés (in both senses of the term) is uncontested, but there seems to be no ambivalence over possible metropolitan condescension, over an aesthetic recuperation of basic economic deprivation. Indeed, Lifshitz's comments on filming northern France in the AFCAE (*Association française des cinémas d'art et d'essai*) promotional literature do smack of the middle-class getting a kick out of poverty:

> One day on location I came across a supermarket dating from the 1970s, where nothing had really changed since. It had been left to ruin . . . I was moved, full of a bygone era. The same thing happened in a church and a school . . . These places were all like open graves.
> (Un jour de repérage, je suis tombé comme cela sur une supérette des années 70. Rien n'avait changé vraiment. Elle était juste à l'abandon . . . J'étais ému, rempli d'un temps révolu. La même chose est arrivée dans une église, une école . . . Tous ces lieux étaient comme des tombeaux ouverts.)[43]

Such images of social decline are effectively drawn as human metaphors for the characters' emptiness rather than as vehicles for political arguments in themselves.[44] Whilst Lifshitz and Godard are cautious about how to film sexuality to avoid charges of voyeuristic intent, the endless repetition of deserted streets makes the beauty of these anti-realist shots ultimately hollow. Put crudely, filming class seems to hold fewer precautions than filming sex, though, strictly speaking, you need to film human beings – not just barren landscapes – to get a comprehensive feeling of a social milieu. Class tourism ends up as the unfortunate flipside to dissident sexuality.

The downward gaze works better in the urban setting where, given the scarcity of shots of Mikhail's immigrant community and workplace, there is less room for grand romanticism and more room for precise detail. His arrival in Paris sees him trawling around immigrant tenements in search of his uncle, coming across a busy Russian woman who is preparing food for the workers; the precision of Godard's camera picks up the details of her labour as she dices tomatoes and kneads meat. A later scene shows Mikhail given hospitality by her 'family' of construction workers, the documentary naturalism of their meal cut by Mikhail watching disturbing television archives of violence against children in Russia (presumably the war in Chechnya). Likewise the earlier pan shot of *banlieue* tower blocks that introduces images of Djamel's alienation from his social milieu and the snapshots of Belmadi's childhood are effective because not repeated, but they are let down by Jocelyn Pook's cloying musical refrain whose recurrence throughout the film again works to over-promote middle-class sympathy as the project's dominant mode. There is a variant strain of this off-putting condescension in Denis's social outlook in which speaking on behalf of others is meant to imply the filmmaker's own generosity. Lifshitz's very first project was an interviewed documentary, *Claire Denis la vagabonde* (1995) (the title an obvious nod to Genet), in which he filmed his mentor in close-up talking about her early career up to *US Go Home* (1994). Her political vision of the fiction film is both traditionally republican and unashamedly utopian in nature: cinema as a medium through which to give a fictional voice to those who are denied social equality or recognition – 'de leur prêter le temps d'un regard' ('to grant them a look'), she says in all sincerity, without apparent awareness of her own social positioning, or even of the way her films actually tend to resist an imperialist gaze of black men (Mercer 1994; Marriott 2000).

The editor of *Wild Side*, Stéphanie Mahet, was not shown the original script, only discovering the finished product through the rushes, and was given carte blanche by Lifshitz to cut up the first edit to produce the final elliptical structure, in which sequences are organised by thematic and poetic order rather than chronological logic. Whilst this technique enabled Lifshitz to experiment with the narrative simplicity, *Wild Side* was later criticised for its apparent incoherence and for the final cut not being the sum of its parts – too many trendy mini-ellipses, according to *Cahiers du cinéma*;[45] it is all style and beauty, its look at marginality scarcely provocative, according to *Positif*.[46] Critic Emmanuel Burdeau even situates *Wild Side*'s silent fragmentation within a certain French art-house cinema chasing after its own formal radicalism.[47] Lifshitz's penchant for verbal understatement likewise places him at the opposite end of the spectrum from Catherine Breillat, who similarly negotiates the difficulties of explicit sexual representation, but who in contrast drowns them in ideological declaration (*Romance* (1999), *Sex is Comedy* (2002) and *Anatomie de l'enfer* (2004)).[48] Lifshitz defends the hybrid structure of *Wild Side*, contrasting the stylised visual (anamorphic wide-screen photography and controlled framing) with naturalistic acting in often-improvised scenes.[49] Such spontaneity is purposefully meant to thwart the over-riding lyricism of the mise en scène.

Bouquet, who sees social identity as the film's preoccupation, wrote it with a view to evacuating conventional psychological cause and effect.[50] But in Lacanian mode, he sees Lifshitz as occupying an ambiguous position between the desire to organise and represent his vision of reality and his desire for film to resist a flat transcription of reality, based on the premise that actuality would elude attempts at representation (the supposedly insuperable barrier of the real). Lifshitz himself more prosaically mentions the need to slot artistic imagery into the material society in which he lives and works. Jean-Luc Godard's quirky marginal threesome in *Bande à part* (1964) is said to be of historical (not simply formal or thematic) interest, representing an air of 1960s France beyond Godard's own aesthetic stamp, the precise movements of bodies (the basic function of mise-en-scène) situated in their precise historical moment. The attention given to the mores of contemporary society by recent US TV production is also cited as an inspiration for *Wild Side*.[51] Conversely, the international success of the regressive 1940s remake *Les Choristes* (Barratier, 2004), with its quaint comforting fantasy of a bygone France, its old-fashioned composition and its audience figures of 1.5 million in two weeks, is offered as an example of the rise of derivative commercial cinema. Lifshitz positions *Wild Side* in reaction to this widespread disavowal of French society and its unresolved anxieties and conflicts over race, immigration and sexuality, but he stops short of spelling out the exact oppositional mode of representation in which to incite queer disturbance.

Whilst admiring the European cinematic tradition of sexual dissent (Genet, Pasolini and Fassbinder), Lifshitz sees the possibility of a radical update as inconceivable, describing it as the dilemma of his generation, evolving in the fall-out of actually existing socialism. What is left is the melancholy of art films like *Wild Side*, in which the marginal victims of ruthless neo-liberalism are the primary vehicles for this modest brand of queer cultural production. The limitations of gay pathos are nothing new of course: Richard Dyer drew on Walter Benjamin's idea of 'left-wing melancholy' to address the political affect of Fassbinder back in the 1970s, including excessive dwelling on the victim state, denying empowerment outside of oppressive emotional entanglements, the brutalisation motif used to represent the lower classes, and the recourse to a purposefully static framing device to visualise entrapment (Dyer 2002 [1979]: 175–86). Likewise, Lifshitz's constant preoccupation with Oedipal resolution (dying mothers and ill or absent fathers cropping up every time) might be considered by some a retreat in queer film, though *Wild Side* is after all pointing to family reconfiguration through an oppositional *horizontal* mode of interpersonal commitment outside traditional models of kinship, a strand of the recent French queer cinema explored later in Chapter 4. *Wild Side* stands strategically at the centre of this book because it combines the thematic concerns of the previous chapters – Arab masculinity, queer migrations and the crossovers between ethnic identities and sexual dissent in the French context – with those of the following chapter – the relations between transgender and gay identities. *Wild Side* is also important for its attempt to address dissident sexualities in tandem with ethnic exclusion and social deprivation, but it is, I have argued, let down by a complacent reliance on middle-class sympathy, part of a local formation of class tourism, an argument also developed in Chapter 4 in relation to other queer films such as Honoré's *Ma mère* (2004). Lifshitz and Bouquet's decision to tackle transgender identity, sexual dissent, ethnic context and class hierarchy in one narrative is on balance ambitious and sits well with the broader cultural politics of a renewed queer critique that engages with non-normative sexualities across lines of race and class. I began with two media snapshots that called into question the apparent polarised opposition of queer sexuality and immigrant poverty. What is actually going on in between? The challenge of *Wild Side* is precisely its attempt to answer that question.

NOTES

1. Sylvie Pierre-Brossolette and Michel Schifres, 'L'Interview de Nicolas Sarkozy: "Je revendique la rupture"', *Le Figaro Magazine*, 2 September 2006, pp. 40–5.
2. Nicolas Sarkozy, quoted in Pierre-Brossolette and Michel Schifres, 'L'Interview de Nicolas Sarkozy', *Le Figaro Magazine*, 2 September 2006, p. 44.
3. Of some 30,000 applications, Sarkozy regularised the first 6,924. See Catherine Coreller, '6,924 sans-papiers régularisés et "une immense déception"', *Libération*, 19 September 2006.
4. For details of the BVA-Le Figaro-LCI poll, see *Le Figaro*, 8 June 2006, pp. 1, 7, 17.
5. See David L. Eng, Judith Halberstam and José Esteban Muñoz (eds), *Social Text*, special issue 'What's Queer about Queer Studies Now?', nos 84–5, Fall/Winter 2005.
6. For details of the word on the street, mostly from appreciative teenagers, see Agnès Dalbard and Alain Grasset, 'Chouchou fait mouche', *Le Parisien*, 20 March 2003, p. 29.
7. Nicolas Sarkozy, ' "Il n'y a pas de sujet tabou"', recueilli par Renaud Dély, Antoine Guiral et Patricia Tourancheau, *Libération*, 19 July 2005, pp. 12–13.
8. Julien Dray, ' "Sarkozy 2, c'est beaucoup de bruit pour peu d'efficacité"', recueilli par Didier Hassoux, *Libération*, 21 July 2005, p. 10.
9. Jean-Jacques Bozonnet, 'L'Espagne et l'Italie réclament l'aide de l'Europe face aux boat people', *Le Monde*, 23 August 2006, p. 6.
10. Michèle Tribalat, 'L'immigration choisie, la régularisation et le bal des hypocrites', *Le Figaro*, 4 May 2006, p. 18.
11. For activism against the law, see www.contreimmigrationjetable.com (accessed 30 August 2006).
12. Attac, 'POUR LE RETRAIT DU CONTRAT PREMIERE EMBAUCHE (CPE)', flyer distributed at the anti-CPE demonstrations in Paris, March–April 2006. On intern exploitation, see 'Stagiaires: Visa d'exploitation légale', cover to *Libération*, 27 April 2006.
13. Catherine Coroller, 'Immigration: un PS bien discret sur le projet Sarkozy,' *Libération*, 1–2 April 2006, p. 16.
14. 'En 2006, les Français n'attendent pas de miracle', *Métro*, Paris edition, 15 December 2005, p. 1.
15. See Hugues Lagrange, 'An outcast generation', *The Observer*, 6 November 2005, p. 13.
16. See Act Up's collective article, 'L'insécurité des minorités/Minorities in danger', *Action: La lettre mensuelle d'Act Up Paris*, no. 81, July 2002, pp. 18–19.
17. For sympathetic coverage by *Le Monde* of minority insecurity and the state-sanctioned repression of street prostitution, see Pascale Kremer, 'Des Associations dénoncent l'Amalgame entre Insécurité et Prostitution', *Le Monde*, 6 June 2002, p. 12.
18. See 'Le gouvernement veut explulser les prostituées étrangères', *Le Monde*, 12 July 2002, p. 8.
19. 'Le tapin sur le tapis,' *Libération*, 19 July 2002, pp. 1–5.
20. Anne Hildalgo quoted in Pascale Kremer, 'Le Tribunal de Bordeaux s'attaque aux clients de prostituées – La Mairie de Paris se mobilise contre cet "esclavage"', *Le Monde*, 13 September 2002, p. 11.
21. See Didier Arnaud and Blandine Grosjean, 'Du tapin au pavé', *Libération*, 6 November 2002, p. 2.
22. Nicolas Sarkozy quoted in Philippe Le Cœur, 'Sécurité: les nouveaux interdits de la loi Sarkozy', *Le Monde*, 14 February 2003, p. 8.
23. See Marie-Françoise Colombani, 'Les Français contre la pénalisation des prostitué(e)s', *Elle*, 11 November 2002, pp. 83–8.

24. Nicolas Sarkozy quoted in Florence Muracciole, Michel Deléan and Stéphane Joahny, 'Sarkozy contre-attaque', *Le Journal du dimanche*, 29 September 2002, p. 2.
25. Eric Fassin, 'Panique sécuritaire, panique sexuelle', *Le Monde*, 7 August 2002, p. 1.
26. Jacques Mandelbaum, 'L'insubordination sexuelle contre l'aliénation sociale', *Le Monde*, 14 April 2004, p. 27.
27. Claude Miller in the radio programme *Le Cinéma l'après-midi*, France Culture, 24 April 2004.
28. Yann Gonzalez, 'Lifshitz côté sauvage', *Têtu*, April 2004, p. 20.
29. Lifshitz quoted in AFCAE promotional literature and in radio interview for *Tout arrive*, France Culture, 14 April 2004.
30. Jacques Mandelbaum, 'L'insubordination sexuelle contre l'aliénation sociale', *Le Monde*, 14 April 2004, p. 27.
31. Emilie Bickerton, 'Wild Side', *Sight and Sound*, vol. 15 (4), April 2005, p. 80.
32. Philippe Azoury, 'L'hybride "Wild Side" ', *Libération*, 14 April 2004, cinema section, p. IV.
33. Emilie Bickerton, 'Wild Side', *Sight and Sound*, vol. 15 (4), April 2005, p. 80.
34. Yann Gonzalez, 'Lifshitz côté sauvage', *Têtu*, April 2004, p. 20.
35. Claire Denis quoted in Chris Darke, 'Desire is violence', *Sight and Sound*, vol. 10 (7), July 2000, pp. 16–18.
36. Chris Darke, 'Desire is violence', *Sight and Sound*, vol. 10 (7), July 2000, p. 16.
37. Thierry Jousse, 'Les insomniaques', *Les Cahiers du cinéma*, nos 479/480, May 1994, p. 22.
38. Thierry Jousse and Frédérique Strauss, 'Entretien avec Claire Denis', *Les Cahiers du cinéma*, nos 479/480, May 1994, p. 28.
39. Yannick Lemaire, 'À propos d'Agnès Godard et de quelques autres . . .', *Positif*, no. 471, May 2000, pp. 128–9.
40. Beugnet notes similarly that 'external looks are difficult to read, and, in some of the films, the bodies, obscured rather than exposed, tend to stand "too close" to the camera, sometimes literally blocking out the view' (Beugnet 2004: 38).
41. Yannick Lemaire, 'À propos d'Agnès Godard et de quelques autres . . .', *Positif*, no. 471, May 2000, p. 128. See also Françoise Audé and Yann Tobin, 'Agnès Godard: Regarder jusqu'à vouloir toucher', *Positif*, no. 471, May 2000, pp. 131–6.
42. Emilie Bickerton, '*Wild Side*', *Sight and Sound*, vol. 15 (4), April 2005, p. 80.
43. Lifshitz, quoted in AFCAE promotional literature.
44. Likewise Godard's use of *décadrage* with Denis: 'the void suggested by the image seems like an extension of the sense of anguish that the film's scarce dialogues, isolated heightened sounds and silences generate' (Beugnet 2004: 31).
45. Emmanuel Burdeau, 'Marges silencieuses', *Cahiers du cinéma*, no. 589, April 2004, pp. 31–2.
46. Françoise Audé, 'Wild Side', *Positif*, no. 518 April 2004, p. 49.
47. Emmanuel Burdeau, 'Marges silencieuses', *Cahiers du cinéma*, no. 589, April 2004, p. 32.
48. In the radio programme *Le Cinéma l'après-midi* (France Culture, 24 April 2004) Breillat notably attacked *Wild Side* for its inconclusiveness, only seeing flashes of a film amid the film's fragments.
49. Lifshitz, quoted in Serge Kaganski and Jean-Marc Lalanne, 'L'Amour en tout genre', *Les Inrockuptibles*, no. 437, 14–20 April 2004, pp. 38–41.
50. See Philippe Azoury and Gérard Lefort, ' "Liquider toute psychologie pour qu'il ne reste que les êtres" ', *Libération*, 14 April 2004, cinema section, pp. IV–V.
51. Lifshitz, quoted in Serge Kaganski and Jean-Marc Lalanne, 'L'Amour en tout genre', *Les Inrockuptibles*, no. 437, 14–20 April 2004, p. 39.

3. *MAUVAIS GENRES*: TRANSGENDER AND GAY IDENTITY

This chapter takes up the argument that 'transgender' (the umbrella term for transsexuality and queer forms of cross-gender identification including lesbian and gay gender performances of butch and queen) articulates uncertainty as to the categories of gender and sexual identities. The chapter exposes the strains between transgender and lesbian and gay identities in the French context through coverage of queer community-based documentaries (*Portrait d'une présidente*, 1995; *L'Ordre des mots*, 2007), and narrative cinema – both mainstream (*Mauvais genres*, 2001; *Ma vie en rose*, 1997) and independent (*Thelma*, 2002), now casting transgender actors in transgender roles. This chapter seeks to contrast the emergence of political activism against institutional psychiatry with more intimate projections of transgender by filmmakers such as Patrice Chéreau (*Ceux qui m'aiment prendront le train*, 1998) and Jacques Nolot (*La Chatte à deux têtes*, 2002), who not only project specifically gay fantasies of transgender, but also weave the effects of AIDS and loss on gay love into the social fabric of their films.

Shoot and Run

Border crossing is the topic of an important tribute to the transgender immigrant prostitutes of the Boulevard Ney in Paris, written by journalist and activist Hélène Hazera for *Têtu* magazine in 1999.[1] Hazera's tribute to the 'sisters of the boulevard' captures the predicament of a group of Algerians, whose identifications range from effeminate boys to male-to-female transsexuals. They are perceived and persecuted as homosexuals and sentenced to execution in Algeria, whilst refused refugee status or residents' permits in France, unable to work legally and left to their own devices for survival out on the street. Hazera compares her own story of transgender prostitution in Pigalle in the 1970s and her eventual exit with help from a gay friend, writer and journalist Michel Cressole, whom she had known since their days together with the radical gay movement FHAR (*Front homosexuel d'action révolutionnaire*) in the early part of the decade. He found Hazera work as a television critic at *Libération*, at the time also home to other eminent former FHAR activist and intellectual Guy Hocquenghem. The point of Hazera's autobiographical digression is not so much to express satisfaction at her own luck, but frustration that the issue of immigration and nationality bars these transgendered Algerians from any right to a life other than prostitution.

The Ney girls are generally well received in the few gay Arab venues dotted around the city: by invoking sisters in her title, Hazera is making a point about alliances between gay and transgender concerns. She wonders whether this is an illusion, whether this festive solidarity extends once outside the artificial world of the nightclub. Indeed Hazera is encouraging gay men to question their alleged distance from transgendered people by referring to one moment in a shared history – the moment of sexual liberation; she explains that in the FHAR manifestos first published in the far-left revue *Tout*, there was a camp lexicon of conversational do's and don't's. The entry under 'travesti' read 'Don't say "transvestites", say "our sisters"' ('Ne dites pas "travesties", dites "nos soeurs"'.[2]

Contrary to their reception in gay venues, part of Hazera's exposé concerns the violence the Algerian transsexuals encounter from gangs of young Arab men from the *cités* surrounding Paris, or worse still from tabloid journalists who, hungry for a salacious storyline, have transgender prostitutes beaten up for photographic effect. Indeed, the visual element in Hazera's account is important, for she includes photographs taken by Kader Attia, whom she admires for the complicity and intimacy he establishes between camera and subject. By juxtaposing images of their lives through everyday objects rather than their bodies, Attia attests to their *material* lives – he includes interior shots of fur coats, shoes, furniture, a birthday cake, a political banner bearing the bluntly realistic protest 'Deported from France, executed in Algeria', and exterior shots of the girls' urban playground. Attia is seeking to convey the cultural dislocation of people condemned to exile. Hazera prefers his approach to that of the contemporary American photographer of the sexual underworld Nan Goldin, whose perceived objectification of transsexuals, is, in Hazera's opinion, offensive and verging on the voyeuristic. Her experience as Goldin's object leads her to describe Goldin's technique as a case of 'shoot and run'.[3]

Transgender photographer Del LaGrace Volcano, whose work documents the growth of an urban, drag-king subculture in New York, San Francisco and London – from the underground clubs of the early 1990s to mainstream press attention by the end of the decade – thinks Paris is dull. However, one of his set pieces is a moody shot of a Parisian brasserie, in which the kings smoke philosophically, an apparent ode to Brassaï, who famously recorded the secret sexual underground of 1930s Paris, including soirées at the lesbian venue *Le Monocle*, catching the tail-end of the legendary, gay drag parties called the 'Inverts' ball' (*Le Bal des invertis*) at *Magic City* in 1933 (Brassaï: 1976). In his introduction to an illuminating visual and written testimony to the world of drag kings, simply entitled *The Drag King Book*, to which LaGrace provides the photographs and Judith Halberstam the various interviews and accompanying text, LaGrace recounts an unpleasant experience of Paris. 'Of all the urban centres I've been to,' he asserts, 'in my opinion, Paris is the most reactionary and regressive of European cities, and yes, I'm talking specifically about the lesbian and gay "community"' (LaGrace 1999: 25). French lesbians are perceived as overwhelmingly hostile to LaGrace's photography on account of his incorrect subject choice: instead of depicting feminine lesbians, he favours butch dykes and female-to-male transsexuals. In LaGrace's anecdote, the kings' tour of Parisian nightspots ends in disaster when some 'lipstick lesbians' physically assault them. 'They simply did not like us crossdressing in their clubs and felt we were doing their cause a disservice,' he surmises. 'Some French lesbians seem to be deeply resentful of anything that throws them off their precarious pseudo-feminist perch, which we obviously did' (LaGrace: 25). According to this account, gender dissent is suggested to be taboo in French queer communities.

LaGrace is pointing to ideological conflict around transgender in lesbian and gay milieus, undermining any neat pact between non-normative sexual and gender identities. The ideological work of the films covered in this chapter focuses primarily on issues of transgender dissent, a preoccupation familiar to Anglo-American queer theories. How is effeminacy systematically pushed into issues of same-sex desire rather than taken as part of the transgender dynamic? If we reconfigure effeminacy as tantamount to transgender rather than as a subset of homosexual desire, we might then ask how easily male femininity inhabits the same ideological space as transgender. Alan Sinfield has argued that transgender in gay and lesbian milieus, in the guise of effeminacy and butchness has been, since gay liberation, historically subsumed into sexual identity, rather than set apart as gender identity – that is to say, the formation of Western metropolitan sexual identities has been hiving transgender off as a subcategory. Sinfield is urging us to recognise this pattern to clarify what gay and lesbian, and later on bisexual, identities have been over-simplifying or worse excluding.

> In gay liberation, it is lesbians and gays who could pass who gained the option of coming out, because now they were defined fully as homosexual. In other words, sexual orientation became prior, and gender identity was subsumed, more or less uneasily, into it. Transgender demands reconsideration of that model. (Sinfield 2000: 157)

The extent to which cross-gender identification is a widespread form of transsexuality was of course taken up by canonical queer theory – much of the critical thought in the light of Butler's *Gender Trouble* (Butler 1990) articulated such troubles. Criticising orthodox forms of psychoanalysis for fixing sexed positions around correct identification, Butler argued that identifying as a man or woman involves refusing feminine and masculine identifications respectively, presupposing that the loss of aberrant gender ties is present in all sexed identity. What interested Butler at this time was 'a very *mundane* sense of transsexuality', how cross-gendered identification 'could be understood on a continuum with transssexuality, [making] transsexuality into something less aberrant and other' (Kotz 1992: 88). Transgender, at least in this context, has as much to do with subculture; social alliances between sexual and gender identities can (or not) put transsexuality on a continuum with lesbian and gay gender dissent. If so, this would counter the more widely held tendency to regard transsexuals as identified above all by bodily parts. Judith Halberstam's work is important in this respect, for she has been insisting on the overlap between transsexual men and masculine women, but not necessarily on a straight continuum of gender dissent – the complication being that not all masculine women or feminine men are in the initial stages of transition. Halberstam comments that 'it would not be accurate to make gender dysphoria the exclusive property of transsexual bodies or to surmise that the greater the gender dysphoria, the likelier a transsexual identification'. We are quite obviously not all transsexuals,

> but many bodies are gender strange to some degree or another, and it is time to complicate on the one hand the transsexual models that assign gender deviance only to transsexual bodies and gender normativity to all other bodies, and on the other hand the hetero-normative models that see transsexuality as the solution to gender deviance and homosexuality as a pathological perversion. (Halberstam 1998: 151, 153–4)

Critics of queer approaches to transgender have argued that the material context of transsexual life tends to get overlooked. Jay Prosser has made an important case against the critical tendency to knock transsexuals for being the dupes of gender fiction, for wanting to pass socially as real men and real women; he accentuates gendered realness and the importance of the body's surface for ego formation (Prosser 1998). Prosser points to transsexuals as agents in their own narrative construction, rather than the monster creations of much traditional psychiatric discourse. Feminist critic Lynne Segal takes up Prosser's argument to explain how transgender 'and all the other attempts to combine and repackage gender and sexual signifiers, might be thought to keep us all the more in thrall to their now multiply exhausting demands and anxieties, fears and pleasures' (Segal 1999: 62). Segal is keen to underline the psychic pain (a testimony to the ever-present fixity of binary gender) and personal cost in attempts to escape ones assigned gender. The following materialist-inflected account of transgender politics in the French context points to the collective struggle for a fairer society in which it would be easier to cross gender or reject gender binary altogether, with less institutional interference from medicine and psychiatry. The following section aims to document the emergence of a 'trans-pride' movement in French queer subcultures.

GET THERAPY

In the French context, the struggle for trans-pride has seen the recent formation of an annual political rally, Existrans, launched in 1997 by Tom Reucher's association L'ASB (L'Association du syndrome de Benjamin). The annual march assembles the more radical queer groups and associations (Act Up, Résistrans, le Mag, les Flamands Roses, le PASTT) with an agenda that aims to explore the exclusions and silences surrounding transgender dissent in the movements for sexual liberation, the type of agenda for radical change squeezed out of the normative lesbian and gay rights movement and absent in its commercial manifestation as 'gay pride'. The 2007 Existrans demonstration declared resistance to the psychiatric stranglehold ('Contre la psychiatristaion. Résistrans!'). The formation from within Act Up Paris of the GAT (Groupe activiste transgenre), whose political video output is covered in Chapter 5, was intended as an empowering backlash against French psychiatric hegemony. Hazera has expressed similar concerns in the context of libertarianism – to unchain the body, all identity cards, those fixed markers of biological power, must be burned. The libertarian position – Hazera's article appeared in a special 1999 gay pride edition of *Le Monde Libertaire*, issued by the French Anarchist Federation, the headline of which was 'Our bodies are not commodities!'[4] – argues for the withdrawal of the psychiatric machine classifying transsexuals as real or false, a halt to the psychic damage caused by forcing all transgender people in France to undergo sex reassignment therapy, still a difficult and often dangerous operation, as the only means to obtain revised identity papers and social security rights. The insight here is that transgender is not intrinsically radical, but plainly illustrative of the social investment of the state in moulding gender – 'how, through its doctors, its judges, its administration, its police, the State assumes the right to an invasive control of people's lives'[5] ['comment l'Etat s'arroge, par ses médecins, ses juges, son administration, ses flics, une mainmise accablante sur la vie de quelques individus']. Hazera argues for a more thorough emphasis on the material lives and situations of transgender people in specific medical, psychiatric, legal and administrative schema, so as to bypass the predictable theoretical wrangling in the fall-out from queer theory as to whether transgender is, or is not, in itself politically progressive.

Activist groups like the GAT attack the French psychiatric institution for not only restricting personal freedoms but also policing the ideological boundaries and social possibilities of identity formation. An example given by Hazera of psychiatric abuse is Colette Chiland's theoretical tract, *Changer de sexe* (Chiland 1997), which advocates therapy as the suitable cure to deviant fantasy. The biographical cover blurb lists Chiland's academic credentials as a philosophy-major, doctor, psychiatrist, psychoanalyst and teacher of clinical psychology at the Sorbonne; a crude outline of her present argument would read: head change, not sex change. The doctor is out to prove her own credibility – whether social, personal or intellectual – at the expense of the objects she has spent years treating at the specialised clinic at the Fernand-Widal hospital in Paris. (This hospital, however, has a generally progressive reputation in the field of social politics, as the first methadone distribution centre for drug users, the first to pioneer a drug risk-reduction policy in the fight against AIDS.) Chiland speaks disparagingly of her transsexual patients as having a simplistic notion of gender, and at one point, mid-way through, ventures haphazardly into social politics, claiming that female-to-male transsexuals are generally more intelligent than male-to-female transsexuals, so are more able to overcome the administrative difficulties of identity change; MTFs (male-to-female transsexuals) pass less easily in public and tend to become housewives apparently. The axe she is grinding falls predictably enough on prostitution – she indulges on two occasions in some blatantly insulting rhetoric on the physical appearance of sex workers, and ends by labelling 'transsexualism' a form of mental anorexia. Were Chiland not practising such ideology on a daily basis, inflicting institutional violence by vetting transsexuals for potential pathology, her récit could indeed be brushed off as a parody. As it is, Chiland misleadingly flaunts her debt to influential psychiatrist Robert Stoller (a far more enlightened figure than his French admirers), and fills her book with an array of American clinical theories – a pretty conclusive balance sheet of the psychiatric damage done to transsexuals for some fifty-odd years.

For Chiland, transsexuals hanker after the impossibility of the real gender roles of yesteryear; their supposed illness turns out to be the product of an imbalance in contemporary culture. Wading through some 200 pages of clinical theory, the reader finally gets Chiland's hidden agenda. With bouts of epistemological panic about the breakdown of heterosexual hegemony, her account actually resembles apocalypse now. Accordingly, the death of God means that nothing is forbidden in our culture; by using the prefix trans- to slide transsexuality into transgression, thus isolating trans- as a key value, her rhetorical strategy makes of transsexuality the violation of the law. In reality, not every act of transgression will necessarily violate a law – for example, receptive anal sex for men transgresses a cultural norm in the contemporary western European context, but does not encroach on the forbidden. Chiland's appeals to 'communal consciousness' ('la conscience commune', Chiland: 232) situate her ideology in the late 1990s sexual fears of symbolic disintegration, culminating in the outing of homophobia during the same-sex partnership parliamentary debates – 'where are the boundaries to real power and to the lawful power of homo artifex?' ['où sont les limites au pouvoir réel et au pouvoir licite de l'homo artifex?'], she wonders (Chiland: 232). Behind the abstruse thinking, what Chiland is actually up to is a last-minute conversion of scientific discourse, in the course of which Freud and Lacan get predictably hijacked – in a familiar description of Oedipal law and order – for conservative Catholic ends, which come down to not messing with creation. For Chiland, transsexuals are not classically psychotic, but they present borderline symptoms, the cure for which – and this is Chiland's principal therapeutic weapon – is the acceptance of ontological 'finitude', that is to say, coming to terms with the immutable facts of binary sexual difference and death. Her use of the terms *serenity* and *wisdom* are political stop-gaps to pass sexual difference off as some transcendental or universal law, whereas in actual fact what is hypothetically interesting, if anything, about sexual difference is not the necessity of an unchangeable law at all cost, but how it is used, how it breaks down, what it contains, what values a given culture accords it, and the uncontrollable havoc it can wreak on psychic life. In any case, it is doubtful whether Chiland's prescribed psychotherapy can very well do much to eradicate 'deviant' fantasies. A later vulgarised introduction to Chiland's thesis (Chiland 2003) is more pernicious because her extremist ideology gets packaged as credible scientific truth through the publication of an introductory volume on the subject for the widely diffused (and in this case ironically appropriate) series *Que sais-je?* (*What do I know?*).

The political agenda of the radical movements such as the GAT attempts to free transgender from the dominant prism of psychiatry. The community-produced documentary *L'Ordre des mots* (Cynthia and Mélissa Arra, 2007) likewise attacks the institutional straitjacket of psychiatry through lengthy, in-depth interviews with some of the main French transgender activists. The documentary's structure uses testimony to political effect rather than indulging in the cheap voyeurism of a freak show, by giving the articulate subjects the time and space to recount their personal stories. Free from the generic constraints of liberal pity, and without the anthropological tendency to interpret for a mainstream audience, the directors are able to synthesise the differing conceptions of non-normative genders without reducing the testimonies to pre-established binaries. Activist Vincent He-say gives a politicised account of resistance to a fixed identity as a trans-man. Tom Reucher articulates childhood difficulties and the educational handicap resulting from social exclusion as an FTM trans-man, personal hardship that is shown without pathos or sentimentality, without the generic device of audience manipulation employed by TV documentaries of the sort made by Mireille Dumas, who has for long exploited gender from behind the mask of liberal sympathy. Her 'Travestir' for Arte's *La Vie en face* series in 1996 adopted a maudlin approach to transgender. *L'Ordre des mots*, in contrast, is a breakthrough in the French context simply because it allows its subjects to direct the form of the documentary rather than being subjected to strategic editing techniques that frame transgender people as exotic objects of fascination. *L'Ordre des mots* does not shy away from painful subjects such as suicide and psychological damage, but instead of localising them as individual deficiencies, it points the finger at the institutional psychiatric damage done to citizens whose lives are manipulated by self-appointed experts. It is the documentary's matter-of-factness – combining voice-over narrative testimony with prolonged close-up shots of the speaker in the process of thinking – that gives a synchronic picture of transgender life in a national context of harsh psychiatric repression.

TRANSGENDER SCREENS

Unlike the example of a community-based production such as *L'Ordre des mots*, mainstream and independent narrative cinema, even when sympathetic to transgender, remains critically entrenched within the psychological paradigm. The following selective survey of transgender representation through three narrative fictions (a psycho-thriller, a romantic adventure and a family drama) shows the limited potential for transgender visibility within the generic frameworks of narrative cinema.

The crime thriller *Mauvais genres* (2001), directed by Francis Girod and adapted from Brigitte Aubert's novel *Transfixions*, works within the explicitly Freudian framework of family neurosis, locating masochism as inherent to male-to-female transsexuality. Filmed in cinemascope in the old streets of Brussels to give the production the look of a *grand-guignol* horror film, *Mauvais genres* gives a new spin to the classic female victim by tracing male-to-female transgender to early childhood. Bo (Robinson Stévenin), who wears her dead mother's couture, was abused as a boy by her father, who is arrested for paedophilia at the start of the film, an ideological manœuvre used to explain both Bo's 'wrong' gender identification and her queer sexuality (she is a sex worker). Bo becomes infatuated with the handsome gigolo Johnny (Stéphane Metzger); eager to seduce him, she naïvely compromises her own safety by entering into a situation in which she is violently attacked. Her neurotic dependency on Johnny is such that when he breaks her wrist, she draws a heart on the plaster as a declaration of love. Johnny's own misogyny is channelled into deviant sex acts such as whipping and beating a female prostitute. The film's denial of any agency for its transgender heroine is rendered literal through the exigencies of the crime genre in which the gradual slaughter of transgender prostitutes leaves Bo as both the prime suspect and the prime target (Johnny is indicated throughout the intrigue as the all too obvious red herring). Bo's older and more experienced friend Maeva (William Nadylam) is suggested as a possible mother substitute and, in a reverential homage to psychoanalytical orthodoxy, Johnny turns out to be a prostitute's son (hence the earlier revenge whipping), and the police inspector (Richard Bohringer) turns out to be both his father (Bo even gets to dress up as his mother) and the serial killer.

The crime genre is twisted to expose the warped fantasies of ostensibly straight characters such as the police inspector, whilst preaching tolerance on dissident gender identities. However, whilst Bo is sympathetically drawn, she is hardly a transgender role model for our times. A more engaged production might have provided the character with more to do than suffer the consequences of distorted male fantasies. Indeed, an ironic revenge slash-movie would at least have the virtue of liberating transgender characters from their allotted role as passive victims. *Mauvais genres* ultimately queers its own pitch by attempting to enlighten the crime genre through a laborious psychoanalytical frame of reference, a move that backfires by retaining a regressive sexual politics – Bo is shown to adopt the masochistic position in her imitation of an idealised womanhood. Such liberal representations of transgender for the mainstream market (Girod explains his liberal motivations for the film in the DVD interview) would seem to suggest that the subject remains a primarily psychological 'issue' in the popular consciousness. The more radical vision might gesture to the social development of transgender networks and communities seeking to forge new identities and subjectivities outside this stranglehold of oppressive psychiatry.

A more ambitious approach is to cast transgender actors in transgender roles, a form of social progress in independent film production that is certainly as pressing as debates about positive representations of transgender subjects. In Pierre-Alain Meier's first long feature, *Thelma* (a Franco-Swiss co-production, 2002), the versatile Pascale Ourbih (at the time a model and psychology consultant, since then an underground actor and political activist) made her acting début as the eponymous heroine. Thelma offers a wad of cash to a kind taxi driver she meets by chance, Vincent (Laurent Schilling), to accompany her to Crete to get her revenge on an ex-lover, a married man who cast her aside. Thelma then has to reveal to Vincent, with whom she begins to fall in love, that she used to be a man and still has male genitalia. The revelation scene, a frontal view of Thelma naked, is dealt with early on as a visual shock to Vincent, but obviously not to the viewer for whom the film is explicitly marketed as transgender fare. But Thelma withholds her other Greek secret – her former lover, Fenia (Nathalia Capo d'Istria), who lives there with their daughter, unaware of Thelma's transition. The plot essentially focuses on Vincent's attempts to push Thelma towards reconciliation with her former life. It is Vincent, himself an anguished father, who allows his own heterosexual identification to be undermined by Thelma to help her out.

Whilst Meier's outlook seems globally encouraging with respect to transgender, he does tend to re-inscribe the sexual norm into the action. One such example is reproduced on the publicity flyer: at one point during their long car journey, Vincent asks for some clarifications on Thelma's gender identity – drag queen, drag king, transvestite or transsexual? Thelma tells him she is a woman; he slyly replies that she drives well, for a woman. This neat bit of macho irony is slipped in as a punchline to the otherwise carefully crafted explanatory piece on the variations of transgender. Meier's treatment of the sex scenes is also shaky, again serving the very naturalisation of heterosexuality that the film elsewhere gently unsettles. The film contains two sex scenes: the first between Vincent and Thelma, the second between Vincent and Fenia. The first is a rushed fuck – Vincent jumps from an introductory kiss straight to taking Thelma from behind (will film directors *ever* bother putting condoms into sex scenes?); the second is a softly lit, sensual scene of missionary love-making. Certainly the insulting question Thelma's ex-lover later throws at Vincent (does he fuck her or make love to her?) is indeed revealing. Either the two scenes are intentionally opposed, to show where Vincent is really getting his pleasure, or at least should be, or the visual disparity between the clumsy, over-rushed fuck and the cosy, romantic pairing is just a case of directorial nerves.

Thelma is important nonetheless for what it says about transgender and performance. Vincent's wife, for example, misreads the gender signs, casually informing him that Thelma is quite obviously a prostitute, thus conflating high, stylised femininity with prostitution. This example bears witness to an apparent confusion over issues of gender and genre, the debate over whether transsexuals are already acting or not, familiar to post-modernity's obsession with identities as fictive regimes. Collapsing performativity – lately, gender has been theoretically presented as the citation of a set of socially sanctioned norms – into performance, as Ourbih seems to be suggesting, is risky because it has been the historical reason why trans people have been refused transgender roles on screen – they are thought to be acting already, so cannot approach the role from the outside, as *real* acting. Despite the film's ideological muddle, Ourbih is right to feel proud of her work on Thelma for her activism as the first transgender actor to play a transgender role in French cinema.

Alain Berliner's film *Ma vie en rose* (1997) – a more mainstream Franco-Belgian production, co-written by Chris van der Stappen – engages with childhood fantasies of crossing the gender line, but has trouble sorting out gender identification from potential same-sex passion. This is the story of a little boy who wants to grow up to be a girl. His understanding is that God messed up the chromosome count, throwing his X into the dustbin. Kate Ince has located the film's deployment of fantasy as 'politically enabling' (Ince 2002: 90). I am less convinced of the possibilities for adequate transgender representation within the confines of an old-fashioned problem movie masquerading as post-modern chic. The first scene locates the numbing conventionality of Ludo's suburban, middle-class world – the peaceful, comfortable part of the Essonne, south of Paris – by drawing attention to items of clothing. Hanna and Pierre (Michèle Laroque and Jean-Philippe Ecoffey) are throwing a house-warming party for the neighbours – an open inspection of house and kin. The camera follows the careful preparation in each household – men zipping women into tight dresses, children spying on their parents' bedrooms, lips being adorned in bright red lipstick. The lips on show are Ludo's, for, as his parents proceed to bring on the four children for community appraisal, calling after daughter Zoé, the young Ludo (Georges Du Fresne) puts in his first cross-dressed appearance in his sister's place. Ludo advances precariously in an outsized pair of mother's shoes, much to the admiration of the crowd (for he has no trouble passing) and to the bemusement of his parents, who brush off the incident as part of the child's farce. His youthful-looking, eccentric granny (Hélène Vincent) finds all this gender-bending quixotic and Mother, at this early stage, is far from anxious, having read a comforting article on identity development in *Marie-Claire*. Indeed Berliner uses the subsequent party scenes, described by one critic as 'a sort of sociology of taste'[6] ('une sorte de sociologie du goût') to illustrate Ludo's happiness with the two women, the camera filming them in slow motion, as all three dance together, all the while touching and smiling. The rest of the film serves as a mundane, realistic antidote to Ludo's cross-gender identification, these initial scenes later appearing just about as far-fetched as Ludo's own pink, fantasy world of dolls – the corny, garish television romance of Pam and Ben, fictive European clones of Barbie and Ken.

Unlike the rest of the conventional family, Granny has a rare insight into make-believe. Ludo's imaginary world is presented alongside Granny's: Ludo calls her in to fantasise the moment Pam and Ben appear on screen. Images of the ideal, plastic couple segue back into the living room, where Ludo is entranced by them, lip-synching the theme song, lines of which – particularly 'neurotically obsessed by happiness' – are sung at various stages by the characters as a sort of leitmotif throughout the film. Granny enters, amazed at Ludo's dance, surprising him, only to break the embarrassed pause by imitating his dance routine. Granny explains her own desire to Ludo – she is keen on the idea of eternal youth – and gives Ludo tips on imagining his own ideal world.

Ludo's friend Jérôme (Julien Rivière) also indulges his fantasy of crossing gender – homoeroticism on Jérôme's part is hinted at, figured as a possible attraction to effeminacy, which, since the two strands of gender and sexuality are never straightened out, contributes to a lack of clarity in handling transgender and homosexuality together. The homophobic community stigmatise Ludo for apparently being gay – 'poof out!' is spray-painted over the garage door. Ludo discovers the nursery of Jérôme's deceased baby sister, a veritable hidden gender laboratory, where the two enact a ritual wedding, blessed by a teddy-bear priest, who curiously keeps falling over, and witnessed by Jérôme's meddling mother, who faints on sight. Just as Hanna arrives to scold Ludo, a blond and busty Pam sweeps in through the window to rescue them, blowing magic gold dust to restrain the mothers, all three flying off above the humdrum reality. Berliner's film certainly has some salient and occasionally humorous points to make about the force of individual fantasy (learning the theory of chromosomal deficiency, Ludo waits with baited breath for puberty, jumping for joy at the signs of supposed period pains) through Ludo's rational amazement at the craze of the bourgeois circus around him – at one point, he stares wide-eyed in astonishment at his school teacher as she tries to redirect his identification from Pam to Ben.

The film falls down, however, when it begins to take on the weightier subject of social reality – the question of stigma (the neighbourhood witch-hunt) and the wreck it makes of the family cell, together with the painful degree of institutional violence Ludo faces in his expulsion from school, where he is informed that his tastes are too strange for the establishment, his visits to the, albeit caring, psychologist, and Pierre's unemployment. Middle-class insanity – for it is important to note that Berliner is carefully wrapping 'heteronormativity' up in the specific class concerns of hypocrisy, stifling normalcy and relational destruction generally tending to representations of the bourgeois milieu – is ultimately a worthy subject, but far less visually entertaining than Ludo's gaudy fantasies. Indeed, the fantasies enacted early on in the film serve as a mere pretext to address the degree of social disturbance they provoke. This underscores a certain ideological confusion throughout the film, explaining Ludo's fantasies not as specifically transsexual, but more as symptomatic of his desire to be a (possibly) gay, effeminate boy, thus pushing him from a transsexual to a gay identification.

Beneath what Lucille Cairns has described as 'the film's strategically ludic and conspicuously postmodern style' lies the more disheartening question of how individuals are damaged, or cut up, to fit the mould of social norms. So the remainder of Ludo's story turns into an old-fashioned problem movie addressing what the filmmakers perceive as a controversial theme. Again, as Cairns puts it, 'the film does encode the popular conflation of transgender and homosexuality, and it does reflect the stranglehold of heteronormativity in which France, as much as any Western country, is caught' (Cairns 2001: 119, 127). Chantal Nadeau voices frustration at the film's foreclosure of politics, at how gender identity is pictured in the idealist tradition as a unique attribute of the individual, mixed up with the dubious biologism of the chromosome solution; yet Nadeau admires the film's humanist spirit, concluding that '*Ma vie en rose* allows a certain openness toward political selfhood and subjectivity . . .' (Nadeau 2000: 143).

There are at least two, albeit brief, instances of something verging on the political, vaguely broaching notions of the potential power of collective action. Contrary to the pop-psychological analysis of Ludo's case shared by the neighbours – the overbearing Christian fundamentalist's homely wife voices the received wisdom that if society weren't so degenerate, we wouldn't need madmen to take care of other madmen – Granny suggests an alternative therapy: let Ludo live out his fantasy to see whether he tires of it. Following Ludo's melodramatic suicide attempt in the freezer, the parents' guilt drives them to grant Ludo a wish and he chooses to go to a neighbourhood birthday party in a skirt. Thus a joyous image amidst the previous and subsequent scenes of melodrama is of Ludo, in his kilt, promoted by his proud Granny and pursued by the self-conscious parents, marching triumphantly to the party, to the theme of a camp chanteuse, Sheila's hommage to three other figures in drag – the Three Kings. Ludo's arrival dampens the neighbours' fun somewhat. Hanna awkwardly explains the therapeutic strategy – transgression loses its cachet when anything goes (shades of Chiland's God is dead and anything can happen). Ludo's trans-pride is short-lived as it turns out, for his employer, Albert, Jérôme's father, who fears Ludo's corruption of his son, lays Pierre off and the family are forced out. As they drive off, Ludo gets one last glimpse of his friend in the front yard: Albert is shearing the hedge ominously close to Jérôme's head.

Gazing up at a huge billboard promoting *Pam's World*, bored and lonely in his new alien neighbourhood, Ludo is set upon by an older-looking boy, introducing himself as Chris and looking for a willing and able playmate. Chris's boyish bravado is demolished however the moment she shamefully hears her mother calling for her – Ludo has met Chris(-tine), the generic tomboy. At her fancy-dress birthday party, Chris is paraded, in drag as it were, as an impressively butch-looking Queen, with Ludo complementing her as a musketeer. Chris's admiration for Ludo's apparel is such that she forces him to exchange costumes, to the fury of Hanna who lashes out at Ludo, and chases after him, climbing a ladder propped up against the billboard, through the door into Pam's fantasy world. To be sure, Hanna's fantasy enlightenment – she figuratively enters her child's psyche and finally accepts Ludo's situation – is a rushed attempt to tie up the loose strands of the family drama. Yet, as the camera pans out over the party, as the children run off in a chain, Ludo tagging along, the unsettling play-out music and the dark clouds overhead undercut any coherent idea of a happy ending, or at least suggest that a resolution to gender is inevitably provisional.

FROM TRANSGENDER TO AIDS

Darren Waldron has argued that mainstream images of male homosexuality and gay forms of transgender such as camp and drag have recently revived the popular temporary transvestite narrative, a staple ingredient of popular comedy (Waldron 2006). Drawing on Marie-Hélène Bourcier's notion of 'passive visibility' in which queer subcultures are represented by the mainstream (Bourcier 1998), Waldron looks at comic narratives of gay passing in box-office hits such as *Pédale douce* (Aghion, 1996) and *Le Placard* (Veber, 2001).[7] Such passive visibility of queer/transgender subjects is, in the French cinematic context, dominated by *La Cage aux folles* (Molinaro, 1978), which was also scripted by Veber from a stage play by Jean Poiret, which had been literally trashed by a group of gay activists furious at Michel Serrault's grotesque performance of the trans-queen Zaza Napoli.[8] Overshadowed by this hugely popular lampooning of gay transgender (followed by two limp sequels in the 1980s), underground films (examples of active queer visibility) such as Spanish-expatriate filmmaker Adolpho Arrieta's *Les Intrigues de Sylvia Couski* (1974) have disappeared from commercial circulation and critical interest. A notable exception is Richard Dyer's passing reference to the film in his account of gay political underground film production in France in the 1970s (Dyer 1990: 223–7). Arrieta's film was made in 1973 around the dissolution of *Les Gazolines* (the drag element of the FHAR), whose members notably included legendary chanteuse Marie-France and activist Hélène Hazera.

AIDS activism is perhaps the most powerful example of how camp and drag have been used as political weapons in the French context to contest the inactivity of the state in matters of health-care, particularly the social exclusion of people with AIDS.[9] Cleews Vellay, president (*présidente* in the feminine) of Act Up from 1992 until shortly before his death in 1994 at the age of thirty, was one such 'folle atteinte'. A documentary film produced by Canal Plus and

Artefilms in 1995, made by Act Up activist Brigitte Tijou, *Portrait d'une prési-dente*, is a montage of archive material (AIDS benefits, Act Up's weekly meeting, Vellay's filmed kidnapping of health minister Philippe Douste Blazy) together with accounts from friends and fellow activists, and private interviews at the time of Vellay's presidency. The press dossier accompanying the release of Tijou's film describes its subject in the following terms:

> Cleews was not a hero and never wanted to be an AIDS star. However, he was well aware that his own personal experience revealed quite well the forms of injustice and exclusion brought on by the epidemic.
> (Cleews n'était pas un héros et n'a jamais voulu être une star du sida. Il a toujours eu conscience en revanche que son expérience personnelle révélait assez bien de quelles injustices et de quelles formes d'exclusion l'épidémie a pu se nourrir'.)[10]

The first sequence in Tijou's portrait shows Vellay coming on stage into the glaring spotlight amid the cheers of encouragement from supporters at some AIDS benefit or other, camply trying to hush the audience so he can introduce himself. Tijou splices her presentation of Vellay's background – telling of early family rejection, comically recounting how he came out to his father by announcing that his boyfriend was a transsexual – with a traditional docu-mentary use of archive material such as school photos, reports and leaving cards. Tijou films Vellay at home without artistic artifice, with only the naked camera on him, giving the illusion of an intimate conversation with the specta-tor or director.

The political sequences, Vellay in combat with government representatives, show how agilely he used his own camp rhetoric, his personality, honesty and effeminacy to disable the political order of things. The film's press release indi-cates the importance of Vellay's effeminacy to his political approach, describing him as undoubtedly the most outrageous queen among the Act Up activists. Tijou's portrait is presented as a sketch of a president whose political practice was deliberately playful. The activists interviewed point out that Vellay was so effec-tive at getting ministers to listen up because he refused to adapt to the formal, impersonal, low-key machismo of the political scene. He had no qualms in informing Henri Paul of the Ministry of Health of his dire material straits, hoping that his truthful account of hardship would pierce the distancing effect of gov-ernment jargon. Tijou cuts in scenes of Vellay in action with his camp star-turns at Act Up meetings and accounts of his hysteria in AIDS associative meetings, where he systematically demanded attention by banging his rings on the table.

Vellay's prize moment in Tijou's film is his intricate manipulation of health minister Douste Blazy: whilst activists cause chaos in front of the ministry, Tijou films a composed Vellay seemingly undaunted by the presence of the haughty minister, who is impatient to wrap up the meeting, business as usual. The pres-ence of the camera, as Lestrade observes (Lestrade 2000: 115–16), is a weapon against an obviously self-conscious minister, who is obliged to appear to accommodate Vellay's demands. These include demands for an explanation as to the absence of any government-funded HIV prevention, and an explanation as to why teenagers are still being mindlessly contaminated – in one moment of desperate rhetoric, Vellay asks when the wall of government disinterest will tumble down. Tijou craftily cuts up the long interview scene with Douste Blazy by sandwiching it between Vellay's victorious re-telling of the earlier events to the Act Up group. Douste Blazy eventually caves in under Vellay's subtle pressure (or perhaps the camera's threatening presence) and agrees to cancel his appointments to pay an impromptu visit to Act Up. He is, of course, unreceptive to Vellay's attempts to explain the material needs of someone suffering from an evolving illness, trying simply to recuperate his visit before the expectant journalists gathered to film him.

Tijou's documentary is an admittedly subjective and sympathetic account of Vellay's activism, effective because she has situated it at a precise moment in the history of French AIDS. Tijou ends this politically informative, yet visually bare portrait of Vellay with his death, pointing out his wish for a political burial, and with images from his public funeral. An activist's voice gravely informs us that his ashes were thrown at a member of the *Agence de Médicaments*, who was stalling the distribution of a new antiretroviral drug at the time. Tijou keeps the most painful and infuriating irony of Vellay's death for the last line, the film's distinctly bitter aftertaste: three months after his death, Vellay received the first payment of the state benefits (*Allocation adulte handicappé*) he had fought to obtain and had needed to stay alive.

Besides the politicised camp of Act Up, filmmakers such as Patrice Chéreau and Jacques Nolot have also taken issues surrounding gay transgender (including both transvestism and transsexuality) in tandem with AIDS, particularly Nolot's *La Chatte à deux têtes* (2002) and *Avant que j'oublie* (2007), and Chéreau's *Ceux qui m'aiment prendront le train* (1998). Activist groups like Act Up have been breaking the silence on transgender communities in HIV prevention and AIDS treatment, and the silence on HIV/AIDS within transgender milieus. In 2006, for the first time, the group of medical experts designated by the Ministry of Health included in its official report ('Le Rapport Yéni') specific recommendations for the medical care of HIV-positive transgender people. Chéreau's *Ceux qui m'aiment . . .* separates out the two strands, subordinating transgender to a fuller exploration of alternative patterns of gay male kinship in the immediate aftermath of medical breakthroughs in antiretroviral treatment drugs from the mid-1990s onwards. Nolot, however, has sought to retain AIDS and (male-to-female) transgender in the same frame by attempting to avoid the mainstream clichés of camp exuberance. His interest in gay fantasies of transgender was already present in his first short feature *Manège* (1986) that showed Nolot's character picking up a soldier at Austerlitz station. The two men go off to the Bois de Boulogne where a transgender sex worker is filmed giving fellatio to a client in a car whilst a surrounding group of voyeurs masturbate – one man even shines a torch through the car window to spotlight the sex worker's body. It remains unclear whether the film is seeking simply to document scenes of transgender prostitution in a quaint anthropological way or whether such images revel in the scenes of lurid voyeurism – a close-up of the girl's breasts suggests the thrill of a body in transition as the turn-on.

This sexual ambiguity also runs through Nolot's second feature, *La Chatte à deux têtes*, which focuses on spectatorship from the angle of the customers of a Parisian porn theatre from a bygone era. Nolot's film harks back to the independent big-screen porn theatres at Pigalle, which showed heterosexual porn to a less than straight crowd and which have since been transformed into sex shops with individual screening rooms to prevent any client contact. The poster for a showing of a film entitled 'Sodomised bourgeoises' with an entrance fee of thirty-one francs points to a nostalgic take on Parisian sex culture. The film feels both claustrophobic – Nolot's initial project was for a stage play and the only outdoor shots are the opening and closing credits – and theatrical, alternating between long static scenes of dialogue between Nolot's everyman character and the wise female cashier (Vittoria Scognamiglio) and the intimate interaction of the customers in the theatre below. Nolot's first extended image of the theatre itself is a slow pan shot across the spectators, who are filmed watching predictable images of hysterical porn actresses, and moving out into the wings, to focus attention on the action off the main screen in the space occupied by the mostly older, transvestite denizens on the lookout for a man. Nolot's assembled cast also includes a fair number of younger transvestites, including a sexy Fouad Zéraoui whose character is fucked in a group session filmed through bars, the routine melodramatic symbol of human entrapment made famous by Fassbinder.

Nolot's enthusiasm for casual sex practices is manifested through a democratic society of male clients that mixes men of different races, classes and ages, a scene resembling the parallel picture of a lost gay sex culture described by Samuel R. Delaney in New York (Delaney 1999). As Japp Kooijman has observed, the film's strength is that it 'neither makes political statements nor passes moral judgments. Instead the film provides often aesthetically beautiful tableaux vivants of sexual acts that are normally hidden in the darkness of seedy porn theatres.'[11] Despite this non-judgemental approach to casual sex (Nolot had also previously had a bit-part as a client in a porn theatre in Claire Denis's *J'ai pas sommeil*), the films runs the risk of showing the male transvestites as ultimately pathetic, binding together male masochism, passivity and femininity through cross-dressing. Femininity is figured as a *pis aller* by the film's finale in which Sébastien Viala is filmed alone, leaving the deserted theatre at the end of the day, followed by a peaceful shot of the sexual detritus scattered across the set. The minor strand of AIDS commentary running through the film is inserted into the upstairs dialogue between Nolot and the cashier and is shown in the sex scenes themselves in which Zéraoui's character refuses point blank the offer of unsafe penetration. This balance of HIV/AIDS and transgender is further developed in Nolot's melancholic self-portrait *Avant que j'oublie*, which shows an ageing writer come to terms with the need to begin a course of antiretroviral medication, and which gives a necessarily honest account of the grieving protagonist's personal progression from hustler to client. The film's magnificent closing shot is a prolonged close-up of Nolot, who is taken in drag by one of his clients to the Atlas cinema at Pigalle, the close-up capturing the character's sense of loss before he drifts off into the darkness, returning to the below-level action of Nolot's previous film.

Chéreau's *Ceux qui m'aiment prendront le train* likewise balances transgender with painful loss and precarious love in the time of AIDS. The film recounts the funeral of Jean-Baptiste Emmerich, painter, teacher, friend and lover, who has died leaving his disparate Parisian circle to set out for his hometown, Limoges, Europe's largest necropolis, where the number of dead exceeds the number of living. Chéreau's film concentrates less on the biography of the deceased, than on a sort of collective life instinct provoked by funerals, the desire to live, laugh, resolve conflict and make love. Emmerich's band of associates meet up by chance and their relationships are chaotic: Jean-Marie and Claire, nephew and wife, who are struggling to cope with drug addiction and the dissolution of their relationship; Jean-Marie sees his estranged father, Emmerich's twin brother, for the first time in years. François, a cynical art critic, for whom Emmerich was a friend, former lover and mentor, is cutting himself off from the others, including those who have disappeared, such as Emmerich's former student, Frédéric. In a complex relational jumble, Louis, François's present partner, falls in love with Bruno, the painter's last secret lover, who also has unfinished business with François. The long-term gay relationship opens up to free Louis to take his chance with the HIV-positive character Bruno. Martine Beugnet has harshly criticised the gay milieu in Chéreau's film as conventional and stereotypical, in particular the characterisation and filming of Bruno (Sylvain Jacques), who is perceived to be 'subjected to the same process of "objectification" traditionally reserved for female characters who are reduced to objects of desire' ('soumis aux mêmes procédés "d'objectification" auxquels sont assujettis traditionnellement les personages féminins qui sont réduits au role d'objet de désir') (Beugnet 2000: 11). Chéreau pictures the film's milieu in personal terms:

> As for drugs, homosexuality and seropositivity, they're part of the landscape, part of the reality of the milieu in which I live . . . And I don't believe in art that would ignore them. Even so, to repeat, my film isn't entirely dark or pessimistic; it gestures towards an opening, a sort of utopian optimism.
> (Quant à la drogue, l'homosexualité et la séropositivité, elles font partie du paysage. Cela correspond à la réalité du milieu dans lequel je vis . . . Et, de mon côté, je ne crois pas à un art qui ne dirait rien. Cependant, je vous le répète, mon film n'est pas entièrement noir, pessimiste. Il tend vers une ouverture, une sorte d'optimisme utopique'.)[12]

This optimism is compared to the bleakness of his early 1980s collaboration with Guibert, *L'Homme blessé*, a film focusing on sexual identity and adolescence, 'which was sad, shut off, redolent of an indulgent sorrow'[13] ('Triste, fermé, impregné d'une douleur complaisante').

'The king is dead, long live the train' ('Le roi est mort, vive le train') is screenwriter Stéphane Bouquet's assessment of the characters' plight in his review for *Cahiers du cinéma*.[14] Chéreau is seen to set up a court system – the chaos of the claustrophobic train sequences (roughly the first third of the film) is attributed to the characters' perturbation faced with their loss of gravity; the human element that linked them is gone. Every micro-society is run much like a court – a situation resembling Chéreau's bloody historical drama *La Reine Margot* (1994) with its covert relationships, its favourites and its courtesans. When the centrepiece, the king of Bouquet's title, is removed, the natural order of things is shattered, sending the particles spinning. This is one of those funerals at which those present are vying for privilege, still playing the same game of seduction that the deceased mastered to perfection. In their attempts to position themselves, the characters ask one another sly questions – the spiteful Lucie, who has for years been in love with her uninterested friend, surprises François by asking if he had indeed known the discreet, last boyfriend. Chéreau never explains Bruno's relationship with Emmerich, but leads us to guess his identity by jumping from Lucie's inquiry to a shot of Bruno's youthful face, as he gravitates towards Louis. Emmerich's final tableau is his funeral, orchestrated through the indirect imperative of the title – *if* you ever loved me, you *will* come to my funeral – a throwaway line, uttered by the painter in a recorded conversation for François's art journal.

Chéreau visualises this human angst by shutting his players up together in an early-morning train. His jerky hand-held camera movements indicate the characters' emotional nausea, intensified by the constant noise, the impossibly tight space and occasional erratic motion of the train. In the intimate corridor conversations, where Bruno and Louis are flung together, the characters' minds often escape out of the window. Claire, whose jagged nerves are minutely captured by actress Valeria Bruni-Tedeschi, tormented by the marriage break-up and the news of her pregnancy, is shown early on desperately putting on make-up in the cramped toilets, ransacking her handbag in search of pills – the camera jumps around the interior following Claire's actions, as if about to collide with her at any moment. Chéreau includes one sharp moment of interaction between the alienated couple: seeing Jean-Marie, Claire goes to greet him; she sits down beside him; he mentions the administrative business of their separation; she goes to touch him and he jerks, as if the contact would wound him. This is the torment, the 'mutual destruction' that the voice-over fragments with Emmerich serve to frame. Indeed, the relief of short, almost slow-motion shots of the painter at work in the calm of his studio break the claustrophobia of the train.

The boundary crossing literalised by the constant motion of train travel also serves as a metaphor for gender transition. The character mentioned in passing by the others as Frédéric, one of Emmerich's protégés, who had disappeared from the painter's circle, no longer identifies as gay, but is transitioning to become Viviane. Absent from the train sequences, arriving at the cemetery by taxi, Viviane is not initially recognised by the others. She views the gathering as Viviane's birth, as Frédéric's funeral, looking to a romantic future of family life, a notion cruelly discarded by François, but to which she is psychologically attached. In the cellar of the ancestral house, Emmerich's twin brother, Lucien, has stored the leftover stock of the family's shoe commerce, which he graciously shows to an eager Viviane, reminiscing on the old days. Twinning is clearly important, for Chéreau recalls that one of the film's models was Guibert's account of Foucault's death and burial in the Morvan, according to which the Parisian cortège was stunned to catch sight of Foucault's almost identical twin brother – an episode from the novel, *A l'ami qui ne m'a pas sauvé la vie* (Guibert 1990; Thompson, Chéreau and Trividic 1998: 11–12).

The critics agree with Emmerich *frère* that the introduction of the transgender 'fairy' Viviane, lightens the film's mode. Pierre Murat, in his review for *Télérama*,[15] sees Viviane as a Chekhovian innocent, whose naïvety is mocked by the more worldly characters, but who provides insight into their lives. In the rounds of publicity for the film in 1998, mainstream media focused on Vincent Perez's transgender performance, locating sexual ambiguity (in actual fact it is *gender* ambiguity) as the film's crux.[16] When transgender slides into performance, as it does here – think of Viviane's camp comedy in the kitchen, or her performance trying on the exquisite red shoes in Lucien's hidden gender storeroom – it is exaggerated transgender as only an actor could imagine it, which seems to be consciously tied to a gay vision – the exaggerated tribute to femininity that is drag. Indeed, transgender as performance, as a comic turn, forms part of the queer aesthetic of art cinema, a trope particularly associated with the work of another filmmaker with perhaps more manifest fantasies of transgender – Pedro Almodóvar, who, in *Todo sobre mi madre* (1999), memorably put a character on stage to fill in for the cancelled show by giving a humorous, improvised rendition of her life and times. The fact that Perez camps it up quite so much in Chéreau's production does tend to naturalise biological femininity: in her role as confidante, Viviane spends long, intense scenes consoling Claire, who is pregnant, who potentially has an element of Viviane's fantasy of happiness.

It is in the company of the former lovers Bruno and François that Viviane verbalises her fantasy of future normality. This follows the harsh father/son confrontation Viviane has been privy to in the cellar. In spite of the emotional manipulation and destruction she witnesses around her, she holds tight to her vision, excusing herself as an ersatz of the 1950s home girl. She tells her chocolate-box dream of heterosexuality, of being a simple baker's wife, serving the people, married for better or for worse. Bruno begins to mock her fantasy, but François, whom he thinks is playing devil's advocate, translates her wish as the beauty of leading an ordinary life. What lies beneath Viviane's sugar-coated vision of domesticity is the chance to love; she argues the importance of rites – love must be witnessed. Viviane is alluding to conventional marriage, François to their own alternative gay arrangements. We infer that he is actually offering his secret lover (Bruno) to his long-term partner (Louis). Bruno misunderstands Viviane's metaphor, reading only allusions to his past affair with François, who, in Bruno's eyes, rejected him because of his seropositivity.

Viviane's soap opera is translated into a potentially more radical queer re-working of kinship relations. As Julianne Pidduck argues in an article on Chéreau's 'homosocial' relations and his queering of kinship, 'Gay and straight couples, fathers and sons, current and ex-lovers, friends and acquaintances all grapple with François' challenge to define the ambivalent bonds of intimacy' (Pidduck 2007: 200). Exchanging performance for spectatorship, Viviane witnesses the actual translation of her soap opera as the gay characters proceed to act out before her their own version of her marriage ideal. In a speech cut from the final version of the film, Chéreau includes a vision of gay relationships that adapts Viviane's 'for better or for worse' discourse to the context of AIDS:

> In fact, it's gay men who marry. Because, for better or for worse is a vague formula. For worse more than for better. That's the crux of a real union today. Marriage as sacred. When for worse is almost guaranteed.
> (En fait ce sont les pédés qui se marient vraiment. Parce que là c'est une vague formule, pour le meilleur et pour le pire. Le pire c'est vraiment le pire. C'est ça, au fond, le vrai mariage d'aujourd'hui. Le mariage sacré. Quand le pire est presque sûr) . . . (Thompson, Chéreau and Trividic 1998: 147)

This clearly situates the text, perhaps written as early as 1996 (considering the film was shot in spring 1997 and released in 1998) marked by the discourse of the AIDS era immediately prior to advanced antiretroviral medication, representing gay relationships as conditioned by a near automatic fear of imminent illness or death.

Only Viviane is present at the three-way telephone conversation, in which the three men negotiate their love for one another. Bruno, who is visible to François in an adjoining room, listens in to his conversation with Louis who is at a nearby hotel, whilst Viviane listens in with the earpiece. François admits that he was scared of not being up to it, not capable of living with AIDS in a sero-different couple with Bruno. The film then flirts with the scope for more radical potential but forecloses its actual development – Louis wishes the male lovers to form a threesome, to make some room for innovation in their lives by 'adopting' the younger man. His suggestion gives voice to the desire many people feel for affective experimentation outside the constraints of the basic one-to-one scenario, however sexually open: that is to say, the complex combination of friends, tricks, buddies, lovers, multiple short-term and long-term partners, the whole palette of queer interpersonal alternatives evermore sidelined by institutional gay culture's rush to the altar – 'new possibilities outside of the "majoritarian" psychosexual order of stable couples and family units', as Pidduck puts it (Pidduck 2007: 201). However, as with much AIDS film and fiction, the couple – however loosely conceived here – is reaffirmed as the natural template for queer love. Chéreau seems to foreclose the more radical option of a three-way relationship (unfortunately, as it would have added an additional layer of intricacy to his tableau of gay male relations), with François leaving the two lovers to their own devices.

What this chance meeting around Emmerich's death has revealed is how haphazard their arrangements for loving are – the actual Emmerich family does not comprehend who is who, or why Bruno (whom they do not recognise) is weeping at the ceremony, invariably attempting to straighten out the complex forms of gay male relations to pre-established fixed models of passion and friendship. These are forms of grief that go socially unnoticed (Watney 2000: 216–27). In the case of *Ceux qui m'aiment prendront le train*, Viviane's corny fantasy and rhetoric of hope serve to put these fluctuant forms of gay love into focus. She encourages Bruno to go to Louis, to grab what happiness he can.

What is perturbing about the film's ideological manoeuvres – gay life seen through the prism of transgender – is that the weight is unevenly distributed between the two. The film argues for complex, mobile modes of gay relations, at the expense of a more sustained exploration of transgender other than as camp or performance, or as a desirable integration into hetero-normality. For doesn't Viviane basically end up as a voice-box for the heterosexual norm, as the ground for what are perceived as the more mobile, more experimental, ultimately more life-fulfilling gay arrangements? The gays get their men (or not, if they choose to), whereas Viviane is left to fantasise alone.

Ceux qui m'aiment prendront le train explores at length the complexities of gay relations in relation to HIV/AIDS, suggesting their institutional fragility at a time when the concurrent conflict around same-sex partnership agreements (the PaCS) located a central contradiction within models of same-sex passion: whilst advocates of greater institutionalisation of same-sex relations were questioning the authority of the heterosexual kinship model, they also prescribed stable coupling as the norm. Chéreau would seem to dissent from this position – in the earlier train sequences, François homes in on the definitional instability of their relationships, pressing Louis, who is unable to put a name to the bonds of love between them. Finally, it is in light of his mentor's death that François withdraws from their relationship in a moving scene in front of the hotel, in which he catches a veiled glimpse of his two lovers embracing passionately in the sunlit reflection of the bedroom window. Chéreau's magnificent coda is an aerial shot of François walking alone among the 185,000 inhabitants of the Limoges cemetery.

Notes

1. Hélène Hazera, 'Les Soeurs du boulevard', *Têtu*, June 1999, pp. 8–21.
2. Ibid., p. 20.
3. Ibid., p. 10.
4. Hélène Hazera, 'Le mauvais genre est dans la rue!', *Le Monde libertaire: hebdomadaire de la Fédération Anarchiste*, supplement to no. 1207, June 1999, p. 3.
5. Ibid.
6. Jean-Michel Frodon, 'Une très sombre bluette', *Le Monde*, 29 May 1997, p. 32.
7. For a full account of mainstream images of gay transgender, see Roth-Bettoni 2007: 562–71.
8. Footage of the activists trashing the stage is included in Yves Jeuland's TV documentary of French gay history, *Bleu, blanc, rose* (2002).
9. For coverage of health issues specific to transgender communities, see 'Personnes trans': quels enjeux de santé?', *Lettre d'information du CRIPS*, no. 84, November 2007.
10. 'Résumé producteur', *Portrait d'une présidente* (Tijou, 1995), *Canal Plus*, 6 June 1996.
11. Jaap Kooijman, 'Glowing eyes (porn theater)', www.outrate.net/outrate glowingeyes, accessed 14 January 2008.
12. Patrice Chéreau quoted in Florence Castelnau-Mendel, 'Un Chéreau nommé désir,' *L'Express*, no. 2445, May 1998, p. 112.
13. Ibid.
14. Stéphane Bouquet, 'Le roi est mort, vive le train', *Cahiers du cinéma*, no. 524, May 1998, pp. 100–1.
15. Pierre Murat, 'Ceux qui m'aiment prendront le train', *Télérama*, no. 2522, 16–22 May 1998, pp. 76–8.
16. *Le Journal 20h*, France 2, 14 May 1998.

4. QUEER SEXUALITY, AIDS AND LOSS

A few months before the release of *Ceux qui m'aiment prendront le train*, novelist Christophe Honoré wrote an angry dismissal of the moralist tendency of contemporary French cinema, published by *Cahiers du cinéma* in February 1998. 'The sad morality of French cinema' was conceived as a pastiche of François Truffaut's critique of the so-called tradition of quality, the staid literary adaptations predominant in the 1950s.[1] In his eclectic international pick of the ten best films released in 1997, Honoré did not select a single French production, rejecting the populist social politics dominating realist film, notably Robert Guédiguian's popular fable *Marius et Jeannette* (Guédiguian, 1997), dismissed as sublimated social work, and Anne Fontaine's *Nettoyage à sec* (Fontaine, 1997), trashed as a complacent wash-out. The climax to *Nettoyage à sec* came under attack for its lurid image of gay sex as brutalisation, Honoré detecting voyeuristic intent on the part of filmmaker Anne Fontaine, and also its failure to show the exciting image of 'two men making love because it suddenly becomes their whole reason for living' ('deux hommes faisant l'amour parce que c'est soudain leur seule raison d'être au monde').[2] To situate Honoré's polemic, he was reacting against the movement of filmmakers and actors (known as the the citizen filmmakers, lead by Pascale Ferran and Arnaud Desplechin) who had mounted a campaign the previous year in protest at the Pasqua/Debré immigration reforms. Following Pasqua's law of 1987, these reforms had sought to increase the expulsion of so-called 'undocumented' immigrants and to tighten up on immigration by suspending 'le droit du sol' – the automatic right to French nationality for the children of immigrants born in France (Prochasson 2000: 13). Honoré sympathised with the filmmakers' political cause, but was sceptical about their opportunism.[3]

Honoré's ambitious cry for unlimited artistic freedom came before he had even made his first film. The polemic was used by the editors to express distaste at a politically committed form of filmmaking associated with the so-called *cinéastes citoyens*, and his standing as a novelist not a filmmaker (and thereby outside the professional frame) positioned his article as a timely wake-up call for a film establishment seen to be particularly pleased with its previous year's production. Three months later Honoré found a French film he actually liked. Called on to give his reaction to the release of *Ceux qui m'aiment prendront le train* in an intimate diary format, as part of a monthly column designed to chronicle a film's effect on a spectator's life, Honoré recounts falling in love with Chéreau's film, being haunted by the characters' predicament, and excited by Chéreau's frank treatment of serological differences within gay milieus. Honoré goes on to document annoyance at Chéreau's perceived objectification of male youth and beauty in the form of the androgynous Bruno, a tormented object of desire who only seems to exist through his serological status. Honoré points to the ghost of Hervé Guibert overshadowing the production, glimpsing him in the character Louis, the central figure in the threesome that the film sets up as an alternative queer form of kinship. As the preceding analysis of *Ceux qui m'aiment prendront le train* attempted to show, the film foregrounds a psychic attachment to traditional heterosexual structures on the part of the transgender character, the same institutional form of family and kinship that is contested by the gay male characters, who are seeking to negotiate unorthodox emotional commitments across differences of social standing, age and HIV-status. In *Ceux qui m'aiment prendront le train* Honoré found what he considered lacking in contemporary French cinema, that is to say an artistic vision of the real – in this case a queer bourgeois artistic milieu – without recourse to run of the mill naturalism or didactic political realism. I want here to use Honoré's interest as a template for the central preoccupation of this chapter, which takes up the film's engagement with non-sanctioned arrangements for loving in the time of AIDS, and its effects on representations of queer sexuality.

Families and Form

Appearing as a guest on the radio programme *Le Cinéma l'après-midi* for the highbrow *France Culture* in April 2005, Honoré took issue with Olivier Ducastel and Jacques Martineau's vaudeville farce, *Crustacés et coquillages* (2005), criticised for its lazy format and predictable politics. Agreeing with fellow filmmaker and critic Pascal Bonitzer, Honoré dismissed the film's perceived vision of a queer sexuality harmoniously accommodated by a modified family structure as conventional and didactic. Charlotte Garson writing in *Cahiers du cinéma* likewise criticised the film for being over-written, but nevertheless admired its pastel fantasy in the style of Jacques Demy.[4] Indeed, Honoré and Bonitzer's disdain may simply misunderstand the film's mode of fantasy farce. *Crustacés et coquillages* sees Béatrix (Valeria Bruni-Tedeschi) and Marc (Gilbert Melki) take their two teenagers off to a seaside retreat in the south of France, where they are joined by their son's gay friend Martin (Edouard Collin), whose own frankness and ease spark off a comedy of sexual errors. Béatrix wrongly assumes that her son Charly (Romain Torres) is also gay and pushes her reluctant spouse to accept the situation; her own free-spiritedness is explained by being half-Dutch, smoking pot and conjuring up a secret lover

(Jacques Bonnaffé), who appears as if in a hallucination to make love to her at will. This sexual idyll, brought on by an over-eager consumption of shellfish (including a cheeky running gag about the solitary pleasure of long showers), goes awry when Marc's sexy former boyfriend, the local plumber (Jean-Marc Barr), turns up, a plot twist that leads Marc to admit to his own former homosexuality. Martineau and Ducastel's technique is to pervert the farce tradition of mistaken identities and false appearances, so as to unsettle its hetero-centric framework. The kinks in their alternative family arrangement include a surprising shot of the father chained to the bed by the plumber.

Crustacés et coquillages ends on a reconfiguration of the contemporary family, one that not only takes account of its messy, recomposed histories but that puts queer and straight variations on an equal footing. Florian Grandena sees progressive potential in the alternative 'community of destiny' outside biological structures in Ducastel and Martineau's *Drôle de Félix* (Grandena 2006: 64–70). Vinay Swamy addresses the issue of traditional and alternative kinship relations on screen (Swamy 2006), arguing that the films covered (alongside *Drôle de Félix*, the broad vaudeville farce *Le Placard* (Weber, 2001), and the TV film *Rêves en France* (Kané, 2002)) 'not only act as a barometer of the debate on the family, homosexuality and kinship structures, but also . . . actively participate in it – along with the demagogues – and, by so doing, help construct the very ideologies that subtend public opinion on these issues' (Swamy 2006: 56). Swamy claims that each film appears to construct its own vision of kinship relations as a coherent discourse – from the predictable bolstering of hetero-normative structures in *Le Placard*, through the privileging of a traditional model of state-sanctioned coupling in *Rêves en France*, to the 'radical re-conception of the family' posited by Ducastel and Martineau, whose *beur* protagonist (played by Sami Bouajila) avoids looking to the state for legitimate recognition of his emotional bonds.[5]

Rather than seeing this more radical potential in *Drôle de Félix*, Kate Ince has argued that the family

> is important because it functions . . . as a metaphor for the state of the French nation. It can do this because the French Republican model of the family as an institution exactly parallels the 'assimilationist' model of unity and difference often observed at work in the discourse and practices of French national identity . . . (Ince 2002: 91)

The idea is that queer disturbance is to be tolerated so long as it can be slotted back into the dominant structure without a radical overhaul. But, in the case of the films under scrutiny, Ince argues that 'the universalist conception of the family extends to incorporate gay and queer sexualities, and undergoes telling changes in the process' (Ince 2002: 91). The wider cultural context between the making of *Drôle de Félix* in 1999 and *Crustacés et coquillages* in 2004 is the post-PaCS moment, heralding the same-sex marriage debate within gay/queer subcultures. The advocates of same-sex marriage argue that queerness is to be readily accommodated within the parameters of state universalism and republican individualism, with the effect that to conform to the state-sanctioned norm would enable queers to transform it from the inside.

Such enthusiasm for the family within the framework of same-sex marriage and parenting provides the agenda for recent efforts by French intellectuals to kick-start the gay marriage debate. One of the most ardent defenders of same-sex union, Didier Eribon, who with Daniel Borillo wrote the manifesto calling for equal rights – 'Manifeste pour l'égalité des droits et l'égalité devant le mariage' (Manifesto for equal rights and equality in marriage)[6] – sees its potential to destabilise the social order. Eribon has defended the value of same-sex marriage in his monthly column in *Têtu*, arguing that by conforming to exclusionary norms, LGBT citizens are therefore able to shake the scheme of things from the inside. Continuing his earlier transposition of Anglo-American queer theory to the French context (Eribon 1999), Eribon here argues for the dissident potential in re-signifying norms from within the very institutions that wield their power. It could be argued that this political strand is part of what Maxime Cervulle sees as a local 'homo-normative' formation (Cervulle 2008), in which making marriage the central tenet of queer relations risks extending the regulation of sexuality by making private conjugal sex the only legitimate expression of sexuality. The widespread adoption of the watchword 'equal rights' is a rhetorical trap because equality is not limited to a simple equivalence of rights between homosexuals and heterosexuals. Implementing a one-size-fits-all juridical model fails to take account of larger structural inequalities, which ensure that the same law does not produce the same effects for every citizen. The 'universalist' rights package lacks detail of the socio-economic reality of queer lives and works to favour the juridical rights of state-sanctioned families over those of individual citizens. The extension of social security rights and the authorisation of immigration documentation to non-national partners, as well as the whole deal of fiscal benefits that favour the middle-classes (inheritance, property and so forth) could as well be extended to citizens as individuals outside the state-sanctioned regime of marriage.

At the heart of the 'equal rights' agenda are the interests of predominantly white, middle-class gay men, who tend to have the most economic clout within LGBT subcultures and who tend to gain the most from supporting inclusion within hetero-normative structures. Lurking beneath Eribon's defence of same-sex marriage in the French context is a degree of class prejudice. He illustrates his argument with reference to France's first gay wedding, a political media stunt performed by green politician and mayor Noël Mamère at Bègles in 2004, which according to Yves Jeuland and Jean-Michel Vennemani's revealing documentary, *Maris à tout prix* (2004), saw the politician and his entourage of Parisian intellectuals and lawyers duped by Stéphane Chapin and Bertrand Charpentier, a star-struck couple avid for media attention. They were both subsequently convicted for fraud, having stolen cheques to pay for their wedding reception and elaborate outfits.

What would we all have preferred? A proper middle-class couple, who would have posed for the press in a tender embrace on the settee, their coffee table strewn with artistic books? That would have been more presentable, I admit, but the lived realities of gay life are not limited to the happy few.

(Au fond, qu'aurait-on voulu? Un couple de la moyenne bourgeoisie, qui aurait posé pour les magazines tendrement enlacé sur le canapé du salon, avec des livres d'art sur la table basse? C'eût été plus présentable, j'en conviens, mais les réalités de l'homosexualité ne se limitent pas à ces milieux favorisés.)[7]

Whilst acknowledging actual social diversity, Eribon seems to promote a sanitised version of presentable gayness linking private property, highbrow culture and conjugality, a package suitable for mainstream consumption.

The final tableau of the queer family in *Crustacés et coquillages* is more utopian and less class-driven than the contemporaneous same-sex marriage debate, working as an ideological coda to the preceding farce. The extended family is seen reunited the following summer, each separately declined couple (the parents with their respective lovers, Charly with a girlfriend, daughter and Martin with boyfriends in tow) shown throwing open the shutters to the villa, proudly celebrating their new-found sexual freedom and equality. Ginette Vincendeau has criticised the film for trying 'too hard to be offbeat. It is difficult to be convincingly sexually insouciant when sexual insouciance is, as it were, the rule.' She goes on to question the film's social scheme, which establishes a working-class erotic utopia for the two male lovers, one of whom is a plumber, the other a mechanic, 'in a social space that is entirely bourgeois-bohemian'.[8] Honoré reads the class dynamics slightly differently, arguing that the film serves as a transparent vehicle for some well-meaning liberal sentiment, the final sexual reconciliation read as a mere twist on the routine romantic union through marriage required by the genre of farce. Honoré's verdict is perhaps mean-spirited, since, by following the lofty prescriptions of formalist criticism, it can only assess the merits of the film in terms of artistic value, which eliminates audience enjoyment and misses out on the film's lightness of touch. For example, HIV prevention is deftly slipped into an excruciating moment of parental embarrassment, when Marc, believing his son to be gay, clumsily lecturers his offspring on the importance of safer sex practices. Yet it is true that the film does occasionally indulge in some heavy-going proselytising, such as Martin's claim that Charly is too cute to be straight or his ham-fisted explanation of queer vernacular such as 'coming out' to a supposedly unenlightened mainstream audience. Unlike the couple's first film, *Jeanne et le garçon formidable* (1998), which was inspired by the filmmakers' activism with AIDS organisation Act Up Paris, and which managed to balance a straight heterosexual love story with involvement in radical queer politics, *Crustacés et coquillages* sees them move to the cosy middle-ground of family fun. The fact that the film fails to challenge a queer audience is not something Honoré's critique takes on board, concerned primarily as it is with the film's aesthetic limitations. In actual fact, while the framing itself is unremarkable, there is the odd moment of formal ingenuity such as the use of opposing tracking shots of Marc and Béatrix mentally preparing to admit their infidelities to each other, a sequence carefully edited to speed up to their head-on confrontation.

The film's defiant assertion of equal rights certainly situates it within the contemporary preoccupations of mainstream gay politics, whose focus remains fixed on the gay marriage/same-sex parenting equal rights package, but by championing sexual tolerance and laissez-faire, it also avoids prescribing same-sex conjugal monogamy as the *nec plus ultra* of contemporary queer life. Indeed, notwithstanding the parental infidelities, many of the farcical misadventures take place on the late-night cruising ground. The final plea for sexual diversity simply tries to show the sexualities of both young and less young gay and bisexual men to be plausibly harmonious, which is attractive because it rejects the sad young man cliché and its attendant baggage of gay pathos. However, a queer spectator looking for more innovative or challenging representations of plausible queer relations might feel short-changed, especially by the complacent end tableau of harmonious family integration. This brings us full circle to Honoré's 'cinéma de parent d'élève' (an update of the much-derided 1950s 'cinéma du papa') and his dismissal of supposedly responsible films that flatly transcribe concurrent socio-political realities onto screen. Looking back in 2002 on the diatribe against conformist French cinema that had seen him fired from *Cahiers du cinéma*, Honoré expressed his dislike for 'films in which the camera claims to make itself invisible' ('je n'aime pas les films où la caméra prétend se rendre invisible').[9] He is equally dismissive of films that see desire as harmonious, defending his own brand of unruly, chaotic sexuality, most notable in his 2004 adaptation of Georges Bataille's posthumously published novel *Ma mère* (Bataille 2000 [1966]). While Honoré and Ducastel/Martineau would seem superficially opposed, seemingly attached to opposing formal styles, they both draw inspiration from Jacques Demy, and their thematic concerns are remarkably similar – family re-configuration, queer sexuality, AIDS and loss.

Queer Families

In the interview preceding the TV broadcast of his first short film *Nous deux* (2000),[10] Honoré explained his desire to explore contemporary coupling. The couple are brothers, and one of them seeks to father a child with an English woman who, unable to commit, backs out of the project. The film's energetic opening flourish shows the brothers' hurried departure for London chasing across the *Gare du Nord* in tune to 1980s 'indie-rock' band The Smiths. The 'retro' feel to the piece is complemented by a subsequent sequence set in England, filmed through a faded yellow filter to suggest nostalgia or wish fulfilment as the film's dominant mode. The fraternal relationship toys with homoeroticism in one long scene in which the brothers spend a hot sleepless night at a hotel, talking of girls and prospective children, then play-fighting, the erotic tension pierced by the older brother's cocky suggestion of masturbation in order to pass the time. The contrived narrative which includes a melodramatic scene at the hospital in which the English woman lets the older brother down is set up to frame the brothers' emotional bond, building up to the final cathartic scene in which the younger man comforts his grieving brother, a sequence shot through a glass door without sound, a distancing device used to cut the spectator's sentimental involvement in the drama.

Honoré's first feature film, *Dix-sept fois Cécile Cassard* (2001), described as a poetic manifesto by *Libération*,[11] developed a similar thematic interest in alternative family structures and loss but in a more ostensibly expressionist mode, privileging atmosphere and mood over narrative coherence and spectator identification.[12] Following the death of her husband in a car accident and her attempted suicide, Cécile (Béatrice Dalle) abandons her child with her sister (Jeanne Balibar), and leaves for Toulouse. There she befriends a gay hotel receptionist Mathieu (Romain Duris), with whom she begins to construct a surrogate family. The disorientating framing and dark atmospheric lighting of the first third of the film are used instead of dialogue or psychological cause and effect to express Cécile's state of loss, the night shots said to resemble Léos Carax's first film *Boy Meets Girl* (1984) and the opening sequence of David Lynch's *Lost Highway* (1997).[13] Indeed the 'chromatic', 'sonorous' and 'sensorial' qualities of the film were particularly noted by critics. Alongside stylistic experimentation and expressionism, the 1980s brand of 'cinéma du look', with its rejection of naturalism, and its favouring of mannerism and style, can equally be read into *Cécile Cassard* through the casting of Béatrice Dalle, who had made her name as Betty Blue in Jean-Jacques Beineix's *37°2 le matin* (1986). Dalle cultivates a rebellious rock-star image, moving from her early popular stardom as Betty Blue in the 1980s to more edgy performances such as the vampire-predator in Claire Denis's *Trouble Every Day* (2001), a conscious rejection of her earlier image as an object of desire. In her next film, Honoré chose in turn to showcase her vulnerability. Discussing Dalle's earlier image from the 'cinéma du look' to the apparent change in her career with *Trouble Every Day*, Guy Austin has argued that Dalle 'is represented most consistently as a sexualised and desiring female body' (Austin 2003: 117). Opposite Dalle is Romain Duris, who is known for his versatility, straddling popular genres – acting the leads in the action adventure *Arsène Lupin* (Salomé, 2004), in the heritage biopic *Molière* (Tirard, 2007), and from the start of his career in Cédric Klapisch's popular comedies *Le Péril jeune* (1994), *L'Auberge espagnol* (2002) and *Les Poupées russes* (2005) – whilst holding his own in auteur film, most memorably in Jacques Audiard's neo-noir *De Battre mon coeur s'est arrêté* (2005).

One scene halfway through *Dix-sept fois Cécile Cassard* is filmed as a music video, showing Dalle stoned, sensually dancing with a half-clad Duris to Lily

Margot's rock ballad 'Pretty Killer' before his boyfriend cuts in. The clip exploits both stars' nonchalant sex appeal and cool demeanour, and combines influence from the 1980s pop-video aesthetic with Honoré's expressionist attention to subtle lighting and artificial setting. This is particularly evident in the depth of field as the camera, initially focusing on Duris's lover pensively smoking, inches vertically into the narrow frame towards the couple dancing at the rear. The use of a large mirror allows Dalle to remain within the frame even though the male couple temporarily replace her in the foreground, the lover having reclaimed Duris, leading him with hands placed seductively down the back of his trousers. The smooth inward trajectory of the camera and the slowed-down choreography of the sequence shot, ending with a long close-up of the film's star (Dalle) smoking, capture the three characters' half-cut weariness by the end of the night. The striking effect of the lover's interruption is to reverse the predictable gender positions in slow dancing, as here the male body (Duris) is positioned as the sensual centrepiece – the object of exchange, so to speak – rather than the female character, who escapes the traditional sexual schema and whom Honoré chooses purposefully not to eroticise.

Duris's character Mathieu is a romantic type who follows his boyfriend to Paris but is disappointed when the relationship flounders; he returns to Toulouse to suggest the possibility of fathering a child with Cécile. The prolonged shots of the two male lovers in bed, their estranged bodies no longer fitting together, point to the cracks in their relationship and to the perceived lack in Mathieu's life, carefully juxtaposed with shots of Cécile's abandoned son. This sincere meditation on gay male desire for paternity is far removed from the milieu and mindset of Honoré's next film, *Ma mère* (2004), with its heady cocktail of transgression, morality and religion, updated to take in mass tourism and sexual consumerism in the Canaries. As Ginette Vincendeau found when reviewing the film,[14] the synopsis reduces the action to a mere checklist of sexual perversions, the aim of neither the film nor the original novel. Following the sudden death of her husband, the self-declared 'slut' Hélène (Isabelle Huppert) decides to take care of her son Pierre's (Louis Garrel) sexual initiation by introducing him to her sexually voracious friend Réa (Joana Preiss). Réa deflowers him, before leaving him in the care of the pretty but disturbed Hansi (Emma de Caunes), who engages him in a sado-masochistic three-way with gay boy Loulou (Jean-Baptiste Montagut). The sexual practices range from Pierre's frequent bouts of masturbation (at the start over his deceased father's belongings; at the end beside the lacerated body of his mother) through voyeurism (mother hesitantly watching Réa mount Pierre in public; Pierre subsequently watching mother spoon with Réa) to the later scenes of S/M, in which the submissive Loulou is brutally whipped by Hansi, followed by the film's excruciating finale of self-harm as Hélène cuts herself to death for her son's visual excitement.

Honoré's ploy is to adapt what has been considered Bataille's visually inadaptable novel on mother-son incest and to render its mostly implicit episodes of extreme sexuality 'representable' without recourse to either old-school prudery or hard-core porn. In fact, as Vincendeau notes, *Ma mère* came at the tail end of the series of violent and sexually explicit auteur productions (most notably *À ma soeur*, *Baise-moi*, *Dans ma peau*, *Intimité*, *Irréversible* and *Romance*), a 'French' brand of violent and/or sexual extremism, branded abroad as 'French' at any rate. Read in that context, a contemporary auteur cinema in which explicit sexuality has become pretty much par for the course fits well with the residual legacy of Bataille, the much lauded cultural package of transcendence through perverse sexuality that is now a staple ingredient of the high French philosophical and literary canon. As Vincendeau goes on to argue, far more problematic is the class tourism woven into the update from a novel written in the early 1960s but set in the early twentieth century, to the early twenty-first-century context of hedonism and sexual consumption in a holiday resort in the Canary Islands. Vincendeau is critical of the film's 'facile snobbery,' its 'contempt for "ordinary" tourists' and its 'elitist project'.[15]

The novel, presented as indispensable in the introductory statement issued by the Bataille estate on its posthumous publication and conceived as part of a larger projected cycle of late fiction, is composed of Pierre's narrative fantasies of his mother's drunken, sexual debauchery and his account of his own downward spiral into sin and perversion. He renounces his religious beliefs after his father's death to accommodate his mother for whom he is 'lost in adoration' ('perdu d'adoration', Bataille [1966] 2000: 13). The original mother is considerably younger than Isabelle Huppert – aged thirteen when she first seduces Pierre's father, becoming pregnant and later secretly married abroad to avoid scandal, and aged thirty-two at the start of the narrative. Indeed, the film's broadening of the age disparity between mother and son makes the incest taboo more visibly shocking on screen, as their relationship can be less easily reduced to the closer generational conventions of standard coupling. One way the film tries to retain Pierre's version of events – in virtually every other respect the possessive pronominal *Ma mère* is a misleading title for the adaptation – is through his vision of a youngish woman visibly ageing before his eyes through alcohol abuse: he describes her as 'an old overcome woman' ('une vieille femme accablée') (Bataille [1966] 2000: 20). Acting ability and star value notwithstanding, the casting of Huppert allowed Honoré to make Hélène older (thereby fitting her advanced age with class privilege and personal confidence) but still physically attractive and superficially undamaged by drink.

The film opens and closes with a white screen – the writer's white page here signalling the unfinished status of the novel, which ends abruptly with its most explicit passage binding incestuous lust to the so-called death drive. The startling screen also introduces the overall lighting design of much of the film, alternating between the garish neon of the tourist resort, the spotlighted swimming pool and the glaring sunlight. The sequence – accompanied by religious music in which the camera zooms in on Pierre who is shown to be spiritually lost in the vast expanse of the sand dunes – is a nod to Pier Paolo Pasolini, not only through the 'retro' reproduction of the zoom shot, but also through the spiritual homage to his film *Il Vangelo secondo Metteo* (Pasolini, 1964), filmed in the arid landscape of central Sicily. However, the homage to Pasolini goes beyond this one intertext and points more widely to Pasolini's familiar Freudian interest in Eros and Thanatos, to the interest he shared with Bataille in sex and the sacred, and to the persistent strand of social critique running through his cinema in which class conflict is acted out through deviant sexuality.[16] The religious imagery in *Ma mère* deriving from Bataille includes shots of Pierre praying in the dunes under the surveillance of blank-faced tourists and a scene in which he loses all self-control and runs along in the rain desperately praying for repentance, oddly accompanied by a Cindy Lauper ballad. Even distanced by 1980s pop music, the overwrought Catholic interjections are alienating for the (assumed secular) twenty-first-century audience, who might easily find such overtones outdated or irrelevant. Whilst Bataille's religious preoccupations are incongruous in the context of mass tourism and sexual consumption, Honoré's purposeful references to an earlier filmmaker such as Pasolini gesture to the queer dimension to the European epistemology of death and desire (Dollimore 1998).

By the end of the film, Hélène explains to Réa her weariness with casual sex and the local nightlife. The pair's collaborative – rather than amorous – relationship follows the novel's ambivalence on lesbianism, and the film forecloses the development of female same-sex attachment beyond titillating provocation – take, for example, the sequence in the backseat of the taxi in which she jokingly caresses Réa's breast to provoke Pierre, compared to the more ambiguous comments in the letter of departure in the novel, in which she claims to have been 'twisted' by her relations with Réa (Bataille: 84) – 'tordu' meaning both mad and bent, thus queer by association. The casting of Isabelle Huppert as Hélène built on the critical acclaim she had received as the closet pervert in Michael Haneke's *La Pianiste* (2001), in which she played the daughter in a tortuous and ambiguous relationship with her threatening mother, memorably played by Annie Girardot. In *Ma mère*, Hélène willingly comes out to Pierre in a restaurant, revealing herself as a 'slut', whom no one respects.

The context for the film's perversity is actually established from the start through an aerial shot of rows of uniform holiday villas, used to present the socio-geographical setting for the action. The lengthy sequence of scenes of local nightlife, filmed mostly undercover at the Yumbo resort, work to depict the supposed excesses of sexual consumerism through industrial tourism. Despite Honoré's own lack of prudishness, these scenes are far from ideologically neutral, the downward focus, so to speak, of the camera used to orientate both the characters' and the audience's reaction to this artificial milieu, thereby turning the spectator's gaze against the mostly real-life tourists on show. Joana Preiss and Louis Garrel are filmed walking around the amusement arcade as a beautiful, well-heeled couple, opposed to the predominantly gay male tourists – cut to a shot of a semi-naked man to accentuate the 'anything goes' mentality within the confines of the sex zone. The sequence of shots alternating between the smug, privileged couple and the made-to-look-vulgar tourists continues as follows: a shot of an older local waitress wiping down tables is contrasted by a shot of Preiss and Garrel's youthful vitality as they meander through the resort; this is followed by subjective shots of both characters, enabling us to judge the atmosphere from their perspective. This is followed by a shot of an older, half-naked, deep-tanned man, then it is back to a prolonged close-up of Preiss's appealing thigh. The accumulative effect of this rapid-fire sequence is that it becomes hard to tell how much is scripted and how much just banal documentary naturalism – all tongue piercings and cheap sunglasses, and even one revealing shot of a gay couple kissing before coyly acknowledging the camera's intrusive presence. This sequence appears to follow the narrator's view in the novel of sexual pleasure as a luxury constrained by old age, ugliness and poverty ('Le plaisir génital est le luxe que limitent la vieillesse, la laideur et toutes les formes de la misère') (Bataille [1966] 2000: 101). Pierre's disorientation when Réa ditches him is accentuated by shots of lone, middle-aged men leaving a club. Hélène and Réa, figured as two drunken predators, hook back up with Pierre who has passed out in the middle of the deserted shopping mall. Réa proceeds to mount him under his mother's watchful supervision, then to fuck him in front of passing tourists, Preiss's strategically placed, hip mini-skirt their only form of protection.

This attention to apparel is far from innocent as it points to the casting of Joana Preiss, who alongside acting – notably in Olivier Assayas's *Clean* (2004) and *Boarding Gate* (2007) – is also a classically-trained singer, occasional model (for Karl Lagerfeld at Chanel and Nicolas Ghesquière at Balenciaga) and underground muse, modelling for photographer Nan Goldin.[17] Preiss brings a cool control to her performance as Réa, tinged with a metropolitan haughtiness that suits the class bias of the scenes of local tourism. Her underground art cachet is balanced by a more mainstream image as a fashion model, referenced in *Ma mère* through her signature 'indie' look, comprising of wispy, dishevelled hair and rock-chic, vintage clothing, most visible in the scene in which Réa, Hélène and Pierre, accompanied by Hansi and a male pick-up, stagger home in the early hours. The camera films the group head-on from a distance, parading down the middle of the empty road. While Huppert and Emma de Caunes occupy the right-hand side of the frame (Hélène 'maternally' propping up Hansi who is blind drunk), Preiss nonchalantly strides down the street with the two men in tow.[18] Even in character Preiss is still a model.

The ethical problem with the 'snatch filming' (*à l'arraché*) of the preceding sequence is that by contrasting an elegant established star, an up-and-coming leading man and an underground fashion icon with earlier documentary shots of supposedly real, less physically appealing tourists, the images work to expose the perceived tackiness of the ambient mass tourism.[19] To be fair, despite the patronising sketch of sexual consumerism, Honoré tries at times to be equally critical of his more privileged characters, never making them even remotely sympathetic – clearly one of the formal objectives of the film was to avoid sentimentalism. *Ma mère* also tries to make a minor point in Marxist mode about local patterns of consumption, showcasing the socio-economic disparity between those free to indulge in sexual leisure at their will and those bound to serve them, both categories sustaining the local economy.[20] The precise editing of the earlier scene of taxi titillation leads to a critical engagement with the class dialectic by juxtaposing the principal characters' inane antics (including back-seat fingering) with contrasting images of the couple of French housekeepers as alienated workers, critical of their employers' libertinage. On reaching home, Pierre insults and fires them both for no apparent reason, ignoring their previous concern for his welfare following his father's death. As with the earlier contrasting shot of a local waitress, the film points to the contradiction between the material freedoms enjoyed by the arrogant hedonists and the attendant constraints on a more sympathetic supporting cast of exploited workers.

The masochistic Loulou, originally a girl in Bataille's novel, is also a housekeeper in a hotel residence, shown at work with cleaning apparatus in hand. However, whereas this would seem to bind social subordination to sexual submission, we learn later from Hansi that he actually manages the residence himself. (As in the novel, Hansi's own sexual apparatus of horse-riding boots and whip is conversely derived from upper-class iconography.) Loulou is figured as a gay character transcending homosexuality, in Honoré's view, modelled on the boys in Dennis Cooper's novels who portray a terrorising passivity, making them pliable to the violent fantasies of older men.[21] *Ma mère* includes one such snuff fantasy of extreme masochism, in which Loulou recounts playing a pig in an S/M scenario, being fattened up for the slaughter. The scene of Loulou's account takes place at night around Pierre's spotlighted swimming pool, thereby neutralising the macabre terror of Cooper through a chic transposition. The camera slowly follows the contours of a semi-naked boy (Patrick Fanik) listening to Loulou's story; his lithe, youthful body provides a visual contrast with the narrative carnage, which includes details of frozen, dismembered bodies. The accompanying objectification of the tanned male bodies is suitably erotic, including an extreme close-up of Montagut's intense face, before alternating between Garrel's stunned audience reaction and shots of both boys' skin.[22] Loulou later becomes Pierre and Hansi's 'slave', spat at, tied up and whipped raw. The fact that Loulou morphs from a fantasy lesbian soubrette in the novel to an unfazed sex junkie in the film naturally alters the significance of the S/M three-way. Honoré's subtle queering of *Ma mère* ultimately sees him discard Bataille's hetero-centric fantasy framework, which for all the talk of controversial transgression, builds up to the disappointingly conventional male fantasy of 'girl-on-girl' action.

AIDS Film

Despite being branded abroad as the latest example of the 'New French Extremism' trend, *Ma mère*'s more encrypted debts to Pasolini and Cooper show how Honoré is working within a Euro-American queer aesthetic tradition. Cooper, who now lives in Paris, is consistently part of the selection of contemporary US authors celebrated by Parisian literary authorities, and Pasolini has enjoyed something of an early twenty-first-century revival in France with DVD re-issues and frequent screenings, particularly of *Salò o le 120 giornate di Sodoma* (Pasolini, 1975). In the apocalyptically-entitled *The End*, a dissection of contemporary gay sexual subculture published a few months before the timely update of *Ma mère*, Didier Lestrade linked the renewed interest in Pasolini to not only the widespread acceptance of extreme or hard-core sexual practices as a booming business within metropolitan queer subcultures, but also to the concurrent practice and ideology of 'barebacking', which seeks to lifestyle unsafe sex as acceptable and ordinary (Lestrade 2004).[23] In that light, *Ma mère* can be seen as symptomatic of the broader return of the so-called death drive within queer culture, which has the spectre of AIDS hovering in the background. Within recent Anglo-American critical theory, Lee Edelman's *No Future: Queer Theory and the Death Drive* (Edelman 2004) is perhaps the emblematic text of this turn. Published the same year as Honoré's *Ma mère* and Lestrade's *The End*, Edelman's urge to embrace queer negativity coincides historically (if perhaps not intentionally) with the AIDS revisionism incorporated within the bareback ideology. Lestrade's argument is more difficult to articulate, for it runs the risk of appearing to blame gay promiscuity alone for increases in HIV transmission rates and to bundle together all S/M practices as uniformly disturbed. The hard-core sexual practices Lestrade is pinpointing are not part of the older S/M subculture of controlled anonymous intimacies (the redemptive myth of the sexual democracy of gay liberation) or practices that were formally promoted as safe from HIV contamination, but more a result of the internet boom in gay cruising. This has not only disseminated bareback practices through virtual peer-to-peer contact, thereby propelling a hitherto minority discourse of unsafe sex into a larger popular consciousness, but also installed sexual compulsion, male aggression and relational violence as its modus operandi. Like Cooper's novel *The Sluts* which charts this evolving trend (Cooper 2005), Honoré's queering of the sexually blasé character Loulou works by situating him historically within this potentially compulsive sexual network culture, which, Lestrade argues, is spiralling out of control.[24]

The potential difficulties of anonymous sexual encounters as an HIV-positive gay man are broached in Honoré's first full-length film, *Tout contre Léo*, made for TV channel M6 in 2001, never broadcast and eventually issued on DVD by Antiprod in 2004. In the DVD portrait of Honoré, he explains that he had wanted to avoid the apparently plodding realism of AIDS TV fiction by attempting to play with the codes of the genre, thus introducing elements of art-cinema into the packaged brief from M6. So whilst the film is for the most part conventionally shot and narrative-driven (close to the sort of cinema Honoré had dismissed at *Cahiers du cinéma*), Honoré toys with the use of anti-naturalist fantasy. *Tout contre Léo* is an adaptation of Honoré's first children's novel (Honoré 1995), written to present AIDS to a young readership. Both the book and the film focus on the viewpoint of Marcel (Yaniss Lespert), the youngest of four brothers, one of whom, Léo (Pierre Mignard), is HIV-positive. The film traces the complex patterns of love and the circulation of desire between the brothers and the knock-on effects of AIDS on the family unit. The later stages of the narrative see the action move from Brittany to Paris where Léo (with Marcel in tow) tries unsuccessfully to re-ignite a former flame, before discarding his antiretroviral medication and choosing to die. The one prolonged sex scene between Léo and the night porter at the hotel shows Honoré's measured approach to filming sexual desire as opposed to an opportunistic focus on body parts. Instead of approaching a sex scene from a strictly narrative angle, in which the act is used as a plot device to convey that any two given characters have had sex together, Honoré lays bare Léo's lust and his subsequent incapacity to act on it. The horny porter lures Léo into the dimly lighted back room, the camera filming them tease one another before clumsily undressing – a devise to arouse the viewer's curiosity as to what turns them on. Honoré is attuned to both characters' psychological motivation, filming Mignard lead the action, lying face down on the sofa (the inference is that Léo wants to be fucked), then showing him block as his partner reaches for a condom. Léo stalls either due to the reminder of his HIV-status or the assumed burden of responsibility of having to disclose it to each sexual partner, thereby potentially wrecking the action. Léo panics and leaves, rejecting his partner's offer of a drink during their disjointed verbal exchange, seeking solace in the arms of his young brother. This is captured through the following shot of their bodies clasped together, expressing Léo's need for comfort rather than sex. It was the fact that Honoré chose to broach the difficulties of negotiating HIV-status in a gay sex scene and refused to edit the sequence which M6 used as their reason not to screen the film.[25]

The HIV prevention adverts that Honoré later made for the Ministry of Health and INPES (*Institut national de prévention et d'éducation pour la santé*) conversely contained no erotic sequences and were broadcast widely by all major TV channels across a three-week period in December 2002 (totalling 850 slots for a budget of 3.75 million euros). Honoré was also working to a brief (the campaign's strapline aimed to encourage people to be tested for HIV) but had artistic control over the visual design of the clips. The press blurb from INPES explains the series of ads as an important turning point in state-funded HIV prevention seeking to promote testing and not only safer sex as necessary protection. The difficulty lies in the communication rather than the political scope of the ads because they rely heavily on three main sociological stereotypes that tend to give out the message that HIV testing (as opposed to the use of condoms) is the primary tool in prevention. In reality, a regular HIV test is a basic necessity rather than a reliable means of prevention.

The first spot is set in a run-down bed-sit and shows a young heterosexual couple who run out of condoms. The boy suggests they dispense with protection as they have been together for three months. The ad plays with audience expectation that the girl will then be coerced into unsafe sex by presenting her as unbothered by the situation, simply refusing to have sex until they have both been tested. To get serious means to get tested. The second clip is heavier in tone and moves out of the bedroom and into the library, to a more intense scene of gay coupling and extra-conjugal relations, making negotiations around HIV/AIDS more fraught in the same-sex context than in the heterosexual context. The final spot is addressed to sub-Saharan African immigrants; the setting this time is not in places of intimacy or learning, but in the workplace, thereby defining immigrants primarily in terms of their professional function of upholding France's service economy. The choice of alternating social milieus for the three ads binds gayness to serious endeavour, and heterosexuality to either bohemian freedom or to manual labour, depending on racial and national identity. As in the case of the gay male couple, promiscuity is the source of anxious inquiry in the final clip in which the female character makes allowances for her man's 'good times' back home but demands he be tested before resuming sexual relations. The unfortunate inference is that HIV testing will then inevitably take the place of adequate prevention. Yet whilst the campaign's message (beyond that of urging people to get tested) is problematic, Honoré's abrupt editing and the ironic use of pop music ('Just another love song') avoid both the traditional bland generality and the recent scare tactics of much HIV prevention. The brevity of these spots also enabled Honoré to avoid the trap of pathos, which was the mode chosen for Lifshitz's series of HIV prevention spots made for INPES and first shown at the Paris Lesbian and Gay Film Festival in 2006. These combined scenic art direction, biographical testimony and naturalistic documentary to highlight the individual and interpersonal difficulties of living with HIV. The films also sought to encourage HIV-positive gay men to continue safer-sex practices in light of mutations of the virus.

Arguments on the relapse of high-risk sex among HIV-positive and HIV-negative men since the introduction of multi-therapy treatment drugs in the mid-1990s and the more recent specific practice and ethic of barebacking within gay male subcultures have caused familiar preoccupations with promiscuity, AIDS and death to resurface. The story went overground in 2000 when *Libération* published a shock cover article on barebacking, tracking the development of a supposedly underground subculture of unprotected sex among HIV-positive gay men that has since expanded rapidly through widespread internet use. The notion that gay male subculture could be sexually fragmenting according to HIV-status has since been debated in relation to practices of 'sero-sorting' in which partners are chosen according to known or assumed sero-status.[26] This follows on from developments in community prevention favouring 'harm reduction' campaigns that vary according to HIV status. The idea, now widespread among prevention workers and activists, is that protected sex, whilst the safest message, is apparently not the *right* message for all gay men. Harm reduction strategies have been developed to cater for people already

not using condoms, informing them of perceived statistical risk in sexual practice.[27] Whereas the relapse of unsafe sex signifies reduced prevention of sexually transmitted diseases and HIV transmission, barebacking is more precisely
the ideology and discourse of risk-taking and the explicit promotion of high-
risk sex by HIV-positive men who turn a blind eye to future mutations of HIV,
or by (last-tested) HIV-negative men who effectively deny the very existence of
HIV or at least think they are immune to it. Giving unsafe sex an acceptable
name has removed its cultural stigma, lifestyling it as a liberating and attractive
sexual trend; the liberation is from government education promoting safe-sex
as good behaviour, which is often perceived as patronising or repressive.

Reports of the bareback phenomenon in France came in light of novels by gay
writers Guillaume Dustan (Dustan 1999) and Eric Rémès (Rémès 1999), which
called into question the inevitability of safer sex practices. Both writers sought
to undermine the representation of gay sex as predominantly safe and to with-
draw the responsibility of gay men in HIV prevention.[28] Effectively denying the
reality of AIDS in gay subcultures and the necessity to inform under-twenty-five
year olds of further epidemic cycles of HIV, Dustan even declared that the
condom never existed.[29] The counter-arguments from Didier Lestrade and Act
Up Paris to this discourse of AIDS revisionism are of interest because in Act Up's
1999 prevention campaign and in Lestrade's subsequent personal history of the
organisation, *Act Up Une Histoire* (Lestrade 2000), an explicit anti-bareback
policy was outlined as part of the group's prevention work. In their account of
the formation of Act Up Paris in 1989, Christophe Broqua and Patrice Pinell
describe how the socio-political function of the group was to dominate media
discourse and to reconfigure the balance of power between the different AIDS
groups themselves and in turn their relations with the state.

> Act Up became a major part of the charity sector, which it in turn trans-
> formed by introducing an additional opposition to those existing between
> 'generalist/specialist' or 'public sector/community sector', which marked
> the slit between 'reformist' and 'revolutionary' or rather 'activist' groups
> in the Anglo-Amercian understanding of the term.
> (Act Up devient une composante majeure de l'espace associatif qu'il
> remodèle en introduisant en son sein une ligne de clivage supplémentaire.
> Aux oppositions existantes, 'généraliste/spécialisé', 'service public/service
> communautaire', s'ajoute un partage entre associations 'réformistes' et
> 'révolutionnaires' ou plutôt 'activiste' au sens anglo-saxon du terme.)
> (Pinell 2002: 207)

Rather than buying into the dominant media representation of HIV positive
people as dangerous or invisible, Act Up broke off the pact, seeking instead to
concentrate on the state's inability to contain HIV contamination.

A fictional vision of sexual risk is to be found in *Un moment . . .* (Salvadori,
1996), a short film from the earlier AIDS conjuncture, part of a collection about

homosexuality in the time of AIDS, *L'Amour est à réinventer: dix histoires d'amour au temps du sida*, a collection of ten short films made by the winners of a screenwriting competition, broadcast on mainstream television in December 1996. *Un moment* . . . focuses on casual sex: shot subjectively, it follows two young men through a brief episode of unsafe sex and their subsequent feelings of unease about discussing it afterwards. The narrator's desire is shown to be so overwhelming that he attempts to convince himself that his prospective partner cannot possibly be positive: he reads, does sport and appears too young. The director, Pierre Salvadori, evokes the popular coupling of desire with danger as the film's main preoccupation.[30] Whilst Salvadori claims that the film is stripped of all psychology, the abrupt, embarrassed conversation following sex would suggest otherwise. The sex itself is subjectively shot and very brief, interrupted only by the narrator's rationalisation about unprotected sex. The unexciting portrayal of sex is used to make the film exemplary: 'filming desire without arousing desire so the film can be exemplary' ('Filmer le désir sans susciter le désir, afin que le film puisse être regardé en conscience et avoir une valeur exemplaire').[31]

Ducastel and Martineau similarly work within an exemplary space with regard to HIV/AIDS but are anything but downbeat. As Stéphane Bouquet observed in his review of *Drôle de Félix*, both filmmakers stay true to their protagonist's name by setting out to capture happiness so as to situate AIDS as a commonplace feature of gay male interpersonal relations rather than as a drama in itself.[32] *Jeanne et le garçon formidable* had already discarded the pathos and martyrdom dominating AIDS visual fiction – examples of which include Guibert's *La Pudeur ou l'impudeur* (1992) and Collard's *Les Nuits fauves* (1992) – but their second feature took life with HIV as its structuring thread rather than as its main narrative preoccupation. The historical shift between the two films is from AIDS to seropositivity. 'Affected by a devastating plague, the passengers on this new ship are heading for a predictable death, albeit one that, thanks to research, is often deferred for even greater lengths of time; it is in this sense that seropositivity as a category displaces AIDS to a greater or lesser extent', as Lawrence R. Schehr argues elsewhere (Schehr 2004: 101). Judging by the number of academic articles devoted to the film, *Drôle de Félix* has become something of a favourite among Anglo-American academics of French gay/queer film, who have given it more critical space than it was granted by mainstream cinema criticism in France on its release in 2000 (Grandena 2006; Ince 2002; McGonagle 2007; Pratt 2004; Provencher 2008; Swamy 2006). Denis Provencher describes Félix as a type of 'good French sexual citizen' (Provencher 2008: 52), while Murray Pratt traces the film's investment in the genre of the 'light-hearted gay road movie', a genre of gay affirmation cinema (Pratt 2004). Pratt argues that the film could have engaged with the contemporary debates around unsafe-sexual practices in gay subculture rather than merely opting for 'warm-heartedness' (Pratt 2004: 91–2).

The opening sequence showing the apparently carefree Félix (Sami Bouajila) cycling along the promenade at Dieppe to the tune of 'tout doucement' exposes the film's investment in wellbeing. As Jean-Pierre Jeancolas argues, Ducastel and Martineau engage with predictably heavy-weather subjects such as AIDS, racial violence and unemployment without disrupting the film's lightness of touch. 'L'homosexualité n'est plus une conquête ou une provocation, c'est un état'.[33] Bouquet, however, picks up on the filmmakers' underlying moralistic politics – 'a strange moralism' ('un moralisme étrange'), as he sees it, seemingly at odds with the film's freedom of movement, the episodic structure that sees Félix's journey across France from Dieppe to Marseille, punctuated by random meetings with a surrogate family that includes a teenaged 'brother' who has a crush on him and a 'cousin' with whom he makes love. Bouquet registers surprise at Ducastel and Martineau's responsible choice to show post-sexual detritus in the form of a used condom, but not the erotic action itself beyond the men's initial embrace. The film's vitality and dynamism not only stem from Félix's actual journey across France in his personal quest for family (self-realisation, after all, being the modus operandi of the road-movie genre), but also from the character's HIV status, and a life ordered by the treatment drugs that keep him alive. José Arroyo describes the film as one of the first to show 'an HIV+ protagonist who is offered the expectation of a future, however delimited . . . It would be wrong, though, to label Félix simply as an HIV+ romance. Like so much else in the film, the issue is introduced seemingly sideways and by stealth'.[34] Life with HIV is initially presented ordinarily (Félix is woken up to take his pills and to watch his favourite soap opera) and later comically (he exchanges information with a puzzled woman at the hospital about the ever-growing variety of drug combinations); the film is therefore able to dodge the doom-laden biographical necessity inherent in AIDS fiction which reduces a character's existence to two events – contamination and death.

This maudlin artistic exploitation of AIDS is best exemplified in French cinema by Xavier Beauvois's *N'oublie pas que tu vas mourir* (1995) in which Benoît (played by Beauvois himself), a conventional student, discovers upon enlisting for his military service that he is HIV-positive. The news of his contamination plunges him into a downward spiral that involves substance abuse and unsafe sex. Preoccupied with alternative patterns of the contemporary family, *Drôle de Félix* breaks with the traditional AIDS narrative mould simply by representing a living protagonist whose life is transformed rather than wrecked by HIV. That said, as Arroyo observes, 'we can't forget Félix is dying – it's what the film represses, displaces on to issues of race and plots of murder; it's a structuring quasi-absence.'[35]

Conversely, in Ducastel and Martineau's earlier *Jeanne et le garçon formidable*, AIDS is clearly the structuring presence, pointing to a socio-political landscape entirely transformed by the epidemic, in which radical activism is less a backdrop to the individual romance than a key part of its narrative development. In his compendium of international cinematic representations of homosexuality, Didier Roth-Bettoni cites Paul Vecchiali's anti-naturalist fable *Encore* (1988) as the first AIDS film in France from a gay perspective (Roth-Bettoni 2007: 591–2). Set in the early 1980s, *Encore* offers a stylised representation of clone bar culture with its ideological rejection of 'straight' coupling, making it both politically removed from the preoccupations of contemporary gay assimilation and artistically dated with its purposefully wooden acting, hysterical female character and camp theatrical structure, including long sequence shots giving an appearance of filmed theatre. With the blunt introduction of AIDS, Vecchiali successfully navigated the pitfalls of pathos, preferring a more cynical voice and a camp style that includes a hilarious, synthesized, musical set piece at a wedding, proclaiming the virtues of endless love and future *jouissance*. The encasing of a grave subject matter within a frivolous form is the format chosen for *Jeanne et le garçon formidable*. Though filmed in 1997 and released the following year, the setting precedes the present conjuncture of second-generation AIDS treatments so deftly captured in *Drôle de Félix*, foregrounding an era in which HIV heralded imminent death rather than sustained periods of chronic illness. Although ostensibly a heterosexual love story with mainstream appeal, *Jeanne et le garçon formidable* wears its dissident credentials on its sleeve, balancing the romance between its carefree modern heroine (Virginie Ledoyen) and her HIV-positive activist boyfriend (Mathieu Demy), with the insight and experience of a secondary character François (Jacques Bonnaffé), who has lost a partner to AIDS, who fights for change with Act Up and who is finishing a doctorate on political activism. Needless to say, Ducastel and Martineau, both former activists themselves, based the character's personal situation and political motivation on their own surrounding milieu. Stéphane Giusti's TV film *L'Homme que j'aime* (1997), a co-production for Arte and la Sept, also showcased Act Up Marseille, drawing on the filmmaker's prior experience as an activist with the group in Paris. The bitter-sweet tone of the film drew on Act Up's striking combination of confrontational politics, camp theatricality and black humour; this distinction is diluted in Giusti's subsequent film, the nonetheless sharp 'coming-out' comedy *Pourquoi pas moi?* (1999).

In an interview with a late 1990s gay magazine *Ex Aequo*, Martineau explicitly argued the case for political, as opposed to artistic, images of AIDS.[36] The scenario's novelty was to represent HIV-positivity from a heterosexual female perspective, whilst simultaneously drawing on gay male experience. Jeanne is young, promiscuous and careful. Unable to track down her missing lover, she makes a desperate appeal to Act Up for help (involving shots of actual former Act Up presidents Philippe Mangeot and Victoire Patouillard), only to hear of Olivier's death later by chance, hours before the funeral. The film's final shot encapsulates her state of flux: hurrying to the *Père Lachaise* crematorium, she trips and falls on the cobbled pathway, remaining on the ground, facing the camera in despair.

Much of the film takes place in north-east Paris, with memorable sequences along the *Canal de l'Ourcq* in the nineteenth arrondissement, harbouring a thriving multicultural mix. The explicit critique of contemporary immigration politics is presented in the film's early stages, as Jeanne leaves work for the weekend, handing over to the non-white immigrant workers employed to clean. As Camille Taboulay commented in *Cahiers du cinéma*,[37] their sung complaint that the only reward for dutiful service is the threat of expulsion echoed the undocumented immigration affair and the protests of the 'citizen-filmmakers' in 1997. The use of song and dance not only works as a distancing effect, but also as assistance when the dialogue becomes dysfunctional. The gay activist character François exposes Ducastel and Martineau's political vision of the intertwined political and personal knock-on effects of AIDS in an accordion ballad that displaces the cosy notion that love could act as a remedy to loss. François's more committed response is to channel his grief into activism, to challenge a status quo that denies the relevance of waves of gay deaths. Yet whilst such an explanatory piece could appear didactic to a politically aware audience (Jeanne is figured as the ideal heterosexual listener standing in for the assumed mainstream audience), the no-nonsense vision contained within the lyrics expands the boundaries of the musical beyond individual coupling and romantic clichés of doomed love. The traditional Parisian accordion sound is used contrapuntally to the lyrics to mark the gap between tradition and actuality, a device that is particularly effective in Olivier's explanation to Jeanne of his HIV-status. The frantic pace of the clipped lyrics fits well with Olivier's curt response to Jeanne's romantic idea that true love will save the day. The person who contaminated him is not to blame, but rather the negligent political class both left and right; Edith Cresson and Charles Pasqua are both singled out in this tirade against the nation.

Gérard Lefort praised the film's strident protest in his review for *Libération*, remarking on 'the contemporary whirlwind of protestation whose noticeable feature is its political engagement from a troubling minority perspective' ('le tourbillon protestataire contemporain dont la singularité est de faire de la politique de manière embarrassante et minoritaire').[38] Ducastel and Martineau were seen to have transformed the staid genre of musical comedy by injecting it with first-hand grassroots knowledge of oppositional politics. As Claire Vassé argued, the film's strength at that time was documentary in nature; it was inscribed within its precise historical moment, proving 'the extent to which the musical is at present able to capture something of the zeitgeist' ('combien la comédie musicale est aujourd'hui capable . . . de saisir quelque chose de l'air du temps').[39] Indeed Jeanne's own sexual freedom and frank sex-talk could be said to derive from the filmmakers' own gay milieu: their vision of contemporary France effectively entailed translating a dissident cultural dialect into a dominant one without compromising their sharp-edged critique of sexual politics both straight and queer. The personal insights of engagement in radical politics are minutely captured through the secondary character François, the generic AIDS activist hard-hit by years of loss, who is articulate (though writing his thesis on activism, he refuses to be the specialist of the dying), but doubtful of his own abilities when confronted with the death of his friend Olivier.

THE DEMY REVIVAL

The 'personal' and the 'political' – the familiar watchwords of sexual liberation – are juxtaposed in *Jeanne et le garçon formidable* in the same way that the film contrasts clashing stylistic sensibilities, succinctly described by Dennis Altman as 'both bitter and very kitsch' (Altman 2001: 81). Actual footage and partial reconstruction of an Act Up demonstration are abruptly edited to follow on from the musical fantasy of Jeanne's declaration of love for the 'wonderful boy', a scene choreographed in a sushi bar with a gaudy artificial backdrop. Jumping from fantasy to reality is part and parcel of the musical's generic remit. In the broader history of French cinema the technique points to the work of Jacques Demy, who, from the 1960s onwards, developed a individual style of musical fantasy. Demy's idiosyncratic but popular output led him to be viewed as more accessible than his New Wave contemporaries,[40] whilst experimenting with similar non-realist distancing effects such as recitative from opera and expressionist choreography from dance. David Thomson has written an appreciative account of Demy's early work, seeing him among the New Wave directors as 'the most faithful to the delights of sight and sound and to the romance of movie iconography' (Thomson 2002: 221) and lamenting his overlooked status among younger generations of *cinéphiles*. Within French cinema, the pastiche of Demy is self-conscious in the case of Ducastel and Martineau through the saturated use of colour, the choreographed use of movement outside the musical numbers, the casting of Demy's son in the juvenile lead, and the recurring use of chance and coincidence as narrative and spatial devises. The critics saw Jeanne as a spin-off Demy heroine, a descendant of the roles played by Catherine Deneuve in both *Les Parapluies de Cherbourg* (1964) and *Les Demoiselles de Rochefort* (1967). Both Vassé in *Positif* and Taboulay in *Cahiers du cinéma* reference the carefree twins played by real-life sisters Deneuve and Françoise Dorléac – like Jeanne both on the look out for true love; and Taboulay refers to Jeanne as both a less ethereal, more down-to-earth *demoiselle de Rochefort* and a modern, busy Lola, a reference to Anouk Aimée's moving portrayal of the character (*Lola*, 1961) as a fragile woman, wounded by love. Thomson points to Lola as the template for Demy's later heroines, an archetype described as 'beautiful, sentimental, hopeful, resigned, gay, nervy, trembling between tears and laughter' (Thomson 2002: 221), an equally accurate all-round description of Jeanne. Whilst the *demoiselles* became something of camp icons in French gay popular culture, showing how queer audiences have historically decoded the work of closeted gay directors and appropriated mainstream culture for their own purposes,[41] the chance meetings and missed opportunities that are also an integral part of Demy's world point to sexual cruising as a key part of both Jeanne's lifestyle and its narrative representation.

Ducastel and Martineau effectively 'out' Demy's trademark aesthetic, revealing its in-built queerness whilst retaining its predominantly heterosexual narrative structure.[42]

The cinema of Demy links Ducastel and Martineau to Honoré, who has likewise claimed the filmmaker as an artistic father figure.[43] Honoré's homage to Demy began with *Dix-sept fois Cécile Cassard*, the appropriation apparent from the heroine's name which amalgamates two of Demy's characters – Roland Cassard from both *Lola* and *Les Parapluies de Cherbourg*, and Cécile from *Lola*. Honoré memorably included a sequence towards the end that lightens the ambient gloom, in which Romain Duris performs a camp homage to Anouk Aimée's sexy lip-sync self-presentation. Duris's number effectively lays bare the repetitious spectacle of gender imitation in the 'original'. As Matthew Lazen points out, Demy's film is 'an intertextual quiltwork of allusions and quotations rather than an entirely original text' (Lazen 2004: 193).

Honoré further developed his thematic mix of family relations, sexual dissent and personal loss in his musical homage to Demy and other New Wave figures, *Les Chansons d'amour* (2007), co-written by Gaël Morel, which takes the sudden death of a female character in a *ménage à trois* as its narrative focus. The film favours the sentimental lightness of pop over the serious pathos of melodrama.[44] The theme of grief is set to a series of love songs taken from Alex Beaupain's album *Garçon d'honneur* (2006) and substantially re-worked for the film's soundtrack, an integral part of the characters' interaction rather than a purely decorative devise. Like Honoré's previous film, his nostalgic hymn to the New Wave, *Dans Paris* (2006), which 'wills the spectator to play the game of spot the reference',[45] *Les Chansons d'amour*'s appropriation of Demy has likewise been criticised as a form of '*cinéphile* karaoke'[46] for its additional pastiche of Jean Eustache's *La Maman et la putain* (1973) and Godard's *Une femme est une femme* (1961) (both of these involve threesomes, and the latter incorporates musical numbers). The film's casting also bolsters the New Wave lineage by including both Deneuve's daughter Chiara Mastroianni and Jean-Pierre Léaud's artistic heir Louis Garrel, who has become particularly associated with Honoré's cinema since *Ma mère*. Unlike the continuing revival of 'quality cinema' promoting a plethora of stars in traditional literary realism – Claude Miller's historical adaptation *Un secret* (2007), also starring Ludivine Sagnier, is emblematic of this trend – both *Dans Paris* and *Les Chansons d'amour* were low-budget productions filmed and released quickly to capture their precise historical moment, a technique reminiscent of the improvised spirit and off-beat charm of early Godard. Honoré's nostalgic New Wave revival also resurrects distancing devices derived from the diverse aesthetics of Demy, Godard and Truffaut. *Les Chansons d'amour* lifts Demy's inter-titles from *Les Parapluies de Cherbourg*, as well as his use of a conveyor belt to slow down movement during song – Ludivine Sagnier, sporting a vintage 1960s white coat and a Deneuve-inspired hair style, is shot gliding towards the camera, a technique borrowed from Deneuve and Nino Castelnuevo's passionate declaration of love. Advertising is referenced to provide an ironic commentary on the action, thereby taking up Godard's critique of consumerism; and arrested motion – the freeze frame, most famously used to capture Léaud at the end of Truffaut's *Les Quatre cents coups* (1959) – is used to block spectator identification during the scenes of death and loss.

Dans Paris performs a continuous citation of the New Wave form, making it very much an early twenty-first-century product through its promotion and re-packaging of vintage memorabilia. Moreover, as Vincendeau remarks, it also reproduces the troubling sexual politics of the New Wave through much male soul-searching and fraternal bonding, at the expense of any insight into female subjectivity, thereby establishing a social milieu in which 'women are inadequate mothers, neurotic girlfriends or easygoing playmates'.[47] Women are superficially less peripheral to *Les Chansons d'amour*, though following Julie's death, the latter stages of the film foreground the male protagonist's loss and emerging love for a wholesome Breton schoolboy (Grégoire Leprince-Ringuet); it thereby neglects a fuller exploration of the subjectivities of either Julie's elder sister Jeanne (Chiara Mastroianni) or her former lover Alice (Clotilde Hesme), who drops out of the emotional – if not out of the narrative – picture. The boys, however, are allowed sex, tenderness and the necessary space to explore their emotional commitment – the romantic conclusion, in which they express their differing expectations, establishes same-sex attachment as the film's narrative resolution. The bitter-sweet salutary sentiment voiced by Garrel ('aime-moi moins mais aime-moi longtemps') is captured in a shot taken from the street below as they climb out onto a narrow ledge to embrace. Female same-sexuality is conversely discarded as a plausible option early on through the initial presentation of the three main characters' design for living (following the heterocentric imperative of Eustache's *La Maman et la putain*) in which Ismaël remains the 'necessary' centrepiece to the relationship, and in which the remote possibility of the two girls not bothering with a boy at all is reduced to the status of 'sister-love' and whimsical experimentation. Lesbianism is disparagingly termed 'le non-sexe' by the girls, hetero-sexist residue from the New Wave that Honoré would have done better to jettison. This regressive vision of female sexuality blithely reproduces the critical move particularly associated with Godard, decoded by feminist critics such as Laura Mulvey as a 'deep-seated, but interesting, misogyny' (Mulvey 1996: 94).

Whilst widely regarded as a companion piece to *Dans Paris*, *Les Chansons d'amour* actually borrows more of the normative politics of heterosexual experimentation outlined in *Ma mère*, in which Huppert and Preiss's 'lesbian' sex scene was for male eyes only. The foreclosure of the more radical possibility of female same-sexuality beyond titillating experimentation, as both viable and pleasurable, points either to individual lack of interest on the filmmaker's part or more plausibly to the wider socio-economic limits of queer representation from within independent production companies that imitate the dominant preference for explorations of gay male over lesbian sexuality, whilst promoting their products as provocative and cutting-edge art. (A rare exception to this 'rule' is Céline Sciamma's intricate exploration of female teenage desire, *Naissance des pieuvres*, a beautiful début, also screened at Cannes in 2007, but out of competition.) In sum, *Les Chansons d'amour* is bourgeois-bohemian cinema, presenting a straightened-out rendition of Queer, strategically deploying bisexuality to indicate the present acceptability of metropolitan nonconformity. The film's bourgeois-bohemian mindset, whilst providing an insouciant vision of multiple bisexual identities in which (male) same-sex attachments are a plausible option, reveals its liberal limitations not only through its lesbian blind spot but also through its half-hearted gestures to a multicultural working-class Paris. While the camera lingers on non-white local inhabitants (Honoré preferring impromptu filming to a closed set, which explains the bemused faces of actual passers-by), they are mere extras in an otherwise white picture.

NOT-ABOUT-AIDS FILM

Les Chansons d'amour was dedicated to a friend whom Honoré and composer Alex Beaupain had loved and lost, and to a fellow filmmaker who had died from AIDS. Critics see loss as the cornerstone of Honoré's cinematic and literary work.[48] His trilogy of fiction – *L'Infamille* (1997), *La Douceur* (1999) and *Scarborough* (2002) – covers similar thematic territory of sexuality, loss and fraternal relations. I want now to position his work following *Tout contre Léo* in relation to a concurrent 'not-about-AIDS' cinema, one that either consciously chooses to banish grey areas around HIV within queer subcultures (central debates around increases in unsafe sex, for example) from its visual production, or one that is unable to address the issue head-on, given the historical precedent for mawkish sentimentalism in the case of influential Hollywood imagery; or of queer martyrdom in the case of French narrative fiction (the continued critical focus on films like *Les Nuits fauves*, *N'oublie pas que tu vas mourir* and so forth). Rejecting the narcissism and pathos associated with much artistic production of AIDS in France, a posture so deftly exploited by Hervé Guibert in his autobiographical film *La Pudeur ou l'impudeur* (1992), I am arguing that films such as *Jeanne et le garçon formidable* and *Drôle de Félix* show that an AIDS cinema eschewing sentimental pathos in favour of bitter-sweet camp (combining a darkness of humour with a lightness of touch) is indeed artistically and politically viable. I am also suggesting that Honoré's structures of loss point less to a conscious decision not to tackle AIDS on principle – there is no purposeful displacement at work here – than to the contextual role played by HIV/AIDS in the social milieus of gay male filmmakers and the oblique effects of queer sexuality and loss on films whose thematic preoccupations are clearly elsewhere.

Chéreau's *Son frère* (2004) and Ozon's *Le Temps qui reste* (2005) both maintain a conscious silence on AIDS, toying with a possible analogy but, particularly in the case of *Son frère*, anxiously denying its thematic presence through the over-insistent reliance on promotional material to closet the subject, a surprising move in light of Chéreau's candid take on gay male sexuality in *Ceux qui m'aiment prendront le train*. *Son frère* captures the fractured relationship between two brothers, one of who suffers from a debilitating blood disease. *Le Temps qui reste* tracks a gay man's acceptance of terminal cancer and his withdrawal from all interpersonal relations. The crossover between fraternal love and sexual passion is an expanding preoccupation in recent queer film, one not only broached by Chéreau and Honoré but also by the small-scale, independent production *Comme un frère* (2005), co-directed by Bernard Alapetite and Cyril Legann, which gives a different take on male intimacy and unrequited love by suggesting a best friend as the ideal unattainable lover.

'Not-about-AIDS' was the title of an article by David Román published in 2000 (the title relating to his analysis of Neil Greenberg's *Not-About-AIDS-Dance*), which probed the continuing AIDS narrative in debates within contemporary gay culture and politics, particularly on the diverse calls for 'post-AIDS' identities and the 'end-of-AIDS' discourse. In the artistic context of queer culture in the US in the 1980s and early 1990s,

> *Not-About-AIDS-Dance* refers to what David Gere calls the 'silent signification' that characterised most dances in the 1980s and early 1990s: the reluctance of choreographers to identify their work with AIDS despite the sense that the work may be about AIDS in some way . . . Not-About-AIDS-Dance extends beyond silent signification to comment on the cultural silence and suppression of AIDS. (Román 2000: 15)

'The sense that the work may be about AIDS in some way' suits the guardedness of films such as *Son frère*, in which AIDS is disavowed rather than included as part of the narrative trajectory or social landscape. Such a disavowal is part of the larger rejection of identity politics from the scope of French auteur cinema, in which the politics of gender and sexuality are shrugged off as either Anglo-American incongruities or else trivial minority-interest concerns impairing a properly formalist, supposedly non-partisan appreciation of film – a manoeuvre revealing the class prejudice involved in safeguarding art from political criticism. A common feature of the queer cinema emerging from the work of filmmakers such as Chéreau, Honoré, Morel and Téchiné is a reluctance to go beyond this modest aesthetic and political form of sexual inquiry for constant fear of adhering to Anglo-American identity politics. This potentially limits the acceptance of their work by mainstream audiences and by fellow filmmakers and critics.

The objective of the strand of queer pathos standard in French AIDS representation is not simply the philosophical penchant for universal human suffering and apolitical art; it is also concerned with financial profit. The commercial exploitation of AIDS-as-art has in recent times included the posthumous publication of Guibert's diaries in 2001 to mark the tenth anniversary of his death (Guibert 2001). The photos, slides and the autobiographical documentary film tracing his physical degeneration have all been used to support his celebrated maudlin fiction that conflated AIDS with the so-called death drive. Whilst the furtive sexuality and teenage angst of Chéreau and Guibert's *L'Homme blessé* was perceived as radical in the early 1980s, Chéreau has since maintained a cautious distance from direct engagement with either radical or reformist gay politics. In Yves Jeuland's documentary *Bleu, blanc, rose* (2002) and in the DVD interview accompanying *Son frère*, he expresses personal reservations about a committed cinema whilst accepting the broader cultural politics of AIDS inscribed within the complex relational entanglements of *Ceux qui m'aiment prendront le train*. His subsequent project was a Franco-British production *Intimacy* (2001), adapted from a novella and a short story by Hanif Kureishi. The film included graphic sex scenes which were celebrated not only for Chéreau's trademark intensity and melancholy but for their unforgiving depiction of imperfect bodies, purposefully filmed against the aesthetics of heterosexual pornography. The affected gloom of Chéreau's cinema is best expressed in his own citation of the popular saying that 'happy people have no history' ('les gens heureux n'ont pas d'histoire').[49]

The son of a painter, Chéreau accentuates his own artistic lineage with reverential nods to Francis Bacon and Lucian Freud; indeed the formal aesthetic of *Son frère* (particularly the controlled sequence in which the protagonist's body is shaved and prepared for medical intervention) provided the focus of critical attention,[50] acknowledging Chéreau as the current master of body representation, the generic body rather than any potential interest in specifically male bodies. Jean-Michel Frodon, writing in *Cahiers du cinéma*, describes the body as the main focus of Chéreau's cinema since *L'Homme blessé*, arguing in idealist mode that the director looks to cinema to represent what is unreachable in drama (Chéreau was for long a more renowned stage director than film director), an intimate relationship between spectator and performer that would transcend mere bodily presence to reach the intersection of love and death.[51] Trite comments about illness as metaphor and the injustices of dying young are indeed difficult to avoid since the film invites this brand of lofty pseudo-philosophy. Adapted from Philippe Besson's literary novel of the same name, *Son frère* is on balance a moving, stark dissection of the re-kindled love between two estranged brothers. The ill brother Thomas (Bruno Todeschini) is heterosexual; the able brother Luc (Eric Caravaca) is gay. After recovering from a haemorrhage, Thomas commits suicide by drowning. The parallel between the heterosexual and homosexual couplings is drawn through the contrastive editing of sequences showing Thomas and girlfriend with those of Luc and boyfriend. The early flashback of the brothers on a nudist beach in Brittany where bathers stare at Thomas's wasted body – another coded AIDS parallel – cuts back to the presentation of Luc's lover (played by Sylvain Jacques, who had played the HIV-positive character Bruno in *Ceux qui m'aiment prendront le train* who is in love with Louis, played by Todeschini).

By elaborating the brothers' intimacy as a couple, the film suggests a provocative analogy with same-sex relations and AIDS. Same-sex intimacy is modestly hinted at, but then underplayed as the peripheral fact of the matter. Frodon draws attention to the use of extreme close-ups that eliminate the claustrophobic environment in order to accentuate individual suffering, a technique in part explained by the film's production for television, only later blown up for cinema. Chéreau admits to having imitated scenes from Guibert's *La Pudeur ou l'impudeur*, particularly the clinical setting of the hospital and the shot of the ravaged body consumed by the sea. Whilst the AIDS references are transparent to some extent, the 'not-about-AIDS' discourse is exploited elsewhere in the marketing spin, a point made by Thomas Doustaly (*Têtu*'s editor-in-chief) in an angry piece on the manipulation of queer audiences by auteur cinema. The fact that the framing of *Son frère* showcases the wasting body of actor Todeschini is not purely an aesthetic concern. Doustaly takes issue with the production's attempts to disguise what he reads as signs of the actor's facial lipodystrophy and alarming weight loss as a form of method acting. Todeschini lost twelve kilos for the role as part of the performance of dying the film seeks to enact. In the DVD interviews, the actors, director, and even the cinematographer all anxiously address the issue of physical degeneration to sustain (what Doustaly claims as) the fiction of performance. His complaint is that *Son frère* updates the tradition of the open secret in artistic milieus, here transposed from homosexuality to seropositivity. Chéreau's pursuit of universal values means that

> AIDS is not AIDS; the gay man is in good health, whereas the ill man is heterosexual . . . So much energy is wasted in establishing inverted screens that only serve to highlight what they are meant to conceal.
> (le sida n'est pas le sida, le pédé est en bonne santé, le malade est hétéro . . . Toute l'énergie du film est gaspillée à construire des fronts renversés qui ne font que souligner ce qu'ils prétendent faire disparaître.)[52]

Doustaly's 'return of the repressed' thesis was supported by reviews of Téchiné's *Les Témoins* in 2007 in which certain critics included *Son frère* in their retrospective coverage of AIDS representation in French cinema.[53] Jean-Marc Lalanne's slip that Chéreau had in fact tackled AIDS directly in *Son frère* points to the inefficacy of the production's earlier attempts to closet its subject matter.[54]

Doustaly ended his tirade asking 'why not AIDS?' Ozon was asked that same question by popular TV presenter Thierry Ardisson with regard to *Le Temps qui reste* in 2005.[55] He situated the film as the second part of a planned trilogy on loss following *Sous le sable* (2000), but expressed personal reservations about tackling AIDS directly on screen. Whilst there are indeed stylistic and thematic overlaps between these two sombre films – Ozon's interest in capturing death through photography had in fact been exposed earlier through his short film *La Petite mort* (1995) in which a son secretly shoots his father's dying body – the vision of queer sexuality in *Le Temps qui reste* refocuses the debates on heterosexual coupling and kinship from Ozon's preceding film *5x2* (2004). *Le Temps qui reste* presents Romain (Melvil Poupaud), an arrogant Parisian photographer who is diagnosed with terminal cancer, causing him to break up with his lover and accept an infertile couple's offer to father a child before embracing death. Ryan Gilbey situates the film between robust French and glossy Hollywood representations of terminal illness, with the film nimbly avoiding the pitfalls of sentimental banality through a distinguished cast (including Jeanne Moreau and Valeria Bruni-Tedeschi in supporting roles), Monica Coleman's abrupt editing style and Ozon's own eye for subversive detail.[56] The basic premise – a gay man's last days – sees the film occupy the same ground of AIDS allusion as *Son frère*, though it is more concerned to reiterate preconceived notions of kinship, death and sexuality, making the entire enterprise shallow despite Ozon's occasional visual quirks. *Le Temps qui reste* showcases Ozon's intriguing mix of banal predictability and off-beat humour – after some heavy-handed shots of Romain walking at night in the woods, cutting to a predictable childhood flashback, Ozon slips in an exchange with Romain's grandmother (Moreau) who lovingly accepts him in her bed, slyly warning him beforehand that she sleeps naked. The film's outcome, however, reproduces a string of artistic clichés through sibling reconciliation (Poupaud is filmed staring at a wilting rose whilst reading his sister's letter), reproductive futurism (the film tries to give Romain a degree of moral virtue by him accepting to father a child) and personal closure (he slowly embraces death as the sun goes down over a beach in Brittany), an idealist agenda that situates the film's post-political pretensions (Asibong 2008).

Ozon also gives a normative spin to gay male sexuality in *Le Temps qui reste*. Romain, the aggressively successful professional who lives in a stylish loft apartment, is complemented by a foreign lover (Christian Sengewald) who is coded as 'feminine' – ten years younger, prettier, paler, blonder, more docile and less professionally secure than the protagonist. Whilst their drug-fuelled passion is realistically raw, complete with erection shots, Jeanne Lapoirie's cinematography tames the action with glossy images of the lovers that resemble homoerotic advertising stills. *5x2* had previously established a straight/queer opposition in which the central heterosexual couple's disintegrating marriage was balanced by a more unconventional same-sex pairing of a pretty boy and his more mature lover who proclaim the merits of a sexually liberated relationship. Romain likewise deserts his boy for some action in a sex club – the same location used for Gaspard Noé's opening sequence in *Irréversible* in which gay S/M is seen as tantamount to hateful violence – but is shown to reject casual encounters as symptomatic of psychological instability or internalised homophobia. After cruising a man at the bar, Romain slowly descends to the basement, the techno soundtrack muted by the use of religious music to symbolise his descent into hell, where he watches the man prepare to be fisted in a sling; a sequence, we learn from the revealing DVD documentary, that employed in-house extras (though not the actor pretending to be fisted). The combination of a close-up of Poupaud's troubled face followed by Romain's mental image of past happiness with his lover reduces gay male sexuality to a choice between relations that are deemed positive and carefree (the mental image of the couple is a bright exterior shot in stark contrast to the dark claustrophobic club) as opposed to others that bind casual sex to anxiety and potential psychic violence. The spatial confinement of the club is clearly meant to be read as a metaphor for the character's own entrapment, the complex significations of S/M rendered literal through the character's subsequent submission to death. The ultimate problem with this return of the 'death drive' in recent queer narrative fiction (in its current 'not-about-AIDS' form) is that it blithely revives (unconsciously or not) the formula equating gay sexuality to death and disease that fuelled so much homophobic discourse around AIDS from the mid-1980s onwards.

WITNESSING AIDS

Téchiné's *Les Témoins* (2007) looks back to the AIDS crisis and social panic of the mid-1980s but instead of contributing to an opportunistic negativity that seeks to rebrand the 'death drive' as the artistic imperative of queer cinema, the film suggests the human potential for renewed passion and political commitment through a dynamic tableau of five interlocking lives affected by AIDS. Novelist Sarah (Emmanuelle Béart) expresses the need to write the story of her husband Mehdi's (Sami Bouajila) passion for the deceased Manu (Johan Libéreau) to testify to the young man's ephemeral presence in their lives. AIDS testimony is also the central preoccupation of Jacques Nolot's autobiographical *Avant que j'oublie* (2007), which looks at seropositivity from the vantage point of an older gay man, and likewise recounts recent history to younger generations before the disappearance of all remaining witnesses. Nolot is Téchiné's friend, collaborator and co-screenwriter of *J'embrasse pas* (1992); he plays a small role as the manager of a run-down hotel frequented by sex workers in *Les Témoins*, the working title of which had been *Avant que j'oublie*. *Les Témoins* begins with the birth of Sarah and Mehdi's child and ends one year later with his birthday. Manu arrives unexpectedly at his sister's (Julie Depardieu) hotel in Paris where she is trying to eke out a living as a classical singer. He befriends Adrien (Michel Blanc) on a cruising ground, and is introduced by Adrien's friend Sarah to Mehdi, with whom he falls in love. Their secret passion lasts till the end of summer when Adrien discovers Kaposi's sarcoma on Manu's body. Responding to Manu's subsequent withdrawal, illness and death, Adrien sets up a charity and becomes a leading medical figure in the fight against AIDS, whilst Sarah struggles to write up her account of Manu.

Bill Marshall has provided a critical survey of Téchiné's sixteen films preceding *Les Témoins*, charting the emergence of same-sex passion in a minor mode from *Hôtel des Amériques* (1981) onwards. This was the first film of five to date with Deneuve: drawing on novelistic narrative techniques from nineteenth-century fiction (particularly the *bildungsroman* archetype of the provincial innocent in Paris) and contributing to Téchiné's dominant reputation as a '*romanesque*' filmmaker. In an interview with Alain Philippon, he retrospectively situates *Hôtel des Amériques* as a break with his genre films of the 1970s:

> From *Hôtel des Amériques* onwards my films are no longer genre films. I do not take inspiration from cinema. Throughout my subsequent production (which I do not see as divided into separate films but rather as sucessive, interlocking chapters), I have asked whether love exists, the leading strand running through all these films.
> (A partir d'*Hôtel des Amériques* ce ne sont plus des films de genre. Je ne puise plus mon inspiration dans le cinéma . . . Au travers des films que j'ai faits depuis *Hôtel des Amériques* (que je ne perçois pas comme des films séparés, mais comme des chapitres qui se suivent et s'enchaînent) je me pose . . . la question: 'Est-ce que l'amour existe?'. C'est le fil conducteur de tous ces films.) (Philippon 1988: 121)

Marshall argues for Téchiné's use of plural narrative strands as 'modern' with its vision of a

> post-traditional world, full of transformation, movement and displacement, in which characters struggle to find emotional meaning . . . Like a realist novel, Téchiné maps the social, economic and even political factors – material urgencies, spatial coordinates, structures of feeling – which determine the protagonists' situation. . . . However – and this is why his films are to be seen as so modern – Téchiné's protagonists are never actually determined by these determinants. (Marshall 2007: 35–6)

This use of multiple narrative strands within a social panorama marks Téchiné's cinema out from the political commitment characteristic of film production in the post-1968 conjuncture. In the interview with Philippon, he recalls his split with *Cahiers du cinéma* when the publication and surrounding milieu took a hard-left turn around 1968 (Philippon 1988: 119). Marshall situates the filmmaker's cinematic bent as broadly 'civilisational' rather than fully political, the constant preoccupation with sexuality and morality more recently seen by Téchiné himself as the common thread running through all his films.[57] This mix of social dynamics and intimate concerns is particularly well suited to the historical and moral context of AIDS in mid-1980s France that is captured in *Les Témoins*, but it had been evident in earlier films such as *J'embrasse pas*, for which, as Marshall explains, Nolot had originally scripted a cruder, darker and queerer version that included the young protagonist's sexual self-discovery with the *beur* character Saïd, and involvement in an underground and violent queer milieu (Marshall 2007: 85, 146). Marshall's analysis shows how the filmed version centres on Pierre's disavowal of homosexuality as structuring his identity and the extent to which money, commerce and class as much as gender and sexual dissent confine the character's emotional life.[58] 'Pierre's itinerary in the film is about what possibilities there are for affection in modernity, in a world of lost tradition and discredited notions of "home", commodified sex, and competitive individualism.' The images of entrapment suggest that 'the young men are the bearers of grids of meaning and boundaries, with little active purchase upon them' (Marshall: 2007: 46, 47).

Older male characters with greater material and cultural capital tend to negotiate their way through the hazardous terrain of Téchiné's narratives with more assurance, though the 'married' characters Romain (Philippe Noiret) in *J'embrasse pas* and Klotz (Jean-Claude Brialy) in *Les Innocents* (1987) both testify to a sense of isolation and dissatisfaction unalleviated by the privileges of wealth or status. In *Les Témoins*, the affluent doctor Adrien criticises divisions of age within the gay community of the era which is proud, in his view, of its ethnic 'melting pot' and social inclusion but less honest about its incessant promotion of youth and beauty. The critical remarks voiced by Blanc point to persistent anxieties over issues of power (disparities of gender, race, class and age) structuring same-sex intimacies (Sinfield 2004). In the film's final section, entitled 'the return of summer', Sarah accepts that Adrien's distance following Manu's death and his reluctance to read her finished manuscript are signs that his new relationship with a younger man is rejuvenating him. In fact Adrien is shown to be more conscious of the social cleavage between heterosexuals and homosexuals brought on by the stigmatising impact of AIDS, one of the film's persistent political points. Adrien is established early on as the voice of post-gay liberation, but Téchiné's discreet depiction of the character's emerging love for the young Manu undercuts any initial pomposity. It is Julien Hirsch's cinematography that expresses more of Adrien's inner life than the character's own declarations, particularly the shots of the two characters visiting Paris on a *bateau mouche* in which they emerge into the bright sunlight: Libéreau's luminous face, shot in close-up, dominates the frame's foreground, supported in the background by Blanc's subtle inflection of awakening desire tinged with amiable curiosity. Likewise, Hirsch's lush images of Sarah's Mediterranean retreat jump from Adrien's declaration to Mehdi that he is 'mad about the boy' to an exquisite tracking shot of Manu bounding across the *calanque*, expressing the character's freedom and vitality, before returning to a static shot of an admiring Adrien. This dynamic pace is in fact established from the film's opening shot of Béart frenetically typing up the manuscript that will provide the intermittent voice-over frame for the narrative, a forward movement further enhanced by Martine Giordano's swift editing style and Philippe Sarde's tense musical refrain.

Racial hierarchy is expressed antagonistically through Mehdi's resentment that Adrien couches his feelings of sexual jealousy in racial innuendo, even if Mehdi's ethnic identity is not singled out for comment elsewhere, surprisingly given he is a *beur* policeman in the mid-1980s. Vincendeau remarks that the film's representation of ethnic integration speaks more of the era of its production than its historical setting.[59] Although both Bouajila and Libéreau are of Maghrebi origin, there is no given indication that the ethnic identities of their characters are meant to be read as formative of their desire for one another, and Manu's mixed-race origins are only later noted in passing after his death when his mother rails against her deceased husband's ostracism as a renegade following the Algerian war. Mehdi falls in love with Manu when he saves him from drowning, a natural awakening shown through a series of sensual images of the men's bodies underwater broken by Mehdi's struggle to pull Manu ashore. Their ensuing passion is framed by hidden trips to a flying club – the repeated images of flying (the plane Mehdi pilots, the helicopter Sarah observes take off) and sailing (the final sequence repeats the earlier motorboat trip but with Adrien's lover replacing Manu) work as both traditional 'literary' metaphors for the characters' journeys and spatial reminders of the film's overall preoccupation with social change and transition.

Jill Forbes ended her section on Téchiné in *The Cinema in France After the New Wave* by detecting a movement through his oeuvre 'from an initial concern to explore the history of the nation to a renewed emphasis on personal history with . . . a consciousness of how the two are inevitably intertwined' (Forbes 1992: 258). Forbes's remark that Téchiné, under the influence of Brecht, 'is concerned with the way a culture represents its own history and how individuals within a culture represent theirs' (1992: 258) is relevant not only to the precise conjuncture of the mid-1980s socio-political trauma of AIDS viewed from a later perspective, but also to the alternative arrangements for queer love and sexuality fleshed out in *Les Témoins*. Forbes ended her coverage of Téchiné with *Les Innocents*, in which, she argued, the immigrant character Saïd (Abdellatif Kechiche) is the central focus for all the other characters' desires (a focus unquestioningly adopted since by the younger wave of gay male filmmakers): 'With his sexual ambiguity, his dual nationality and his ill-defined social status, Saïd undermines the fixed identities that the cinema conventionally projects and explodes our belief in the ideal romantic couple' (Forbes 1992: 257).

One of the leading threads of this chapter has been to show how, despite the differing aesthetic concerns and ideological outlooks, the films covered seek to trouble the notion of a fixed gay identity and community or a received notion of family and kinship, in order to establish alternative templates for visions of same-sex intimacy and queer sexualities. *Les Témoins* brings together these non-normative strands in the context of AIDS and the effects of loss on interpersonal sexual and emotional relations. In short, Téchiné's more explicit gestures towards the socio-political environment of his individual narratives show for the first time in his work how a *sub*culture has been representing itself within and against the dominant culture's norms. Despite the propensity for artistic clichés to portray the novelist Sarah (anxiously smoking; working at home under a mound of typescripts; ignoring her baby), her liberated sexuality and lack of outrage at Mehdi's bisexuality show Téchiné together with co-writers Laurent Guyot and Viviane Zingg avoiding the traps of the traditional hetero-normative narrative – the lack of exclusivity in their relationship is conceived as a form of moral contract by Téchiné, who chose Béart to convey Sarah's erotic allure so that Mehdi's passion for Manu would not be seen conventionally to arise from marital boredom.[60] Mehdi's bisexuality is shown to be a plausible option because the audience, like the character, is surprised by it, due to a tendency to decode characters as either heterosexual or homosexual unless indicated otherwise (though he does add to the presumption of heterosexuality by earlier denying the existence of gays in the police force). His bisexuality is later criticised from a gay viewpoint by Adrien as a convenient means of benefitting from a closeted sexuality by seeing men whilst retaining heterosexual social privilege.

The film also points to contradictions in Mehdi's personal and public personae by documenting the lower-class milieu of sex work that disturbs the heterosexual hegemony that he ascribes to professionally in his job at the vice squad. Marshall has drawn on the inclusion of alternative social spaces in Téchiné's cinema, seen as 'utopia' following Foucault and Hocquenghem's advocacy of sexual non-differentiation against the mainstream assimilation of gay identities by the market; or 'atopia' following Barthes, meant to signal movements opposing the norm (Marshall 2007: 82–3). Nolot's bit-part as the convivial hotel manager (reminiscent of the mother and son couple in J'embrasse pas) is used to establish a positive image of the sexual margins of northern Paris (far from the ambient 'class tourism' noticeable elsewhere in French queer cinema), as he is shown to offer hospitality to Manu, who strikes up a friendship with Sandra, a resident sex worker at the pick-up bar Le Clignancourt, under the constant surveillance of Mehdi and his colleagues. The use of saturated colours (clashing shades of red figure in the early sequences outside the bar in the contrast between Julie's conservative clothing and Sandra's fluorescent wig) points to the erotic vibrancy of a community later threatened by the spread of AIDS and condemned by the vice squad which shuts down the hotel and arrests its occupants. Téchiné's bold visual contrast between early euphoria and later disintegration is particularly insistent in the case of Sandra, who energetically lip-synchs Les Rita Mitsouko's emblematic 1980s hit 'Marcia Baila' (expressing rage at a woman's death from cancer) in a foreboding moment before the onset of AIDS. This is an update of the sequence in which the Brazilian transgender sex workers dance with Pierre in J'embrasse pas, a moment Marshall describes as a 'utopian space before the catastrophe' (Marshall 2007: 63). Sandra's performance for the appreciative Manu – the sequence finishes with a prolonged reaction shot – together with the use of saturated colour again point to Demy's aesthetic stamp on contemporary queer film.[61] However, whereas he tended to incorporate musical numbers as part of the narrative progression, they are used in J'embrasse pas and Les Témoins to punctuate it at crucial moments, a pause before the drama continues – we learn from the film's closing dialogue that Sandra, incarcerated for prostitution, is HIV-positive and unable to obtain suitable medical treatment in prison.

Adrien's comment midway through the film (repeated to Sarah at the end) that a continuing friendship despite their differing sexual identities may be impossible marks out the era of intense homophobia that lead to the launch in 1984 of AIDES, a charity founded in Marseille by Foucault's partner Daniel Defert. Téchiné retains the charity's name and models Adrien on himself, Defert, dermatologist Michel Canesi, and the influential AIDS treatment consultant Professor Jacques Leibowitch.[62] Blanc is filmed lecturing to the medical community and explaining without condescension to Sandra the necessity of targeted HIV-prevention among sex workers. The use of television archive material of the widespread panic around the causes and spread of HIV/AIDS in the mid-1980s accentuates the move from an earlier carefree bohemian society of sexual experimentation to the subsequent outbreak of 'the war' (the title of the second section), the evocation of which borrows elements from documentary naturalism and science-fiction fable – Téchiné reminds us of the frightening atmosphere of social shame and stigma attached to AIDS which accounted for Foucault's much debated silence.[63] Les Témoins is nuanced enough to avoid both a pre-AIDS nostalgia and a reverential portrait of early AIDS activism. Mehdi pinpoints the blind spots in Adrien's political commitment, resenting his refusal to grant him access to Manu and accusing him of ironically coming to life through the epidemic, activism as sublimation. The comments on the potential ideological schism between heterosexuals and homosexuals were later historically transformed by the more radical identity politics of Act Up, transposed to a French context of state inaction by the end of the decade, a form of direct action that highlighted the moralistic opposition between straight, upright sexual practice and a marginal queer sexual politics that forged alliances across sexualities with socially stigmatised groups affected by AIDS, such as injecting drug users.

Philippe Mangeot, former president of Act Up Paris (1997–9), highlights the political limitations of Téchiné's take on the early implementation of community-based mobilisation. Mangeot remarks that Téchiné avoids the inevitable moral and political pitfalls of AIDS cinema from Les Nuits fauves onwards – that is to say, an over-determined treatment of AIDS, the feeling that HIV has at all costs to comply with the familiar tropes of death and desire, rather than, as Mangeot succinctly puts it, 'the disaster of an epidemic from which there is no lesson to be drawn' ('le désastre d'une maladie dont il n'y rien à tirer').[64] The medical and political dimensions of HIV/AIDS are what are missing from the earlier representations of individual suffering and martyrdom. Les Témoins does not, however, completely avoid redemption through the signification of Manu's death as a 'creative' gift to the surrounding witnesses. To that extent, Mangeot argues, Téchiné does not quite go as far as Jeanne et le garçon formidable in locating AIDS as of primary political significance. The gestures towards alternative forms of subcultural relations (the overlap between queerness and sex work in the pre-AIDS conjuncture) are indeed a sideshow to the main narrative threads that remain for the most part within the sphere of intimacy. The collective dimension was fundamental to the emergence of AIDS activism through its production of new relations between the private and the public spheres. Mangeot's sharp critique shows the relative constraints of a radical political praxis within the confines of auteur cinema with its propensity for artistic individualism. The foundation of AIDES shown through Adrien's activism went beyond the singular agitation sketched in the film. Mangeot points to its Foucauldian framework:

> the invention of new forms of relations, the production of techniques of the self that lead to a community-based response to the epidemic . . . The emergence of AIDS historically created new connections between the intimate and the political.
> (l'invention de nouvelles formes de relations, la production de techniques de soi qui permirent d'opposer à la maladie une réponse communautaire . . . Historiquement, l'apparition du sida a opéré des branchements inédits entre l'intime et le politique.)

These are connections that *Les Témoins* alludes to without exploring them further.

Mangeot's verdict is that Téchiné is unduly reticent towards the oppositional politics that support his more familiar intimate narrative structure. Téchiné is indeed cautious about a possible '*communautariste*' division (derived from Anglo-American identity politics) of his work into pre-established categories, less from a reluctance to acknowledge the thematic presence of queer interpersonal relations, and more from a fear of losing the contradictions and complexities at work. His comments for *Sight and Sound* at the time of the British release of *Les Témoins* capture the filmmaker's middle-ground position on sexual politics, keen to explore questions of sexuality in tandem with their socio-political signification, but reluctant to be drawn into the gay artistic pigeon-hole: 'I can never accept that a character be reduced to his or her sexual orientation'; 'I don't think [*The Witnesses*] plays the card of sociological survey'; 'I think it's important to consider the issues on the film beyond the framework of heterosexual vs homosexual'.[65] Vincendeau sees *Le Témoins* as marking a 'watershed in Téchiné's career' by centring the entire project on male homosexuality, a point qualified by Téchiné's own wider-reaching preference for 'radically differing forms of sexuality' for each of the three male characters across the various markers of erotic preference, serological status, age, wealth and ethnicity.[66]

Téchiné's recent reticence towards a 'gay' or 'queer' appropriation of *Les Témoins* is part of both a cultural and intellectual resistance towards critical paradigms derived from the reception of Anglo-American identity politics, and a more local reluctance on the part of filmmakers and critics to accept politicised appropriations of auteur cinema by minority subcultures. Marshall makes this point with regard to Téchiné's previous output, using critical tools from Deleuze and Guattari to position the filmmaker as operating in a minor mode (Marshall 2007: 81–6), emphasising experimental and evolving patterns of 'non-heteronormative' sexualities, as opposed to a major mode predominant in mainstream gay cinema seeking to present a stable representation of prêt-à-porter gay/lesbian identities suitable for mainstream consumption. Such a framework, Marshall suggests, might correlate to the gay/queer opposition used in Anglo-American criticism to separate forms of bland positive imagery from trashier representations of sexual transgression (Marshall 2007: 81–2). Marshall's conclusion that 'Téchiné's films are neither militantly gay nor even coalesce around relatively fixed positions of gay identity and community' (Marshall 2007: 82) is an accurate summary of the filmmaker's preference for a queerness in minor mode, in which same-sex relations are woven into the larger narrative fabric. However, Les Témoins marks a turning point, at the crossroads between minor and major modes of sexual representation, with greater, if over-cautious, attention to a specifically gay history and with more elaborate patterns of male intimacy no longer positioned on the margins but placed at the centre of a more homogeneous social and narrative structure. In that respect Les Témoins is an accurate indicator of the existing 'queer' cinema in the contemporary French context, with its focus on male same-sex relations outside traditional models of coupling and kinship and the effects of AIDS and loss on queer sexualities – an ultimately modest brand of queer cinema within the traditional format and prescriptions of independent auteur production. The political frustrations voiced by Mangeot point not only to the relative limits of individual films or filmmakers, but also to the political temerity of an increasingly fragile independent sector. (Director Pascale Ferran's acceptance speech at the 2007 Césars ceremony attacked the increasing economic polarity in French filmmaking between dominant studio blockbusters and independent low-budget production.)[67] It for this reason that the more radical image-making drawing on post-modern aesthetics and queer politics is now produced on digital video and circulated at local gatherings such as alternative film festivals or via the internet. The final chapter will begin to chart the local proliferation of a digital production influenced by the emerging translations of Anglo-American queer critique, marking the historical transition from a modest French queer cinema to an alternative 'queer underground'.

NOTES

1. François Truffaut, 'Une certaine tendance du cinéma français', Cahiers du cinéma, no. 31, January 1954, reprinted in Antoine de Baecque (ed.), Vive le cinéma français!, Paris: Petite bibliothèque des Cahiers du cinéma, 2001, pp. 17–36.
2. Christophe Honoré, 'La triste moralité du cinéma français', Cahiers du cinéma, no. 521, February 1998, p. 5.
3. For a thorough analysis of the fusion of cinema and politics around the sans-papiers in 1997, see Phil Powrie (1999), 'Heritage, history and "New Realism": French

cinema in the 1990s', in Phil Powrie (ed.), *French Cinema in the 1990s: Continuity and Difference*, Oxford: Oxford University Press, pp. 1–21.

4. Charlotte Garson, '*Crustacés et Coquillages*', *Cahiers du cinéma*, no. 600, April 2005, p. 51.

5. Whilst supporting the more radical vision of queer relations outside the reproductive family and state recognition, Swamy is critical of the film's erasure of the ethnic identity of its half-Arab protagonist whose alternative kinship relations are all with white French people, thus ignoring 'the multi-ethnic origins of the protagonist, and the multicultural reality of contemporary France' (Swamy 2006: 62).

6. Published by *Le Monde*, 16 March 2004.

7. Didier Eribon, ' "Des gens peu communs" ', *Têtu*, December 2006, p. 74.

8. Ginette Vincendeau, 'Cockles and muscles', *Sight and Sound*, April 2006, p. 47.

9. Christophe Honoré, quoted in Jean-Michel Frodon, 'Profil Christophe Honoré, cinéaste au feu de l'écriture,' *Le Monde*, 10 July 2002.

10. Co-written by Gilles Taurand, broadcast on 30 March 2001, France 2, contained in the INA archives, Paris.

11. Didier Péron, 'Sur le fil, "Cécile Cassard" ', *Libération*, 10 July 2002.

12. Indeed the formal attributes of the film were used by Serge Kaganski to dismiss it as promising but too literary and theoretical to be moving, which was surely Honoré's point. See Serge Kaganski, 'trop-plein', *Les Inrockuptibles*, 10 July 2002.

13. Louis Guichard in *Télérama*, 13 July 2002; Didier Péron, 'Sur le fil, "Cécile Cassard" ', *Libération*, 10 July 2002.

14. Ginette Vincendeau, 'Ma mère', *Sight and Sound*, vol. 15 (3), March 2005, p. 62.

15. Ibid.

16. On the critical convergence of Bataille and Pasolini, see Jean Duflot (1970), *Entretiens avec Pier Paolo Pasolini*, Paris: Pierre Belfond.

17. On Joana Preiss, see Françoise-Marie Santucci, 'Joana Preiss, la muse-girl', *Libération*, 30 June 2006.

18. The critics both praised and trashed the film's fashionable allure – *Libération* commented on a glamour rarely seen in French film (Philippe Azoury, 'C'est "Ma mere", son Bataille,' *Libération*, 12 May 2004) whereas *Les Echos* attacked its bourgeois-bohemian credentials, perversion in a chic, glossy wrapper (A. C., 'L'amour à mort', *Les Echos*, 19 May 2004).

19. Philippe Azoury gives an insight into the shoot in late 2003 in the Canary Islands, in Philippe Azoury, 'Honoré au champ de Bataille,' *Libération*, 21 January 2004.

20. Honoré sees the apparent libertarian message in Bataille as important to counter neo-liberal moral and economic hegemony (Michaël Melinard, ' " On est dans une période de puritanisme absolu" ', *L'Humanité*, 22 May 2004).

21. Honoré comments on the influence of Dennis Cooper in the interview accompanying the DVD version.

22. Filmmaker Catherine Breillat particularly praised Honoré's feminising of male bodies in her radio review of the film (*Le Cinéma l'après-midi*, France Culture, 22 May 2004), whereas *Le Monde* criticised the clichéd use of 'gay' imagery derived from advertising, and made a homophobic point of taking Honoré to task for fawning over Louis Garrel rather than overcoming his desire for his leading man (*Le Monde, Aden*, 19 May 2004).

23. Apart from the Pasolini revival, Lestrade also mentions the success in queer cinema of *O Fantasma* (Rodrigues 2000) with its memorable set piece of latex perversion on a trash heap (Lestrade 2004: 155–6). Lestrade earlier links barebacking to the development of extreme sexuality within gay subcultures through the fetish for sperm 'donation' (p. 87). He is also highly critical of the mainstream media in France for latching onto celebrity novelists like Guillaume Dustan who cynically used AIDS revisionism as a commercial pitch (p. 166).

24. This is the argument of Lestrade's subsequent account of contemporary changes in gay male sexuality in Didier Lestrade (2007), *Cheikh: Journal de campagne*, Paris: Flammarion.

25. On the background to the film's production, see Louis Maury, 'Léo le maudit,' *Têtu*, November 2004, p. 46.

26. A comprehensive state of affairs on 'sero-sorting' and the argument that it is simply the more acceptable face of 'barebacking' is to be found in Emmanuelle Cosse, Philippe Mangeot and Victoire Patouillard, 'La Préférence sérologique?', *Vacarme*, no. 40, summer 2007, pp. 42–7. For a counter-argument taking account of relational and emotional factors in 'sero-preference' and 'sero-adaptation', see the radical AIDS prevention collective *The Warning*, particularly 'Sero-sorting, don't act?', www.thewarning.info/article.php?id_article=0227 (accessed 26 September 2007). For a sociological inquiry into 'serostatus' and risk, see Mark Davis, 'HIV prevention rationalities and serostatus in the risk narratives of gay men', *Sexualities*, 5 (3), 2002, pp. 281–99.

27. The harm reduction campaign tested by AIDES in 2002 was influenced by similar campaigns previously developed in Britain by *Gay Men Fighting Aids*. See Watney 2000 for an account by one of the group's founders.

28. Lawrence R. Schehr offers a literary critique of Rémès in Lawrence R. Schehr, 'Reading serial sex: The case of Erik Rémès,' *L'Esprit créateur*, vol. XLIV, no. 3, fall 2004, pp. 94–104. For a frontal attack on Dustan, see the Act Up Paris dossier 'En finir avec Dustan', *Action* no. 77, available on www.actupparis.org (accessed 7 January 2007).

29. Guillaume Dustan, 'La Capote n'a jamais existé', *Libération*, 21–2 October 2000, p. 8.

30. Lesbian & Gay Pride Films (1996), *L'amour est à réinventer*, Paris: Editions Mille et Une Nuits/ARTE Editions, p. 151.

31. Ibid., p. 152.

32. Stéphane Bouquet, 'La mélodie du bonheur', *Cahiers du cinéma*, no. 545 April 2000, pp. 65–6. Thomas Doustaly writing in gay magazine *Têtu*, however, criticised the film as dull and over-burdened by its engagement with minority politics, figuring Félix as gay, HIV-positive, Arab and unemployed. See Thomas Doustaly, 'Triste Félix', *Têtu*, April 2000, p. 20.

33. Jean-Pierre Jeancolas, '*Drôle de Félix*: Un objet incontestablement gentil', *Positif*, May 2000, no. 471, 32–3.

34. José Arroyo, 'Drôle de Félix', *Sight and Sound*, January 2001, pp. 47–8.

35. Ibid. One might take issue with Arroyo's assessment that the film reminds us that Félix is dying, since it more obviously shows him alive and in ostensibly good health. Thank you to Florian Grandena for this point.

36. Olivier Nickaus, 'Le sida en chanté', *Ex Aequo*, no. 17, April 1998, p. 55.

37. Camille Taboulay, 'Attendez que ma joie revienne', *Cahiers du cinéma*, no. 523, April 1998, pp. 72–3.

38. Gérard Lefort, ' "Jeanne et le garçon" c'est formidable,' *Libération*, 22 April 1998, p. 28.

39. Claire Vassé, '*Jeanne et le garçon formidable*: L'amour à mort', *Positif*, no. 447 May 1998, pp. 35–6.

40. For a social history of the New Wave, see Mary 2006.

41. Philippe Colomb examines the queer audience reception of Demy in France in Philippe Colomb, 'L'étrange Demy-monde', in Bourcier (ed.) (1998), pp. 39–47.

42. See interview with Honoré, 'Christophe Honoré: "Je n'accorde aucune importance au scénario", propos recueillis par Isabelle Regnier', *Le Monde*, 23 May 2007, p. 27.

43. Christophe Honoré, quoted in Philippe Lançon, 'Le coup de la grace', *Libération*, 21 May 2007, p. 33.

44. Honoré presents his pick of influential pop music in an interview for *Télérama*: see Laurent Rigoulet, 'Chant contre champ', *Télérama*, no. 2993, 23 May 2007, pp. 20–4.
45. Ginette Vincendeau, 'Dans Paris', *Sight and Sound*, vol. 17, issue 5, May 2007, p. 59.
46. Hervé Aubron, 'Connaît-on la chanson?', *Cahiers du cinéma*, no. 624, June 2007, p. 29.
47. Ginette Vincendeau, 'Dans Paris', *Sight and Sound*, vol. 17, issue 5, May 2007, p. 60.
48. See, for example, Jacques Morice, 'Chants magnétiques', *Télérama*, no. 2993, 23 May 2007, p. 55.
49. Chéreau quoted in interview, Yann Gonzalez, 'Chéreau, L'Homme à côté', *Têtu*, May 2004, pp. 74–5.
50. Sue Harris provides an appreciative critique of the film in *Sight and Sound*, March 2004, 14 (3), p. 63.
51. Jean-Michel Frodon, 'A fleur de corps', *Cahiers du cinéma*, September 2003, pp. 24–6.
52. Thomas Doustaly, 'Le Marketing honteux des cinéastes gay', *Têtu*, May 2004, p. 72.
53. Jean-Loup Bourget surveys the treatment of AIDS on screen by comparing Téchiné's novelistic style to Chéreau's '*intimiste*' style: see Jean-Loup Bourget, 'Les Témoins: In illo tempore', *Positif*, no. 553, March 2007, pp. 42–3.
54. Jean-Marc Lalanne, 'Les Témoins d'André Téchiné', *Les Inrockuptibles*, no. 588, 6–12 March 2007, pp. 48–9.
55. Thierry Ardisson, *Tout le monde en parle*, France 2, 19 November 2005.
56. Ryan Gilbey, 'Time to leave', *Sight and Sound*, 16 (5), May 2006, pp. 74–5.
57. Gérard Lefort and Didier Péron, ' "Faire le film avant l'oubli" ', *Libération*, 7 March 2007, Cinema section, p. 2.
58. Alain Brassart's chapter on Téchiné traces the filmmaker's preoccupation with diverse forms of masculinity (Brassart 2007).
59. Ginette Vincendeau, 'A time to love and a time to die', *Sight and Sound*, vol. 17 (11), November 2007, pp. 46–7.
60. Dominique Borde, 'André Téchiné, un devoir de mémoire', *Le Figaro*, 7 March 2007, p. 30.
61. In the TV documentary, *Territoire Téchiné* (Jean-Jacques Bernard, 2005), Téchiné mentions the influence of Demy and the more common New Wave technique, whereby actors would take a break from their characters, even in the stylisation and choreography of Lola's dance sequence. The musical number in *J'embrasse pas* (like Sandra's dance in *Les Témoins*) signals 'a moment of unexpected release' ('un moment d'abandon, de dérapage').
62. See the interview with Téchiné in *Têtu*, March 2007, pp. 22–3.
63. Téchiné mentions Foucault in an interview for *L'Humanité* , 7 March 2007, p. 21.
64. Philippe Mangeot, 'Sida: 2007–1984,' *Cahiers du cinéma*, no. 621, March 2007, p. 27. Same reference for the subsequent quotes from Mangeot.
65. Téchiné quoted in Ginette Vincendeau, 'A time to love and a time to die', *Sight and Sound*, 17 (11), November 2007, pp. 46–7.
66. See the interview with Téchiné in *Têtu*, March 2007, pp. 22–3.
67. 'Discours prononcé par Pascale Ferran à la cérémonie des Césars 2007', *Positif*, no. 556, June 2007, p. 17.

5. THE EMERGENCE OF QUEER DIY VIDEO

In his comprehensive overview of both international gay/queer cinema and homosexuality represented through mainstream cinema, Didier Roth-Bettoni mentions not only the filmmakers (Chéreau, Ducastel/Martineau, Lifshitz, Nolot, Ozon, Téchiné) whose output has been covered throughout the preceding chapters, but also lesser known, less mainstream visual artists such as Vincent Dieutre, Alain Guiraudie and the joint output of Pierre Trividic/Patrick Mario Bernard (Roth-Bettoni 2007: 614–18). Roth-Bettoni argues that such peripheral figures offer more radical visions of gay sexuality than is possible within the auteur framework despite their varying forms and preoccupations.

> Beyond the straightforward issue of representing homosexuality through the specificity of gay sexuality, what distinguishes these works from more mainstream production is their radicalism and their unique strangeness, be it thematic and/or aesthetic.
> (Au-delà de la simple question de la représentation de l'homosexualité dans ce qu'elle a de plus spécifique (la sexualité homosexuelle), ce qui distingue ces oeuvres d'autres plus grand public, c'est leur radicalité, leur étrangeté unique: que celle-ci soit thématique et/ou formelle.) (Roth-Bettoni: 615)

Guiraudie's highly distinctive, if timidly sexual, films look to establish alternative social milieus – rural and working-class – for same-sex intimacies across generational differences, particularly in *Ce vieux rêve qui bouge* (2000) and *Pas de repos pour les braves* (2002). Dieutre's personal and lyrical film essays (*Rome désolé*, 1995; *Leçons de ténèbres*, 1999; and *Mon voyage d'hiver*, 2002), also discussed as part of the cinema of sensation (Beugnet 2007: 1–9, 122–4), are sexual travelogues, which, though couched in lofty references to Schubert and Caravaggio, also include images of the filmmaker out cruising for boys, figured as an integral part of his piece of artistic self-fashioning. *Rome désolé* contrasts grim images of the city (focusing on graffiti, pavements and passers-by) with a detached literary voice-over recounting personal episodes of cruising and drugs, making for a downbeat account of queer sexuality. Trividic and Bernard prefer to incorporate elements of visual fantasy into the humdrum life of a couple, whilst actually shooting their own sex lives in graphic detail. Their opaque art film *Dancing* (2002) works against the grain of habitual gay male representation by showing a 'bear' couple in an anti-realist fantasy of intimacy based on sameness, providing a concrete template for Leo Bersani's abstract conception of all-male relations (Bersani 1995). Their earlier video *Ceci est une pipe (journal extime)* (2000), playing on the double-entendre of *pipe* meaning both a pipe and a blow-job, was a queer nod to René Magritte's *La Trahison des images* (1929), which shows an image of a pipe, accompanied by the strap line 'Ceci n'est pas une pipe' ('This is not a pipe'). The point was to deny the reality of representation – an image of a pipe is not an actual pipe, in short. Trividic and Bernard adapt Magritte's point to pornography, consciously looking to weave their documentary interest in the history of gay pornographic representation into social fabric of their everyday lives.

The list of gay/queer avant-garde film production would not be complete without reference to Rémi Lange, who has been developing low-budget 'auto-visions': his two super-8 films *Omelette* (1994) and *Les Yeux brouillés* (2000), both blown up for the big screen and later released on DVD, work as blow-by-blow accounts of his coming out in real-time to a potentially hostile family, followed in the second film by the separation from his partner Antoine (Parlebas). Stéphane Bouquet has favourably compared Lange's own personal charm and disregard for film style (he has a haphazard aesthetic that includes quick-fix montage, approximate framing and poor sound quality) to the more blatant video narcissism of celebrated literary figure Hervé Guibert (*La Pudeur ou l'impudeur*, 1992) or of conceptual artist Sophie Calle (*No Sex Last Night*, 1996).[1] Another critic hostile to Lange's second film for its assumed technical incompetence accepts his unpretentious self-display and his penchant for amateurism,[2] illustrating the extent to which Lange has been developing a DIY cinema that queers the aesthetic codes of dominant narrative realism, and likewise has established a financial basis for the production and circulation of local material.[3] This chapter takes a look at the sort of video production promoted by Lange, which goes beyond the concerns of individual filmmakers, to document the network of queer artists and activists currently working in Paris.

Formal experimentation and personal testimony combined with the constraints of self-financing and a sharp awareness of radical politics point to the work of Lionel Soukaz, the pioneer of French queer video, who directed *Race d'Ep!* (1979), a project jointly conceived with Guy Hocquenghem, comprising of four fragments of gay cultural history. *Race d'Ep!* combined documentary footage with a fictional enactment that staged the ideological clash between French and North-American models of gay male identity politics (Dyer 1990: 277–9). Richard Dyer locates drag, porn and pederasty as the three main faultlines running through French oppositional gay imagery of the 1970s, all three seen at the time as threatening to the established social order:

> drag as a refusal of male privilege [a tenuous idea argued by feminists to be context-dependent since drag can just as easily bolster male social privilege by biologically referring back to the real thing beneath the frock], porn making present the polymorphous perversity of desire, pederasty undermining the authority of the bourgeois family. (Dyer 1990: 223)

Dyer situates the type of politicised avant-gardism pioneered by Soukaz as illustrative of the uniformly marginal status of both homosexuality and avant-garde film, particularly because the latter's

> use of the idea of the 'home movie' had special significance for gays seeking to explore and develop new forms of intimacy and sexual community. . . . Moreover, the particular form of avant-gardism favoured – montage, based on a mixture of original footage and images from the mass and gay media – was particularly appropriate to a style of politics that sought simultaneously to analyse and celebrate the construction of homosexual desire. (Dyer 1990: 224)

Dyer goes on to discuss Soukaz's retrospectively daring blend of porn and pederasty, eliciting a libidinal response form the viewer, particularly *Boy Friend 1* (1977), *Boy Friend 2* (1977) and *Le Sexe des anges* (1978). Images of camp, sex and boys also dominate Soukaz's *Ixe* (1980), a self-portrait, the initial sequences of which show him making up and dragging up for the camera. Camp and drag feature in his subsequent short video portraits of performance artists Copi and Cunéo: *Copi je t'aime* (2002) and *La Cuisine de Cunéo* (1991). The visually eclectic *Ixe* mixes popular new wave music with opera, the soundtrack broken by images of male masturbation. The rapid-fire editing follows the disjointed rhythms of the jumpy soundtrack, accompanied by provocative images that alternate between the Pope and male erections, pointing to the opposition between the personal intimacy of gayness and the public nature of homophobic discourse. Soukaz situates his work somewhere between 'affective cinema' and 'activist cinema' ('cinéma affectif' and 'cinéma militant').[4] His more recent prolific output of experimental digital work (thirty-three videos of varying lengths produced between 2000 and 2006, according to IMDb internet listings)[5] blends sexuality with radical politics, and includes the patently sexual *Notre trou du cul est révolutionnaire* (2006) and *Porno industriel* (2006), and the pieces of political commentary *Le Problème de Chirac* (2004), *I Live in a Bush World* (2002) and *Texas Political Chainsaw Massacre* (2002). This last example recycles political propaganda by using pixilated images and repetitive rhythms to combine a lapidary commentary on US international imperialism (including footage from demonstrations against both capital punishment and the imminent invasion of Iraq), with more local attention to AIDS activism in France, including images of an Act Up demonstration from 2001 that situated AIDS in a global context (the banner for the World AIDS Day march of December 2001: 'Sida: l'autre guerre' – 'AIDS: the other war').

In contrast to the nebulous quality of 'unique strangeness' admired by Roth-Bettoni in recent avant-garde film production, this chapter tracks parallel developments in a more rough-and-ready form of DIY digital video production, to situate an emerging 'underground' visual culture, which politicises sexuality outside traditional highbrow notions of the avant-garde. This current tendency marks a critical return to the lowbrow politics of pleasure that formed the post-gay liberation image production (still combining camp with porn though not with pederasty) as exemplified by Soukaz.

A collection of essays on the emergence of a 'New Punk Cinema' in recent years, 'indebted to the punk spirit of experimentation, do-it-yourself ethos and an uneasy, often defiant relationship with the mainstream' (cover blurb to Rombes 2005), provides a useful description of the 'post-punk' attitude of some of the local video production covered in this chapter. In his introduction to the collection, Nicholas Rombes situates 'a do-it-yourself ethos that suggests that anybody can make a film, anybody can be a director' (Rombes 2005: 2) in the wider global context of digital image making. While the visual techniques of independent film (most notably non-linear narrative) have been incorporated by mainstream US cinema to contain 'indie' production as a safe commodity, it is the multinational providers that facilitate the proliferation of experimental DIY digital technology, making an old-school notion of the politically oppositional 'avant-garde' difficult to sustain in the era of 'post-cinema' – Graeme Harper's term for the effects of DVD technology on the 'mode of production and reception of the moving image' (Harper in Rombes 2005: 100–1). The output of this international tendency of new punk cinema is by now familiar and often quite far removed from the strange and perverse queerness of old punk cinema such as Derek Jarman's *Jubilee* (1978) – the book provides an account of the effects of late 1970s Anglo-American punk subculture on a generous range of contemporary filmmakers including Mike Figgis, Harmony Korine, Lars von Trier and the *Dogma 95* movement. However, the overall approach outlined by Rombes fits well with the political defiance and spirit of contestation animating the little-known French DIY production tracked through the rest of this chapter.

> Digital cameras and desk-top editing have made it possible for a greater number of people than ever before to make films. Although we need to be sceptical of Utopian claims about the democratisation of film-making (especially claims that ignore the underlying economics that allow and deny access to these digital technologies), digital cinema has opened up striking alternatives to Hollywood's multimillion dollar productions, in the same way that 8 mm and 16 mm film had done in the past. Although

the punk movement was not the first, nor the last, to exploit the do-it-yourself aesthetic for artistic means, its cultural stamp on film has largely been neglected. (Rombes 2005: 2)

Rombes accepts that 'the emergence of new digital and web-based forms in many ways extends the logic of punk even deeper into cinema' (2005: 17), citing the model of online 'micro-cinemas' as the space for possible DIY production, experimental work done from within the host platforms of sites onto which digital work can be easily uploaded and disseminated. The early user-generated potential of the internet, documented in the 2005 introduction to *New Punk Cinema*,[6] has since spread to DIY uploading onto a range of user-generated platforms, including social networking sites, which can be seen to provide an wider audience for video-makers such as Soukaz, much of whose output has been uploaded onto his personal page on www.dailymotion.com.[7]

This chapter traces the local proliferation of queer digital video production in France, whilst not claiming to be entirely comprehensive or to group together all this work under one rubric for reasons of stylistic, thematic, political and personal difference. The survey includes the recent work by Rémi Lange, the Queer Factory collective, the first French lesbian/trans porn flick made by photographer Emilie Jouvet, and the cheeky post-porn shorts from Panik Qulture, a pastiche of the early work of John Waters, whose own early brand of queer filth took a political stand against normative 'American' values in a DIY format that looked purposefully tacky and included gloriously 'bad' performances. I will end this chapter with an assessment of how the prime areas of cultural contest and contradiction running through contemporary French queer cinema (notably issues of gay *beur* masculinity and subjectivity, transgender identification, and queer sexualities and HIV/AIDS) have also been addressed by small-scale, no-budget digital video, taking as examples both the spoof pilot episode for a *beur* soap opera (*Beurs Appart'*, 2007) and the agit-prop videos of trans-activist group the GAT, which document the ongoing struggle for transgender rights in tandem with AIDS activism.

POST-PORN

The emerging queer digital video not only includes sexually explicit imagery within its remit, but also challenges the whole epistemological framework of traditional pornography through the production of a local brand of 'post-porn'. France's leading queer intellectual activist Marie-Hélène Bourcier, who spearheaded the group *Le Zoo*, actively queering a recalcitrant French academy in the late 1990s,[8] subsequently published two collections of essays that set the agenda for translating queer theoretical approaches to the French socio-cultural context (Bourcier 2001, 2005a). Both collections include essays on France's breakthrough heterosexual post-porn film, Virginie Despentes and Coralie Trinh Thi's much-debated *Baise-moi* (2000), a film that serves to a certain extent as a template for the more 'underground' forms of video production covered through the rest of this chapter. *Baise-moi* is every bit as notorious for its explicit content (simulated violence and hard-core sex) and genre-bending form as for the ensuing legal imbroglio and media scandal. I will now briefly summarise the details of this well documented affair: the film's general release in June 2000 was heralded by one critic as 'the most talked about film of the moment' ('le film le plus débattu du moment').[9] Adapted from Despentes's earlier novel (Despentes 1994), the film is a fantasy spin on the feminist rape revenge movie of the sort made popular by *Thelma and Louise* (Scott, 1991), and it casts porn actors in the explicit sex scenes, hence the overwrought critical brouhaha over how to classify it according to the pre-established genres of art and pornography. Due to the obsolescence of the X rating and in the absence of an '18' rating, the film went on general release on 28 June 2000 bearing a '16' certificate. Provoked by intense lobbying from a far-right child-protection pressure group, the *Conseil d'Etat*, a cross-party juridical committee with wide-reaching constitutional powers to overrule government decisions, took the unprecedented step of 'X-ing' the film on grounds of violent and pornographic indecency. The symbolic violence of censorship was overlooked by a commission whose function, ironically enough given the denial of free speech in this case, is to protect public order with due respect to civil liberties, notably the freedom of expression.[10] A year after the film's quarantine, Catherine Tasca, the minister for culture, altered the certification laws, settling the controversy surrounding the case by creating an '18' rating. *Baise-moi* was re-released in August 2001.

The critical ramifications for film studies have since been covered in detail in the various journalistic reviews and academic articles, notably in important pieces by Lisa Downing on both genre and ethics in *Baise-moi* (Downing 2004, 2006), and by Scott Mackenzie writing in *Screen* on the contentious censorship debate and the film's troubling position within feminist cinema (Mackenzie 2002). Bourcier's writing on the *Baise-moi* affair is itself compelling for the more local, inside account it gives of both the uproar created by the film's initial short-lived release in June 2000 (Bourcier 2001: 23–46) and the slow-burning recuperation of its sexual politics through the highbrow promotion of a so-called French pornographic new wave, mocked by Bourcier in the title of her piece 'The Auteur Blow-job' ('Pipe d'auteur') (Bourcier 2005a: 187–206). Bourcier defines post-porn itself as:

> The emergence of a post-pornographic movement and aesthetic (*post porn*) at the end of the twentieth century constitutes a critique of modern Western pornographic reason (seventeenth to twentieth centuries). It can be thought of as a 'reverse discourse', according to Foucault, coming from the margins and from the minorities within dominant pornography: sex workers, prostitutes, gays, lesbians, BDSM (bondage, discipline and sado-masochism), queers, trans people and a host of gender deviants of all sorts.

(L'émergence d'un mouvement et d'une esthétique post-pornographique (*post porn*) à la fin du XXe s. constitue une critique de la raison pornographique moderne occidentale (XIIe–XXe s.). Elle peut être analysée comme un 'discours en retour', pour reprendre les termes de Foucault, venu des marges et des minoritaires de la pornographie dominante: les travailleurs(ses) du sexe, les individus qui se prostituent, les gays, les lesbiennes, le BDSM (bondage, discipline & sado-masochisme), les queer, et les trans, les déviants du genre en général assumés comme tels.) (Bourcier 2005c: 378)

Bourcier situates the primary characteristics of the modern pornographic regime as the separation of sexual and gendered roles, the predominance of active male heterosexual voyeurism and the imperialist eroticisation of racial difference. This last point is relevant to the apparent threat *Baise-moi* posed to the French cultural establishment because of its casting of *beur* actress Raffaëla Anderson. The reaction of publications such as the *Nouvel Observateur* folded standard male heterosexual fears of sexual passivity (editorialist Laurent Joffrin expressed his profound discomfort at the film's *pièce de résistance* in a sex club, in which the girls dispense with all the clients in a gory bloodbath before penetrating and blowing away the remaining survivor with their handgun, playing up to the supposed horror of anal penetration for straight men)[11] into wider social, specifically postcolonial anxieties, and into more widespread fears of the dissolution of the republican pact and the invasion of identity politics. Linking the formation of post-pornography to emerging post-integration *beur* identities, Bourcier comments that the outlawing of *Baise-moi*, a film with a beur actress, Raffaëla Anderson, stemmed from the threat it posed to both republican universalism and white male heterosexuality (Bourcier 2005a: 195).

The hostility towards *Baise-moi* also revealed the in-built class prejudice in critical judgements of the film's generic boundary games. The film posed a problem precisely because it could not be written off as mere heterosexual pornography, revealing the rigid social hierarchy structuring realist fiction. Laura Kipnis has observed the proximity between 'pornography' (comprising the multifarious sexual images our culture heaps together under one rubric) and more lofty forms of cultural production such as art – 'pornography' is accordingly made up of imagery that violates bourgeois aesthetics (Kipnis calls this an 'antiaesthetic'), the reason for official middle-class aversion being 'its failure to translate one set of concerns into another' (Kipnis 1996: 85). The offence taken by anti-porn feminists is, Kipnis suspects, as much about class hierarchy as gender imbalance, a critical distaste that derives from porn's downward focus, historically formed through the middle-class fantasy of the ideal consumer as a lower-class man, 'brutish, animal-like, sexually voracious. And this fantasy is projected back onto pornography' (Kipnis 1996: 175). There is more at stake than pleasure, Kipnis argues, making pornography a corrosive to the bourgeois ideals of sexual aesthetics.

Much of the aversion towards *Baise-moi* likewise stemmed from such a fear of the downward gaze: not only is female desire the central focus (expressed through erotic pleasure, but also through the protagonists' shared anxieties and mutual friendship), but the women in question are two poor women of mixed race, not the white, middle-class subjects of feminism. Whilst the ethnic origins of the actors went unnoticed in the narrative itself (Despentes later put this down to her own unconscious censorship of the issue),[12] journalists concentrated exclusively on the gender vertigo, subsuming it into wider fears of social disintegration. When the minister of culture organised a conference to settle the affair, Catherine Breillat was invited to represent the film rather than either Despentes or Trinh Thi, anecdotal evidence that provides an insight into a profoundly elitist political culture in which established middle-class auteurs are invited as interpreters for the silenced lower classes. In her autobiographical essay *King Kong Théorie* (Despentes 2006), which includes a retrospective account of *Baise-moi*, Despentes rails against the entire press manipulation of her co-director Trinh Thi, an *ex-hardeuse*, who was denied any airtime whatsoever. Despentes argues that porn actresses have no control over their image should they choose to change career; the logic is that porn sullies women more than men, denying Trinh Thi any legitimacy as a director. Despentes argues that her co-director could not be credited with having been a sex bomb and also be seen to show creative intelligence elsewhere. Trinh Thi was made to disappear from the public sphere altogether (Despentes 2006: 104).

The apparent threat posed by both Despentes and Trinh Thi was, in short, social as much as sexual. Taking the long view of representations of sexuality (including the influence of US pioneers of post-porn such as Candida Royalle and Annie Sprinkle), Bourcier argues that *Baise-moi* counts as the first French post-porn production through its denaturalisation of the modern pornographic regime, with Despentes and Trinh Thi as the 'agents' rather than the 'objects' of representation (Bourcier 2005c: 380). It is the male performers who are sexualised, particularly in the scene in which Manu (Raffaëla Anderson) and Nadine (Karen Bach) engage in a foursome with two men, a macho *beur* performer Karim Sabaddehine credited as 'le grand mec' ('the big guy') who brashly suggests the girls comply to the 'lesbian' fantasies of straight porn, and the bisexual performer Titof, 'le petit mignon' ('the cutie'). It is the unknown *beur* performer who is predictably allotted the traditionally macho role whilst the international porn star Titof is shown to be winsome and compliant. Titof is the star of some eighty gay, straight and bisexual French and US flicks released since 1999. Initially supporting other well-known European performers such as Rocco Siffredi and Ovidie in star vehicles such as *Rocco Ravishes Prague 4* (Siffredi, 2001) and *Ovidie mène l'enquête* (Cabanel, 2001), Titof has gone on to star in a made-to-measure feature *Titof and the College Boys* (Bodilis, 2006).

During the foursome in *Baise-moi*, the girls' visual pleasure is partially directed at one another, hinting at possible same-sex attraction or more plausibly at the stimulation of watching each other have sex, which is not necessarily the same fantasy. Lisa Downing charts the complex patterns of a plausible queer gaze in this sequence, which works to reject the inclusion of images of 'lesbian' sex within straight porn (Downing 2006: 60–4). Lucille Cairns also examines this scene in the context of possible 'lesbian sub-texting' (Cairns 2006: 141). In a later sequence between Nadine and the hotel receptionist, she is shot observing his erection. This pushes the spectator to acknowledge the film's libidinal focus on lower-class, often mixed-race, virile men, a manoeuvre which shows not only the film's obvious distance from standard heterosexual porn that minimises pleasure in male bodies, but also its proximity to other local forms of queer production such as the cheaply produced and naturalistically shot digital gay porn made by Citébeur (at least in its more self-consciously ironic mode). To argue that *Baise-moi* turns the tables on male heterosexual spectatorship also suggests that there are other visual pleasures on offer from within such dissident images of heterosexual sex, suggesting that gay male responses to the film might also share the female protagonists' interest in male sex objects – a response that may also point to the larger question of widespread gay and bisexual consumer pleasure in straight porn.

Other critics have concurred with Bourcier that the film's conscious deployment of the post-modern battery of formal devices (intertextuality, collage, recycling, performativity and so forth) is illustrative of its knowingness and sense of playful irony, part of a queer strategy to denaturalise straight pornographic tropes. Mackenzie points to the self-reflexive violence – the heroines' rampage includes humorous discussions about how to conclude a shooting spree with a 'proper' form of suicide, what would make for good headlines, and how their story would conclude if it were a film narrative itself, and they even chide themselves for not being creative enough in their actions and dialogues. 'This self-consciousness on the part of Despentes and Trinh Thi signals an awareness about the ways in which critics and the public interpret and react to violent images. Furthermore, it points to the fact that *Baise-moi* is self-reflexive about its status as *grand guignol* cinema' (Mackenzie 2002: 318). Downing looks at *Baise-moi* in relation to its use of 'generic collage and the dislocation of ideology from genre' (Downing 2004: 265). Whilst acknowledging the film's 'postmodern cinematic mode' through its use of textual effects such as citing other cinematic moments (the designer violence of Tarantino, the nods to Gaspard Noé's *Seul contre tous*, the perversion of *Thelma and Louise*), Downing expresses scepticism as to whether the film's more ideological project is not foiled by its attachment to sexual realism, 'by putting in focus sexual intercourse, which is presumed, within the heterosexual genital economy, to the "thing itself" of desire' (Downing 2004: 268). Put more bluntly, beyond an attachment to graphic acts of heterosexual intercourse, and despite its brief flirting with possible mutual desire between the two women, *Baise-moi* may indeed be compromised by its own heterosexuality.

Lesbian Porn

In a review of Despentes's autobiographical essay *King Kong Théorie* for *Les Inrockuptibles* in 2006, accompanying a joint interview with controversial rapper Joey Starr, journalist Jade Lindgaard noted Despentes's turn to lesbianism, particularly the personal and intellectual influence of queer philosopher Beatriz Preciado.[13] Preciado's *Manifeste contra-sexuel* (Preciado 2000) was conceived at the time of its publication as a theoretical tract that sought to replace Lacanian kitsch with synthetic sex. The starting point for the book was Preciado's collaboration with the Zoo group and particularly with Bourcier, who translated the text into French. Preciado situates her book in the local context of routine protests by anti-S/M and anti-sex toy lesbians at the *Cineffable (Quand les lesbiennes se font du cinéma)* festival. Detractors of sex toys argue against the perceived male imposition on 'natural' lesbian sex; Preciado in contrast cites such contestation as illustrative of the rejection of penetration by lesbian-feminist culture. The familiar argument that dildos are fake penises whose phallic signification reproduces oppressive straight norms, much like butch/femme gender performance and S/M role-play, is one Preciado efficiently disposes of. Claiming sex, after Foucault (1976), and gender, after de Lauretis (1987), as bio-political technologies, ideologically and materially constructed to control and repress the lesbian body, Preciado argues that the dildo is not an imitation of the penis, not an object whose referent is the real thing, but a displacement of the perceived organic centre of sex (Preciado 2000). The historical map of synthetic sex, as Preciado illustrates in examples of anti-masturbatory devices and instruments used to treat hysteria, would show the dildo as a technical descendant of the hand, rather than an imitation of a specifically male body, an alienating machine threatening the penis with redundancy. Like Donna Haraway's post-gender cyborg, which 'has no truck with bisexuality, pre-oedipal symbiosis . . . or other seductions to organic wholeness' (Haraway 1991: 150), Preciado avoids the critical impasse of phallic substitution in favour of a material history of the lesbian body. Preciado argues that the body has been worked over by machinery, from the speculum and the penis, which are seen as the emblematic devices of 'phallocratic' control, to the hand, the fist and the dildo, which are said to mark a shift in sexual technology (Preciado 2000: 110).

Preciado's insistent promotion of lesbian sex as raunchy fun certainly paved the theoretical way for France's first lesbian/trans porn flick, Emilie Jouvet's *One Night Stand* (2006). Asked in an interview for *Têtu* what she thought was wrong with straight industrial production, Jouvet replied:

> Some things annoy me, like, for example, the fact that gender norms are strictly upheld: men with big cocks, women with long hair, enormous nails, silicone breasts and so on. Straight men make porn films in which the actresses pretend to be lesbians. They don't ever cum and what they get up to is clearly not representative of queer/lesbian sexuality.

(Certaines choses m'agacent comme, par exemple le fait que les normes y soient super rigides: hommes à grandes bites, femmes à cheveux longs, ongles gigantesques, seins siliconés, etc. Les pornos sont réalisés par des hommes hétéros et les actrices font semblant d'être lesbiennes. Elles ne jouissent pas et ce qu'elles font n'est absolument pas représentatif de la sexualité queer/lesbienne.)[14]

Jouvet situates *One Night Stand* as a direct political response to such porno archetypes:

This film will allow me to resolve a number of issues I have with contemporary pornography. It's 'queer' because it's a FTM transgender film too. The term 'queer' is representative of the political dimension to this sort of project; it makes visible sexual practices that are usually closeted. I longed to see a French lesbian porn flick, so I made one!
(Ce film va me permettre de pouvoir répondre aux questions que je me pose concernant la pornographie actuelle. Il est 'queer' car il est également transgenre FTM. Le terme 'queer' est représentatif de la dimension politique d'un tel projet, c'est un acte de visibilité sur des sexualités habituellement passées sous silence. J'avais envie de voir un porno lesbien français alors, je l'ai fait!)

The rejection of dominant imagery of 'lesbian' sex ensures the film's place among forms of cultural production that Bourcier has termed 'dyke' or 'guerrilla' porn (Bourcier 2005b: 375), comprising of independent, community-based production that includes previously taboo images of lesbian sexuality, not only both vaginal and anal penetration, but also S/M role-playing, fantasy substitutions and flexible gender performance.[15] Unlike in the history of gay male porn, lesbians have had to break with the stock voyeuristic fantasy of two women making out for the benefit of the male performer and spectator, in order to revoke erroneous stereotyping of their sexuality by the mainstream. Jouvet's *One Night Stand* seeks to wipe clean the slate, to provide a fresh template for contemporary erotic practice, one that, true to its provocatively promiscuous title, has no time for anything old-fashioned like cosy romanticism. The title is no doubt less ambiguous for a francophone audience, though a one-night stand is as likely to convey a sleazy combination of drunken fumbling and morning-after regret, as it is the heady cocktail of casual sex and raw intensity promoted by the film.

Overall the performers appear to belong to young, urban, 'indie-queer' subcultures that are indeed politically oppositional or which co-opt some of the codes and attitudes of punk. This would suggest proximity between *One Night Stand* and international forms of 'alt-porn' (alternative and often female-friendly pornography channelled through the internet, born out of audience boredom with the predictability of industrial production values), in which the performers tend to form part of subcultures such as skaters, Goths or punks (indicated through fashion, style and body modifications such as tattoos and piercings).[16] One criticism of the film may indeed be its uniformly hip self-consciousness, showcasing only young and slim performers who fit the film's mould. However, avant-garde artists have always filmed their own milieus, and Jouvet was simply filming friends who were happy to collaborate, though she does claim to have aimed for a diversity of styles, not selecting performers according to either physical or sexual criteria.[17] Given the dearth of lesbian self-representation in French cinema and culture more generally, the call for a wholly adequate representation of lesbian identities and sexualities in all their diversity exceeds the brief of a single film. The five individual sex scenes may repeat the same variation on the theme of coupling, but Jouvet's aim is to provide enough erotic diversity (fucking, fisting, light S/M) from within each pair to arouse her audience.

The first shot is of a girl descending a staircase to the basement of a club. This is followed by images of other girls dancing and socialising, the camera positioned right up close to their bodies to such an extent that the spectator is given very little idea of the location itself. Jouvet tracks her performers' bodies rather than expanding to include their actual surroundings, a fact that points to the overall ideological project to film lesbian and FTM bodies from within their space, given their cultural-wide absence outside overblown male fantasies. The fact that the camera often seems randomly positioned during the sex sequences suits the unpolished DIY look that takes pleasure in the supposed realness of the scenarios, the jerky camerawork resembling the brand of naturalism associated with Citébeur in French gay porn. The fact that (according to the accompanying DVD interviews) these filmed sequences often capture the performers' first meeting suits the promiscuous brief of the one-night stand. Whilst Jouvet focuses predominantly on her performers' bodies (naturally enough given the generic remit), the initial sequence ('Underground'), shot in a Parisian club, works as an act of public foreplay to the following scenes of sexual intimacy, all of which are shot in private. Even the sex-toy saleswoman does home delivery.

The club images focus a great deal on the DJ (Elodie Nelson) at work creating the right musical atmosphere for the ensuing seduction narrative of the opening sequence. The client filmed earlier entering the club is figured as an active cruiser, shown smoking as she surveys the action. Jouvet's camera is more interested in her active spectatorship than in the surrounding scene itself – many of the faces of the actual customers are purposefully distorted by the post-production, again highlighting DIY filming in practice. Yet while the rough-and-ready form is part of the erotic realism of the sex scenes, Jouvet includes touches of more traditionally cinematic mise-en-scène in the basement club. The sequence cuts to a low angle shot from the cruiser's perspective of a pair of knee-length leather boots turning to come down the stairs in slowly exaggerated strides. Freeze-framing the image as the rest of the girl's body comes into view shows the screen split into two halves: a spotlighted shot of the girl pausing on the stairs for dramatic effect occupies the right-hand side; her body is positioned at the same height as a small neon exit sign containing the standard iconography of a man running to escape, the visual contrast providing a witty commentary on the semiotics of gender. The sequence continues from the perspective of the cruiser below, observing her partner take out a cigarette and wait for a light. The entire sequence is set up as a camp take on classical cinematic realism, ironically aping the noir glamour of the femme fatale who never had to light her own cigarettes, in order to represent the codes of queer butch/femme gender play. The difference between the two performers is manifested by the teasing positioning of the camera (the cruiser's head is now at the level of the other girl's groin), and by the editing of high and low tilt angle shots alternating between the two viewpoints. The performers' mutual attraction is thereby expressed through their diametric opposition. This is an induction scene, however: having found a light, the girl brusquely brushes off her suitor. The scene cuts back to the bar upstairs where she is shown dancing intimately with her girlfriend again, the inference at this stage being that she is a flirt and that the lone smoker will have to be satisfied to watch. In a surprise turn of events, they hook up in the toilets, thereby kick-starting the action proper.

The following sequences offer a variety of erotic possibilities, disposing of the vanilla cliché of lesbian sexuality dominant among many heterosexuals and gay men. Most of the performers are versatile, sexually and otherwise ('Wendy' is also a writer, academic and cabaret performer (Delorme 2007)) and two scenes include trans-men, showing a range of possible queer desires and fantasies beyond a straight framework of fixed identity positions. Overall, the performers' enjoyment seems spontaneous or at least less obviously faked than is often the case in studio porn. Many forms of gay porn, though said to offer sexual flexibility and generic diversity through an endless expansion of niche markets, are often lazy, formulaic and drug-induced, a factor that might account for the success of the naturalistic style of user-generated internet porn, in which users can upload images of themselves appearing as performers without the industrial setting or generic constraints. The attraction of user-generated content is that it contains fewer of the illusions of performance, obvious staging devises such as studio sets and lighting, or post-production editing that form part of the visual construction of porn itself as representation. *One Night Stand* mixes influences from 'gonzo porn', which sees the camera right in the action mixing tight close-ups with full-body framing, but without any active participation on Jouvet's part; 'amateur porn', using first-time performers; and 'reality porn' in which the unobtrusive editing of sexual sequences is preceded by a staged prologue. Free of the constraints of mass-market production, new forms of DIY porn (Jouvet made her video for the 'indie' queer/porn festival circuit and only later commercialised it through limited DVD distribution as a result of its success)[18] and user-generated amateur porn are also innovative in style because they do not take themselves seriously as slick, marketable products. This means that alongside the main event in *One Night Stand*, there are also fun parodies of all the inevitably stiff acting – the third scene includes knowing nods to *Baise-moi*'s post-porn mode of irony (but without the gore), in which the employee from 'Rapid Sex Toy' does home delivery, conceived as a campy prelude to the business at hand, including an educational survey of the range of dildos on offer (safer-sex, aerodynamic, free gift, you name it).

POP PORN

The emphasis on camp performance discernible in minor mode in *One Night Stand* is the dominant aesthetic code of other local DIY production including work by the Queer Factory collective, a group of contemporary artists set up in 2003 and whose video output has thus far included a collection of shorts, *Queer Factory Tales – Les Contes de Queer Factory* (2004) that included a piece, *BlancX* by Jouvet. Local production has also included live cabaret work by Madame H, a drag act that combines the retrograde look of former first lady Bernadette Chirac (all prim pearls and Chanel couture) with the lewd tongue of a leather queen, an unlikely concoction filmed by Rémi Lange as *The Sex of Madame H* (2005). The short videos made by activist collective Panik Qulture (produced between 2004 and 2006, and shown intermittently on the 'indie' queer and porn festival circuits),[19] whose aim is to destabilise normative heterosexuality, wear their subversive credentials on their sleeve by acting out public displays of queer insurrection such as 'zaps'. Panik Qulture members include queer theorist and activist Maxime Cervulle, and Wendy Delorme from *One Night Stand*, who has also acted in one of their pieces, *BricoPorno* (2005). Their filmed public intervention *Zap les Superhé(té)ros* is a blatant dig at cartoon superheroes whose designs to save the planet are attacked for their reliance on ultra-straight identities (macho, racist, super-bourgeois and so on). Four of Panik Qulture's other offbeat shorts turn the knowing irony of post-porn into plain silliness by making stridently political points through mock-sexual imagery, a means of updating the mode of 1970s gay liberation and 1990s queer politics as expressed through direct action. The point is not to excite the audience but to denaturalise the history of sexuality through ironic detachment by drawing humorous attention to the heterosexist ideologies underpinning dominant culture. *La Culture hétéro, vous savez où je la mets?* (*Guess where I shove straight culture*) is a sharp skit demonstrating quite literally how to dispose of the entire corpus of French structuralist anthropology, written off by the collective as imperialist and heterosexist, suggesting a novel way for Lévi-Strauss to conquer uncharted territory. *How to Ass Ejaculate* is a spoof of Deborah Sundahl's best-selling primer video *How to Female Ejaculate* (1992), together with demonstrably sticky moments and cutesy performers with insider-joke names like Fassbimbo and Mies Van der Pute; and *Pop Porn Party*, which won a 'PorNO award' at the first Berlin porn festival in 2006, shows how to pleasure one's guests by wrapping a boy in adhesive tape then fixing multiple dildos all over his body for hours of fun and games.

Panik Qulture's most sustained piece of critique is their perversion of the supremely normative *Le Fabuleux destin d'Amélie Poulain* (Jeunet, 2000), attacked by hostile critics at the time of its release for its ultra-conservative vision of a bygone era. This retro-kitsch Parisian fantasy, glossing the working-class 'parigot' culture of Marcel Carné's pre-war poetic realism (Higbee, in Hayward 2005: 300), was used by commentators to trash the concurrent images of contemporary culture produced by the first season of French reality TV in 2001 (TF1's *Loft Story*). Despite attracting two million viewers in two weeks, the film was criticised by the liberal-left press for peddling a white, nationalist image of French culture; Serge Kaganski even thought it fascist.[20] *Amélie* turned out to be a versatile performer, particularly embraced by the right. François Fillon, president of the Gaullist RPR party in 2001, forecast in fully populist mode that the party would henceforth be adopting the film's 'enlightened patriotism' – the softer, more carnal France of Amélie Poulain.[21] Panik Qulture disposes of this reactionary nonsense in a vicious copy of the saccharine original (*Le Fabuleux destin d'Amélie Putain*), in which the costly computer-generated imagery from Duran-Duboi that created a mythical Montmartre (Higbee, in Hayward 2005: 299) is ditched in favour of cheap, hand-held naturalism, showing the actual, eighteenth arrondissement in north Paris (including the run-down, local metro station). The irritatingly wholesome Amélie, originally played by Audrey Tautou, is transformed into the 'whore of Montmartre' ('la putain des Abbesses'), who gets her kicks from caressing the statue of camp icon Dalida, and from eating her own excrement, a reverential nod to Divine's famous turn in *Pink Flamingos* (Waters 1972), situating John Waters as the pioneer of this brand of queer filth. The acronym for Panik Qulture – PQ is slang for toilet paper – is a nod to this dirty queer heritage; the group's North American influences also include Bruce LaBruce, Annie Sprinkle and Todd Verow. Subverting the girls-meets-boy agenda sees the perverse heroine paired off with a passive heterosexual boy who is filmed studiously reading Despentes's novel *Baise-moi*. The parody of the cheeky postcards shows dildos planted around the globe to map out the girl's travels and exposes Amélie as a dominatrix, who is attracted to the boy's posterior. She handcuffs then penetrates him, the passive heterosexual male deflowered in every position possible. Beyond the video's smutty content, Panik Qulture's sharper point is to queer homophobic representations (remember the original Amélie shirks at the thought of lesbianism) by illustrating the more dissident erotic practices of het-erosexuality than those allowed within mainstream narrative cinema.

CONCLUDING REMARKS AND EMERGING TRENDS

Queer novelist and filmmaker Cécile Bailly, who with Laetitia Blanquer made a short documentary *Paris was a King* (2002) about the Parisian drag king scene, has complained about an increasingly institutional gay and lesbian culture (in her description, bourgeois, trendy, and integrated according to the dominant model of French republicanism). This culture, she believes, pushes its own embarrassing minorities to the margins of cultural representation, particularly the *beurs*, bears and punks she lists in the title to her article, but also the communities formed around S/M, transgender and physical disability.[22] Bear subculture, formed by groups of corpulent, hairy gay men, can arguably challenge the physical norms of gay male culture – its commercial obsession with youth, beauty and perfection – but it can equally slide into a facile reassertion of straight-acting masculinity, thus repeating the dominant alienation of effeminacy. This is to be interpreted as a timely reminder to situate subcultures according to local context, rather than as a blanket renunciation of any possible forms of contestation, according to which subcultures would be doomed to mime oppressive power structures ad infinitum – a position associated with the myth and writings of Genet in French queer history (Bersani 1995: 151–81; Dyer 1990: 47–101; Sinfield 1998: 129–45). On the contrary, the corpus of film and video production covered so far illustrates the emergence in the French context of a politicised DIY formation, which is influenced by popular genres such as pornography, represented through alternative outlets such as local DVD distribution and marginal cultural festivals and venues, and channelled through recent technological developments in cheap digital video and user-generated internet exposure. I ended the previous chapter's coverage of independently financed but culturally institutional gay cinema on a downbeat note due to the form's inability to generate an oppositional cultural politics, the constraints of its highbrow remit limiting it to a modest brand of queer cinema, fleshed out by Téchiné's *Les Témoins*. The experimental film and video charted through this chapter, however, goes further by pointing to a contemporary revival of the brash sexual politics associated with gay liberation of the 1970s, which mixed porn with politics (Soukaz's queer cinema *avant la lettre*), and a translation of the Anglo-American queer insurrection of the late 1980/early 1990s to the contemporary French context.

As a coda to the present review of emerging forms of queer cinema, I would like to indicate a couple of videos that engage directly with the areas of cultural contest located in the previous chapters as primary faultlines in contemporary French identity politics, namely persisting anxieties around issues of postcolonialism (post-integration identities and *beur* gay subjectivities), transgender (the sidelining of gender dissent from institutional LGBT political movements) and AIDS (through HIV prevention directed at gay men, trans communities and sex workers). The bulk of this book has argued that a recent cluster of films by gay auteurs, however contested the labels gay or queer within the French cinema industry, has actively sought to engage with the cultural politics of queer identities and sexualities. The corpus of French gay cinema certainly includes individual films that tackle the intricacies of same-sex relations and even gesture to a more affirmative political vision of gay and queer subcultures: Chéreau's complex web of relations in the time of AIDS in *Ceux qui m'aiment prendront le train*; Ducastel and Martineau's stylish yet frontal take on AIDS in *Jeanne et le garçon formidable*; Lifshitz's attempt to chart marginal queer sexualities across national, ethnic and gender differences in *Wild Side*; and Téchiné's historical coverage of early AIDS activism from within gay communities in *Les Témoins*. However, the overall synchronic picture could be said to illustrate uneven cultural change through limited active visibility, ultimately confined by the consensual demands of art-house film distribution and by a pervading 'French' unease with the space allotted to alien identity politics. To be fair, such an assessment might seem overly harsh given that the French market is the only sustainable European film industry to have a clear variety of (admittedly gay male and not lesbian) sexual representation, a feature of cinematic production that mirrors the overall state of European cinema, in which only France has an industry able to sustain a variety of popular genres, a star system and independent *auteur* production. Quantity is not the issue in the French context, rather the institutional or cultural setting and the relative political reserve of gay/queer independent production. However, like the postcolonial porn production of local studio Citébeur, this final cluster of examples is intended to show how experimental forms of DIY video are also being used by marginal subcultures in France as active forms of cultural empowerment, used to set the agenda according to their terms, rather than accepting invisibility in mainstream heterosexual culture, or passive visibility on the terms of institutionalised gay male subculture.

The video clips made by the GAT transgender collective from 2004 onwards include documentary footage of the group's radical work fighting for institutional medical and legislative change together with a queer spoof of the psychiatric control of gender reassignment.[23] From a strictly historical point of view, these clips provide invaluable documentation of political contest in France in the early 2000s, with footage of the group's vocal interruption of a conference at the Saint-Anne hospital where all the influential psychiatrists policing gender reassignment were assembled in June 2004. Other clips show protests at transgender invisibility within the institutional framework of LGBT politics, and protests at parliamentary refusal to enshrine specific transphobia alongside homophobia, sexism, racism and anti-semitism in recent legislation.[24] The footage from the annual trans-pride march documents the growth of a social movement emerging into public consciousness, the GAT's imagery collating the diverse social networks and mapping out the early formation of a political movement through queer demonstrations ('zaps' and 'die-ins' to raise awareness of escalating HIV rates and a lack of targeted prevention or medical specificity regarding transgender communities).

The GAT's one satirical clip (*Le Doigt de Dieu ou la bite à Lacan*) is aimed at lampooning the psychiatric and psychoanalytic institutions by turning the tables on their self-assumed theoretical construction of 'transsexualism', notably the clinical and theoretical work of Colette Chiland and Catherine Millot (Millot 1993 [1983]), according to whom all possible gender identifications are straightened out to fit the pre-existing phallic paradigm, whereby one can never be a man without the real thing. The GAT adapted its scenario from the transcription of Bourcier's public intervention in 2003, which gave a suitably scathing account of the recalcitrant psychological control of transgender through films such as Bertrand Bonello's regressive update of Greek mythology that takes in a Brazilian transsexual in Paris, *Tirésia* (2003); and through theoretical psychoanalysis and institutional psychiatry (Bourcier 2005a: 251–71). Three of the GAT members adopt clinical disguise to mull over the troubling cases of patients Lacan, Chiland and Millot, cutting between excerpts from their offensive texts and mock prescriptions to cure psychoanalytic imbalance.[25]

This use of techniques from documentary naturalism provides a transition to a final example of queer DIY video that includes a fair amount of explicit cultural debate within its ideological remit. The project of *Beurs Appart'* (2007) is to voice issues concerning gay *beur* men that are invisible or trivialised elsewhere. The video is the first in a planned series from the collective L'Iskander, filmed by Hugo di Verdura. The brief is to include fresh imagery of gay *beur* men from within the format of a spoof soap opera, rather than accepting the stereotypes imposed upon them by mainstream and independent cinema. The novelty of *Beurs Appart'* in the wider context of French cultural representations of *beur* men is twofold. First, it is primarily a collective project performed by gay *beur* men themselves (actors Rachid Adjane, Ilmann Bel, Slimane Mostefa-Châa, Jimmy Nour and Guillaume Quashie-Vauclin). The video points accurately to friendship networks as much as sexual ones as the affective backbone to queer subcultures. The piece makes use of the stock comedy devise of character typology but without including standard images of young *beur* men as hooded rappers. Their Myspace profile describes the characters as fashion-victim (Ryad), fit boy (Salman), sporty but scholarly straight boy (Karim), shy romantic (Seif), and sophisticated Lebanese neighbour (Jad).[26] Secondly, *Beurs Appart'*, though filmed by a white director, is not auteur-led: the narrative structure, ideas, personal recollections and gags all come from the 'out' gay performers themselves. This gives the project a subjective, inside viewpoint lacking in films directed by white filmmakers (Lifshitz and Ozon) who employ straight-identified actors (Kechiouche and Belmadi) to pass as gay. *Beurs Appart'* does not aspire to be an exercise in narrative realism, and this gives it relative generic freedom from traditional criteria of good acting and realistic representation. This helps lift the inevitable 'burden of representation' (Mercer 1994: 233–58), enabling the audience to glimpse the actors' own personalities beneath the veneer of ironic performance.

The project began as a pilot episode for the cable channel Pink TV but never attracted sufficient funding, so the finished product was community-funded, shot mostly indoors without sets or costumes, by a director and a technician with one camera. *Beurs Appart'* was first presented at the Paris Gay and Lesbian film festival in 2007, prior to a DVD release. Influenced in part by the actors' favourite US TV programmes (both the sitcom *Friends* and the series *Sex and the City* are cited as examples), the humour arises from the discrepancy between these glamorous models and the amateur technique (due to expediency as much as choice); and between the over-the-top gestures to popular divas and the inclusion of current ideological contest around issues of ethnicity and same-sexuality. *Beurs Appart'* twists the sitcom formula of a flat-share, tracing the characters' friendships, attractions and animosities, copying the serial cliff-hangers of Anglo-American soap operas, and even making half-hearted gestures towards the more garish, melodramatic fantasies of the Latin-American *telenovela*.

Beurs Appart' begins with the familiar device used in documentary of a direct testimonial address to camera: Rachid Adjane presents his character as half-Moroccan, half-French, speaks in a grave voice and wears a baseball cap. His subsequent grand entrance as the raving queen, Ryad, however works in direct contrast to both the establishing shots of tower blocks and this initial clichéd image of *banlieue* masculinity: he arrives, adorned in dark sunglasses, a diamante cross and a fur stole, at the flat of Salman (Ilmann Bel), whom he has met via an internet chat room. The comic value comes from Salman's disappointment (we infer that he was eagerly expecting a manly hunk) and compromising nudity. Bel also acted in Lange's *Statross le magnifigue* (2006), a twenty-two minute short video that updates visual devises from silent film, including inter-titled dialogue, to recount the sexual fairy tale of Statross, a mixed-race bisexual baron (Jann Halexander), who rents out his estate to visitors. The character played by Bel is filmed masturbating to a climax in a scene in which Lange inserts visual techniques from gay porn by positioning his camera below the performer to capture the money-shot. Salman in *Beurs Appart'* is depicted as persistently horny but well aware of the imperialist stereotype of *beur* male sexuality as bestial: unable to find work even with a degree (an economic detail reflecting the endemic racism of the French employment market), Salman resorts to hustling on the sly, pleased to earn some easy cash but ashamed of conforming to the imposed cliché.

In contrast to Bel's virile charm is Adjane's insouciant acting style, which though imitating the grandeur of a Beverley Hills princess (and intentionally failing to get it quite right) is equally close in style to the bawdy routines of camp stand-up comedy and the tradition of smutty innuendo. Adjane's technique is to acknowledge the camera's presence through subtle pauses and sly glances, even incorporating a routine associated with drag artist Madame H, who likewise has a prying off-stage mother. *Beurs Appart'* re-appropriates the stock one-sided telephone gag in which the humour is derived from the comedian's selection of information and a similar use of intermittent pauses. (The telephone gag was also used to great effect by earlier queer performance artist Copi in his surrealist one-man show *Le Frigo* in 1983, in which he donned multiple drag disguises to play both caller and recipient.) Adjane's tone of voice also highlights the gap between the character's class pretensions – through an affected Parisian accent – and the lewd content, showing camp to be as concerned as much with class confusion as with gender trouble. Ryad's anxious mother inopportunely calls to check that he has reached his destination safely, and Adjane's curt response suggests a cosy scenario by referencing the history of the sissy-boy syndrome on film. (Hitchcock's *Psycho* is even more pointedly parodied in a later shower scene – in post-modern style as much a parody of the endless recycling of the shower scene as of the original itself.)

Beurs Appart' also breaks new ground simply by including effeminacy within its range of gender representation: Adjane's flamboyant image of *beur* effeminacy works against the grain of popular heterosexual narrative cinema (*Chouchou*, for example) that merely updates inversion theory (effeminacy equalling transsexual fantasy). Adjane's defiant performance of femininity includes a studied combination of drag homage to *femmes fatales* (smoking as glamour) and more contemporary manifestations of narcissism such as pouting for effect while photographing himself with a mobile phone. Competition arrives in the shape of 'easy' neighbour Jad, who calls by to seduce the new-comers. The two actors not only make effeminacy sexy, which is rarely the case in gay self-representation, but manage to breathe new life into the tired routine of diva-worship by downgrading the existing repertoire of icons through their devotion to 'Saint Anna Nicole Smith'. Adjane's half-nods to the camera (to defer expected audience laughter, almost defying an imagined interruption) self-consciously ape the history of wooden acting and garbled dialogue in quick-turnover serials and soap operas, which in the context of French television have included *Salut les musclés*, *Premiers baisers* and *Hélène et les garçons* in the 1990s, and more recently *Plus belle la vie* (broadcast since 2004 by France 3) which had attracted daily audience figures of over six million by early 2007.[27]

Plus belle la vie is rooted in social reality, addressing contemporary social issues such as homosexuality in an educational, 'problem-of-the-week' fashion. Given the generic freedom of *Beurs Appart'*, it manages to slip in whole chunks of dialogue tackling key social issues affecting gay *beur* men, whilst momentarily putting the narrative on stand-by. Thanks to the DIY format, these didactic pauses do not jar in the same way that they would do in conventional narrative realism, allowing such ideological debates more airtime because of the generic freedom on offer. Salman is shown to be attracted to the only white flatmate, later explaining his sexual preferences along ethnic lines (finding relations with other *beur* men too complicated for cultural reasons) and refuting the idea of true love, which leads to a confrontation with Ryad, who believes in settling down with another *beur* man. They do not quite unravel the intricate factors accounting for cross-race and same-race attraction, because the intensity is broken by Ryad's autobiographical interjection recounting the loss of his virginity when he was raped by an uncle at the age of thirteen, a potentially painful anecdote rendered hilarious by Adjane's milking of the tragic moment and his co-performers' stunned reaction. The ideological exposé is later resumed through a broader discussion tackling homosexuality in Muslim contexts with the attendant difficulties of negotiating religious obstacles, coming out to hostile parents and their awareness of HIV/AIDS, the performers again slipping out of character to talk more naturalistically about the particularities of *beur* gay men in France.

As I conclude this survey of emerging queer video work in early 2008, the *Beurs Appart'* team are preparing the next instalment of the series (the first ended on a nail-biting cliff-hanger involving Salman's pernicious attempt to break up the straight boy's relationship). The emerging success of *Beurs Appart'* illustrates the present conditions and future potential for queer image-making on digital video, promoted through online, user-generated, social networking sites (the casting for the second instalment was done through the group's Myspace 'friends'), distributed alongside, rather than in opposition to, gay/queer representation in the institutional art-cinema format. The recent renewal of a politicised queer underground through community-based, digital video production, the early stages of which I have sketched through this chapter, is ultimately still work in progress. Or, to adapt the serial vernacular of *Beurs Appart'*, it is a story to be continued . . .

NOTES

1. Stéphane Bouquet, 'Omelette', *Cahiers du cinéma,*' no. 520, January 1998, p. 66.
2. Jean-Sébastien Chauvin, 'Les Yeux brouillés', *Cahiers du cinéma*, no. 547, June 2000, p. 76.
3. Lange's production company *Les Films de l'ange* was set up in 2004 to promote local independent queer film and video production and in parallel the distribution of foreign independent queer films through a DVD collection 'Homovies' – see www.lesfilmsdelange.blogspot.com (accessed 20 January 2008). Lange was also co-curator of the thirteenth annual Gay and Lesbian Film Festival in Paris in November 2007, which included a large amount of locally produced short films, together with rare French work from the 1970s. This work foresaw the recent revival that mixes porn with cultural politics, notably Jean Estienne's humorous take on telephone sex in which the receiver is mistaken for a dildo, *Et Dieu créa les hommes* (1977), and his gruelling sequence of fisting which played with the generic conventions of horror films, *Poing de force* (1976).
4. Soukaz comments on his method in *Court-circuit: le magazine du court métrage*, ARTE, 26–7 May 2003.
5. See www.imdb.com/name/nm0815772/ (accessed 20 December 2007).
6. Rombes lists www.microcinemascene.com, describing itself as a 'digital filmmaking revolution' as an example (accessed 28 January 2008).
7. See www.dailymotion.com/videos/relevance/search/soukaz/1 (accessed 20 December 2007).
8. *Le Zoo*'s seminars are published as Bourcier (ed.) (1998).
9. Olivier Seguret, 'Sex shots', *Libération*, 28 June 2000, p. 39.
10. See Olivier Schmitt, 'Le dernier mot au Conseil d'Etat', *Le Monde*, 2–3 July 2000, p. 28.
11. Laurent Joffrin, 'Pornographie, violence: la liberté de dire non', *Le Nouvel Observateur*, no. 1862, 13–19 July 2000, pp. 62–4.
12. Philippe Azoury, 'Une ressortie pour faire le deuil', *Libération*, 29 August 2001, p. 26.
13. 'King Kong et le Jaguar', *Les Inrockuptibles*, no. 568, 17–23 October 2006, pp. 34–9, quotation at p. 37.

14. Emilie Jouvet, quoted in Tatiana Potard, 'Rencontre avec Emilie Jouvet, artiste engagée', *Têtu*, October 2005, available at www.tetu.com/rubrique/mag/mag_dossier_detail.php?id_dossier=6X (accessed 10 January 2008). This is the same reference for the second Jouvet quotation.
15. For a history of lesbian and dyke porn, see Heather Butler, 'What do you call a lesbian with long fingers? The development of lesbian and dyke pornography', in Williams, 2004: 167–97.
16. The first Berlin porn festival in 2006 showcased the international trend for 'alt-porn'.
17. Jouvet, quoted in the *Têtu* interview in 2005 (see note 14).
18. For information on the film's screenings and festival distribution, see Jouvet's professional and personal internet profiles www.20six.fr/emyphotografy (accessed 15 January 2008) and www.myspace.com/emyphotography (accessed 15 January 2008).
19. Panik Qulture's output has been aired on French cable channel Pink TV in 2005, and internationally screened at established LGBT film festivals such as Paris (2005, 2006, 2007), London, Lisbon and Turin (2006), the Pink Screen Festival in Brussels (2005, 2006), MIX (2006) and NewFest LGBT Film Fest in New York (2006); at porn festivals in Berlin (2006) and Athens (2007, 2008); and at other queer independent or anarchist festivals including the Revolution and Sexual Revolution Festival, Tokyo (2007) and Busting Outgames! Trans-lesbo-fag-anarcho-queer-event, Montreal (2006). Thank you to Maxime Cervulle for providing me with this information.
20. Serge Kaganski, 'Amélie pas jolie', *Libération*, 31 May 2001, p. 7.
21. Denis Boulard, 'Fillon et la "France d'Amélie Poulain" ', *Le Journal du dimanche*, 8 July 2001, p. 4.
22. Cécile Bailly, 'Beurs, bears, punks: ces minorités qui dérangent', *360°*, no. 24, July/August 2002.
23. Thanks to GAT founder member Carine Boeuf for providing me with the complete set of the group's clips.
24. The National Assembly adopted the law to implement the HALDE (*Haute autorité de lutte contre les discriminations et pour l'égalité*) in December 2004, which saw sexist and homophobic hate speech sanctioned by law.
25. The GAT was made up of Carine Boeuf, Vincent He-say, Maxime Zitouni and Tom Reucher.
26. See www.myspace.fr/BEURSAPPART (accessed 25 January 2008).
27. These statistics come from the show's detailed entry on Wikipedia that gives the precise statistic as peaking at 6.34 million viewers for 13 February 2007: www.fr.wikipedia.org/wiki/Plus_belle_la_vie (accessed 22 January 2008). These unofficial statistics are confirmed by the *Médiamétrie* database that includes *Plus belle la vie* among its 'palmarès des émissions 2007': www.mediametrie.fr/resultats.php?rubrique=tv&resultat_id=490 (accessed 24 January 2008). Thank you to Joseph McGonagle for directing me to these official statistics.

BIBLIOGRAPHY

Agacinski, Sylviane (1998) *Politique des sexes*, Paris: Seuil.

Alderson, David and Linda Anderson (eds) (2000) *Territories of Desire in Queer Culture: Refiguring Contemporary Boundaries*, Manchester: Manchester University Press.

Altman, Dennis (2001) *Global Sex*, Chicago: University of Chicago Press.

Asibong, Andrew (2005) 'Meat, murder, metamorphosis: the transformational ethics of François Ozon', *French Studies*, 59 (2), pp. 203–15.

Asibong, Andrew (2008) *François Ozon*, Manchester: Manchester University Press.

Austin, Guy (2003) *Stars in Modern French Film*, London: Arnold.

Barkat, Sidi Mohammed (2005) *Le Corps d'exception: Les artifices du pouvoir colonial et la destruction de la vie*, Paris: Editions Amsterdam.

Bataille, Georges (2000) [1966] *Ma mère*, Paris: 10/18.

Benshoff, Harry and Sean Griffin (eds) (2004) *Queer Cinema: The Film Reader*, London and New York: Routledge.

Bersani, Leo (1995) *Homos*, Cambridge, MA: Harvard University Press.

Beugnet, Martine (2000) *Marginalité, sexualité, contrôle dans le cinéma français contemporain*, Paris: L'Harmattan.

Beugnet, Martine (2004) *Claire Denis*, Manchester: Manchester University Press.

Beugnet, Martine (2007) *Cinema and Sensation: French Film and the Art of Transgression*, Edinburgh: Edinburgh University Press.

Borrillo, Daniel, Eric Fassin and Marcella Iacub (eds) (1999) *Au-delà du PaCS: l'expertise familiale à l'épreuve de l'homosexualité*, Paris: Presses Universitaires de France.

Bourcier, Marie-Hélène (ed.) (1998) *Q comme Queer: Les Séminaires Q du zoo (1996–1997)*, Lille: Cahiers GKC.

Bourcier, Marie-Hélène (2001) *Queer Zones: politiques des identités sexuelles, des représentations et des savoirs*, Paris: Balland.

Bourcier, Marie-Hélène (2005a) *Sexpolitiques: Queer Zones 2*, Paris: La Fabrique.

Bourcier, Marie-Hélène (2005b) 'Porno lesbien', in Philippe di Folco (ed.), *Dictionnaire de la pornographie*, Paris: PUF, pp. 374–6.

Bourcier, Marie-Hélène (2005c) 'Post-pornographie', in Philippe di Folco (ed.), *Dictionnaire de la pornographie*, Paris: PUF, pp. 378–80.

Brassaï (1976) *Le Paris secret des années trente*, Paris: Gallimard.

Brassart, Alain (2007) *L'Homosexualité dans le cinéma français*, Paris: Nouveau monde éditions.

Burch, Noël (2007) *De la beauté des latrines: Pour réhabiliter le sens au cinéma et ailleurs*, Paris: L'Harmattan.

Butler, Judith (1990) *Gender Trouble: Feminism and the Subversion of Identity*, New York: Routledge.

Cairns, Lucille (2001) 'Gender trouble in *Ma Vie en rose*', in Lucy Mazdon (ed.), *France on Film: Reflections on Popular French Cinema*, London: Wallflower, pp. 119–31.

Cairns, Lucille (2006) *Sapphism on Screen: Lesbian Desire in French and Francophone Cinema*, Edinburgh: Edinburgh University Press.

Cavitch, Max (2007) 'Sex after death: François Ozon's libidinal invasions', *Screen*, 48 (3), pp. 313–26.

Cervulle, Maxime (2007) 'De l'articulation entre classe, race, genre et sexualité dans la pornographie ethnique', in B. Darras (ed.), *Etudes Culturelles et Cultural Studies, Médiation et Information*, nos 24–5, Paris: L'Harmattan, pp. 221–8.

Cervulle, Maxime (2008) 'French homonormativity and the commodification of the Arab body', *Radical History Review*, 100, pp. 171–9.

Chedgzoy, Kate, Emma Francis and Murray Pratt (eds) (2002) *In a Queer Place: Sexuality and Belonging in British and European contexts*, Ashgate: Aldershot.

Chiland, Colette (1997) *Changer de Sexe*, Paris: Odile Jacob.

Chiland, Colette (2003) *Le Transsexualisme*, Paris: Presses Universitaires de France.

Cooper, Dennis (2005) *The Sluts*, New York: Void Books.

Cooper, Sarah (2001) 'Je sais bien, mais quand même . . .: Fetishism, envy, and the queer pleasures of *Beau Travail*', *Studies in French Cinema*, 1 (3), 2001, pp. 174–82.

Debray, Régis (1998) *La République expliquée à ma fille*, Paris: Seuil.

Delaney, Samuel R. (1999) *Times Square Red, Times Square Blue*, New York: New York University Press.

Delorme, Wendy (2007) *Quatrième génération*, Paris: Grasset.

Deltombe, Thomas and Mathieu Rigouste (2005) 'L'ennemi intérieur: la construction médiatique de la figure de l'"Arabe" ', in P. Blachard, N. Bancel and S. Lemaire (eds), *La Fracture coloniale: La société française au prisme de l'héritage colonial*, Paris: La Découverte, pp. 195–202.

Derbyshire, Philip (2001) 'Homosexual politics in the wake of AIDS', *Radical Philosophy*, no. 109, pp. 22–6.

Despentes, Virginie (1994) *Baise-moi*, Paris: Editions Florent-Massot.

Despentes, Virginie (2006) *King Kong Théorie*, Paris: Grasset.

Dollimore, Jonathan (1998) *Death, Desire and Loss in Western Culture*, London: Penguin.

Downing, Lisa (2004) 'French cinema's new sexual revolution: postmodern porn and troubled genre', *French Cultural Studies*, 15 (3), pp. 265–80.

Downing, Lisa (2006) '*Baise-moi* or the ethics of the desiring gaze', *Nottingham French Studies*, 45 (3), pp. 52–65.

Ducastel, Olivier and Jacques Martineau (1998) *Jeanne et le garçon formidable*, Paris: Arte Editions/Hachette.

Dustan, Guillaume (1999) *Nicolas Pages*, Paris: Balland.

Dyer, Richard (1990) *Now You See It: Studies on Lesbian and Gay Film*, London and New York: Routledge.

Dyer Richard (1993) *The Matter of Images: Essays on Representations*, London and New York: Routledge.

Dyer, Richard (2002) *The Culture of Queers*, London and New York: Routledge.

Dyer, Richard (2007) *Pastiche*, London and New York: Routledge.

Edelman, Lee (2004) *No Future: Queer Theory and the Death Drive*, Durham: Duke University Press.

Eng, David L., Judith Halberstam and José Esteban Muñoz (eds) (2005) *Social Text*, 'What's queer about queer studies now?', nos 84–5.

Eribon, Didier (1999) *Réflexions sur la question gay*, Paris: Fayard.

Falconer, Colin (2006) 'Why did the banlieues burn?', *Radical Philosophy*, no. 136, pp. 2–7.

Fassin, Eric (2005) *L'Inversion de la question homosexuelle*, Paris: Editions Amsterdam.

Forbes, Jill (1992) *The Cinema in France After the New Wave*, London: Palgrave Macmillan.

Foucault, Michel (1976) *Histoire de la sexualité I: la volonté de savoir*, Paris: Gallimard.

Giles, Jane (1991) *The Cinema of Jean Genet: Un Chant d'amour*, London: BFI.

Giles, Jane (1993) *Un Chant d'amour. Le cinéma de Jean Genet*, Paris: Macula.

Grandena, Florian (2006) 'L'Homosexuel en dehors de l'homosexualité: Expressions de l'identité gay dans les films d'Olivier Ducastel et Jacques Martineau', *Contemporary French Civilization*, 30 (2), pp. 63–86.

Grandena, Florian (2008) 'Du glissement de l'homosexualité', *Contemporary French and Francophone Studies*, 12 (1), pp. 99–106.

Guénif-Souilamas, Nacira (2004) 'Des nouveaux ennemis intimes: le garçon arabe et la fille beurette', in N. Guénif-Souilamas and E. Macé, *Les Féministes et le garçon arabe*, Paris: Editions de l'Aube, pp. 59–95.

Guénif-Souilamas, Nacira (2005) 'La réduction à son corps de l'indigène de la République', in P. Blachard, N. Bancel and S. Lemaire (eds), *La Fracture coloniale: La société française au prisme de l'héritage colonial*, Paris: La Découverte, pp. 203–12.

Guénif-Souilamas, Nacira (2006) 'La Française voilée, la beurette, le garçon arabe et le musulman laïc. Les figures assignées du racisme vertueux', in N. Guénif-Souilamas (ed.), *La république mise à nu par son immigration*, Paris: La Fabrique, pp. 109–32.

Guibert, Hervé (1990) *A l'ami qui ne m'a pas sauvé la vie*, Paris: Gallimard.

Guibert, Hervé (2001) *La mausolée des amants: journal intime, 1976–1991*, Paris: Gallimard.

Halberstam, Judith (1998) *Female Masculinity*, Durham: Duke University Press.

Hall, Donald E. (2003) *Queer Theories*, New York: Palgrave Macmillan.

Handyside, Fiona (2007) 'Melodrama and ethics in François Ozon's *Gouttes d'eau sur pierres brûlantes/Water Drops on Burning Rocks* (2000)', *Studies in French Cinema*, 7 (3), pp. 207–18.

Haraway, Donna (1991) *Simians, Cyborgs and Women: The Reinvention of Nature*, New York: Routledge.

Hargreaves, Alex G. and Mark McKinney (eds) (1997) *Post-Colonial Cultures in France*, London: Routledge.

Harper, Phillip Brian, Anne McClintock, José Esteban Muñoz and Trish Rosen (eds) (1997) *Social Text*, 'Queer transexions of race, nation and gender', nos 52–3.

Hayward, Susan (2005) [1993] *French National Cinema*, London and New York: Routledge.

Honoré, Christophe (1995) *Tout contre Léo*, Paris: Ecole des loisirs.

Honoré, Christophe (1997) *L'Infamille*, Paris: Editions de l'Olivier.

Honoré, Christophe (1999) *La Douceur*, Paris: Editions de l'Olivier.

Honoré, Christophe (2002) *Scarborough*, Paris: Editions de l'Olivier.

Hughes, Alex and Keith Reader (eds) (1998) *Encyclopedia of Contemporary French Culture*, London and New York: Routledge.

Iacub, Marcella (2002) *Qu'avez-vous fait de la libération sexuelle?*, Paris: Flammarion.

Ince, Kate (2002) 'Queering the family?: fantasy and the performance of sexuality and gay relations in French cinema 1995–2000', *Studies in French Cinema*, 2 (2), pp. 90–7.

Jagose, Annamarie (1997) *Queer Theory: An Introduction*, New York: New York University Press.

Johnston, Cristina (2002) 'Representations of homosexuality in 1990s mainstream French cinema', *Studies in French Cinema*, 2 (1), pp. 23–31.

Johnston, Cristina (2008) '(Post-)queer citizenship in contemporary Republican France', *Contemporary French and Francophone Studies*, 12 (1), pp. 89–97.

Kipnis, Laura (1996) *Bound and Gagged: Pornography and the Politics of Fantasy in America*, Durham: Duke University Press.

Kotz, Liz (1992) 'The body you want: Liz Kotz interviews Judith Butler', *Artforum*, November, pp. 82–9.

LaGrace Volcano, Del and Judith Halberstam (1999) *The Drag King Book*, London: Serpent's Tail.

Lauretis, Teresa de (1987) *Technologies of Gender: Essays on Theory, Film and Fiction*, Bloomington: Indiana University Press.

Lauretis, Teresa de (1991) 'Queer theory: lesbian and gay sexualities', *Differences*, 3:2, pp. iii–xviii.

Lazen, Matthew (2004) ' "En perme à Nantes": Jacques Demy and New Wave Place', *Studies in French Cinema*, 4 (3), pp. 187–96.

Lestrade, Didier (2000) *Act Up Une Histoire*, Paris: Denoël.

Lestrade, Didier (2004) *The End*, Paris: Denoël.

McCaffrey, Enda (2005), *The Gay Republic: Sexuality, Citizenship and Subversion*, Aldershot: Ashgate.

McGonagle, Joseph (2007) 'Gently does it: ethnicity and cultural identity in Olivier Ducastel and Jacques Martineau's *Drôle de Félix* (2000)', *Studies in European Cinema*, 4 (1), pp. 21–3.

Mackenzie, Scott (2002) '*Baise-moi*, feminist cinemas and the censorship controversy', *Screen*, 43 (3), pp. 315–24.

Mahawatte, Royce (2004) 'Loving the other: Arab-male fetish pornography and the dark continent of masculinity', in P. Church Gibson (ed.), *More Dirty Looks: Gender, Pornography and Power*, London: BFI, pp. 127–36.

Marriott, David (2000) *On Black Men*, Edinburgh: Edinburgh University Press.

Marshall, Bill (1998) 'Gay cinema', in Alex Hughes and Keith Reader (eds), *Encyclopedia of Contemporary French Culture*, London and New York: Routledge, pp. 262–3.

Marshall, Bill (2000) 'The national-popular and comparative gay identities: Cyril Collard's *Les Nuits fauves*', in David Alderson and Linda Anderson (eds), *Territories of Desire in Queer Culture: Refiguring Contemporary Boundaries*, Manchester: Manchester University Press, pp. 84–95.

Marshall, Bill (2007) *André Téchiné*, Manchester: Manchester University Press.

Mary, Philippe (2006) *La Nouvelle Vague et le cinéma d'auteur: Socio-analyse d'une révolution artistique*, Paris: Seuil.

Mayne, Judith (2005) *Claire Denis*, Urbana and Chicago: University of Illinois Press.

Mazdon, Lucy (ed.) (2001) *France on Film: Reflections on Popular French Cinema*, London: Wallflower Press.

Mbembe, Achille (2005) 'La République et l'impensé de la "race" ', in P. Blachard, N. Bancel and S. Lemaire (eds), *La Fracture coloniale: La société française au prisme de l'héritage colonial*, Paris: La Découverte, pp. 143–57.

Mercer, Kobena (1994) *Welcome to the Jungle: New Positions in Black Cultural Studies*, London and New York: Routledge.

Michallat, Wendy (2006) 'Marions-nous! Gay rites: the campaign for gay marriage in France', *Modern and Contemporary France*, 14 (3), pp. 305–16.

Millot, Catherine (1993) [1983] *Horsexe: essai sur le transsexualisme*, Paris: Point Hors Ligne.

Mulvey, Laura (1996) *Fetishism and Curiosity*, London: BFI.

Murphy, Kevin P., Jason Ruiz and David Serlin (2008) 'Editors Introduction', *Radical History*, 'Queer Futures: The Homonormativity Issue', Issue 100 (Winter), pp. 1–9.

Nadeau, Chantal (2000) 'Life with Pinky Dots', *GLQ*, 6:1, pp. 137–44.

O., Rachid (2003) *Ce qui reste*, Paris: Gallimard.

Philippon, Alain (1988) *André Téchiné*, Paris: Cahiers du cinéma.

Phillips, Richard, Diane Watt and David Shuttleton (eds) (2000) *De-centring Sexualities: Politics and Representations Beyond the Metropolis*, London: Routledge.

Pidduck, Julianne (2007) 'A cinema of collisions: Patrice Chéreau and the homosocial', *Studies in French Cinema*, 7 (3), pp. 191–205.

Pinell, Patrice (ed.) (2002) *Une épidémie politique: La Lutte contre le sida en France (1981–1996)*, Paris: PUF.

Pratt, Murray (2002) 'Post-queer and beyond the PaCS: contextualising French responses to the Civil Solidarity Pact', in K. Chedgzoy, E. Francis and M. Pratt (eds), *In a Queer Place: Sexuality and Belonging in British and European Contexts*, Aldershot: Ashgate, pp. 177–206.

Pratt, Murray (2004) 'Félix and the light-hearted gay road movie: genre, families, fathers and the decolonization of the homosexual self', *Australian Journal of French Studies*, 41 (3), pp. 88–101.

Preciado, Beatriz (2000) *Manifeste contra-sexuel*, Paris: Balland.

Preciado, Beatriz (2003) 'Multitudes queer', *Multitudes*, no. 12, pp. 17–25.

Prochasson, Christophe (2000) *Introduction à l'histoire de la France au XXᵉ siècle*, Paris: La Découverte.

Prosser, Jay (1998) *Second Skins: The Body Narratives of Transsexuality*, New York: Columbia University Press.

Provencher, Denis M. (2007) *Queer French: Globalization, Language, and Sexual Citizenship in France*, Aldershot: Ashgate.

Provencher, Denis M. (2008) 'Tracing sexual citizenship and queerness in *Drôle de Félix* (2000) and *Tarik el hob* (2001)', *Contemporary French and Francophone Studies*, 12 (1), pp. 51–61.

Raymond, Gino (2006) 'The republican ideal and the reality of the Republic', in A. Cole and G. Raymond (eds), *Redefining the French Republic*, Manchester and New York: Manchester University Press, pp. 5–24.

Rees-Roberts, Nick (2004) 'La Confusion des genres: transsexuality, effeminacy and gay identity in France', *International Journal of Cultural Studies*, 7 (3), pp. 281–300.

Rees-Roberts, Nick (2007) 'Down and out: immigrant poverty and queer sexuality in Sébastien Lifshitz's *Wild Side* (2004)', *Studies in French Cinema*, 7 (2), pp. 143–55.

Rees-Roberts, Nick (2008) 'Kiffe la racaille: Arab masculinity and queer fantasy in France', *Contemporary French Civilization*, 32 (1), pp. 183–207.

Rémès, Eric (1999) *Je bande donc je suis*, Paris: Balland.

Renan, Ernest (2007) [1882] *Qu'est-ce qu'une nation?*, Paris: Le Mot et le reste.

Rollet, Brigitte (2007) *Télévision et homosexualité: 10 ans de fictions françaises 1995–2005*, Paris: L'Harmattan.

Román, David (2000) 'Not-about-AIDS', *GLQ*, 6:1, pp. 1–28.

Rombes, Nicholas (ed.) (2005) *New Punk Cinema*, Edinburgh: Edinburgh University Press.

Roth-Bettoni, Didier (2007) *L'Homosexualité au cinéma*, Paris: La Musardine.

Saïd, Edward W. (2004) [1978] *Orientalism*, London: Penguin.

Sarkozy, Nicolas (2006) *Témoignage*, Paris: Robert Laffont – Xo éditions.

Sayad, Abdelmalek (1999) *La Double Absence: Des illusions de l'émigré aux souffrances de l'immigré*, Paris: Seuil.

Schehr, Lawrence R. (2004) 'Reading serial sex: the case of Erik Rémès', *L'Esprit créateur*, vol. XLIV, no. 3, pp. 94–104.

Schehr, Lawrence R. (2005) 'Relire les homotextualités', in L. Schehr (ed.), *Aimez-vous le queer?*, Rodophi: Amsterdam, pp. 5–11.

Sedgwick, Eve Kosofsky (1985) *Between Men: English Literature and Male Homosocial Desire*, New York: Columbia University Press.

Sedgwick, Eve Kosofsky (1990) *Epistemology of the Closet*, Harmondsworth: Penguin.

Sedgwick, Eve Kosofsky (1994) *Tendencies*, New York: Routledge.

Segal, Lynne (1999) *Why Feminism? Gender, Psychology, Politics*, London: Polity.

Sinfield, Alan (1992) *Faultlines: Cultural Materialism and the Politics of Dissident Reading*, Oxford: Oxford University Press.

Sinfield, Alan (1998) *Gay and After*, London: Serpent's Tail.

Sinfield, Alan (2000) 'Transgender and les/bi/gay identities', in David Alderson and Linda Anderson (eds), *Territories of Desire in Queer Culture, Refiguring Contemporary Boundaries*, Manchester: Manchester University Press, pp. 150–65.

Sinfield, Alan (2004) *On Sexuality and Power*, New York: Columbia University Press.

Stacey, Jackie and Sarah Street (eds) (2007) *Queer Screen: A Screen Reader*, Routledge: London and New York.

Swamy, Vinay (2006) 'Gallic dreams? The family, PaCS and kinship relations in millennial France', *Studies in French Cinema*, 6 (1), pp. 53–64.

Tarr, Carrie (2005) *Reframing Difference: Beur and banlieue filmmaking in France*, Manchester: Manchester University Press.

Théry, Irène (1998) *Couple, filiation et parenté aujourd'hui*, Paris: Odile Jacob.

Thomson, David (2002) *The New Biographical Dictionary of Film*, New York: Alfred A. Knopf.

Thompson, Danièle, Patrice Chéreau and Pierre Trividic, *Ceux qui m'aiment prendront le train: scénario + entretien*, Paris: Petite bibliothèque des Cahiers du cinéma.

Waldron, Darren (2006) 'New clothes for temporary transvestites? Sexuality, cross-dressing and passing in the contemporary French film comedy', *Modern and Contemporary France*, 14 (3), pp. 347–61.

Waldron, Darren (2007) 'From critique to compliance: images of ethnicity in *Salut Cousin* (1996) and *Chouchou* (2003)', *Studies in European Cinema*, 4 (1), pp. 35–47.

Warner, Michael (ed.) (1993) *Fear of a Queer Planet: Queer Politics and Social Theory*, University of Minnesota Press: Minneapolis.

Watney, Simon (2000) *Imagine Hope: AIDS and Gay Identity*, London: Routledge.

Williams, Linda (ed.) (2004) *Porn Studies*, Durham, NC and London: Duke University Press.

Wilson, Emma (1999) *French Cinema Since 1950: Personal Histories*, London: Duckworth.

INDEX

A ma sœur, 97

A toute vitesse, 25, 27, 28–9

Abdi, Nidam, 17

Act Up Paris, 3, 4, 15–16, 51, 71, 79–81, 93, 104, 106–9, 122, 132

Adjane, Rachid, 146–9

AFCAE (*Association française des cinémas d'art et d'essai*), 62

Agacinski, Sylviane, 3

Aghion, Gabriel, 6

Aimée, Anouk, 110

Alapetite, Bernard, 113

Ali et ses potes, 20

Alloucahe, Merzak, 45

Almodóvar, Pedro, 53, 85

Altman, Dennis, 109

Amants criminels, Les, 1, 9, 10, 27, 31–5

American Apparel, 27

Amis du bus des femmes, Les 51

Anatomie de l'enfer, 63

Anderson, Raffaëla, 135, 136

Angel, 9

Après lui, 29

Arabesque, 20

Ardant, Fanny, 8, 24

Arra, Cynthia, 73

Arra, Mélissa, 73

Arrieta, Alfredo, 79

Arroyo, José, 106

ASB (*L'Association du syndrome de Benjamin*), 71

Asibong, Andrew, 8–10, 31, 34, 116

Assayas, Olivier, 99

Attia, Kader, 68

L'Auberge espagnol, 95

Aubert, Brigitte, 74

Avant que j'oublie, 1, 81, 82–3, 117

Azabal, Lubna, 40

Azama, Michel, 27

Bach, Karen, 136

Bacon, Francis, 114

Bailly, Cécile, 143–4

Baise-moi, 97, 133–7, 143

Balasko, Josiane, 6

Balibar, Jeanne, 95

Bande à part, 63

Baquet, Grégori, 28

Barassat, Philippe, 26

Bardadi, Meziane, 28

Barkat, Sidi Mohamed, 34

Barr, Jean-Marc, 91

Barthes, Roland, 121

Bataille, Georges, 9, 94, 96–100

BBB (Black Blanc Beur), 17

Béart, Emmanuelle, 117–24

Beau Travail, 6, 59

Beaupain, Alex, 110

Beauvois, Xavier, 106

Bedjaoui, Amal, 53, 57

Bégéja, Liria, 24

Beineix, Jean-Jacques, 95

Bel, Ilmann, 146–9

Belle et la bête, La, 31
Belmadi, Yasmine, 27, 31, 35–8, 55, 62, 146
Benamoune, Sihem, 38
Benjamin, Walter, 64
Benshoff, Harry, 6
Berliner, Alain, 76
Bernard, Patrick Mario, 129–30
Bersani, Leo, 130
Beset, Jean-Marie, 28
Besson, Philippe, 114
Beugnet, Martine, 59, 83, 129
Beurs Appart', 133, 146–9
Bidasses: Blacks/Blancs/Beurs, 23
Birdcage, The, 47
Blanc, Michel, 117–24
BlancX, 142
Blanquer, Laetitia, 143
Bleu, blanc, rose, 114
Boarding Gate, 99
Bohringer, Richard, 74
Bolatino, 20
Bonello, Bertrand, 146
Bonitzer, Pascal, 90
Bonnaffé, Jacques, 91, 107
Borillo, Daniel, 92
Bouajila, Sami, 24, 25–6, 91, 105–6, 117–24
Bouchaala, Achmed, 24
Boucherka, Karima, 44
Boucherka, Malika, 44
Bouquet, Stéphane, 55, 63, 64, 84, 106, 130
Bourcier, Marie-Hélène, 5, 6, 79, 133–7, 138, 139, 146
Bowles, Paul, 40
Boy Meets Girl, 95
Boyfriend 1, 131
Boyfriend 2, 131
Brassaï, 68
Brassart, Alain, 7, 8, 31, 32
Brasseur, Claude, 46
Breathless, 20
Brecht, Bertolt, 120
Breillat, Catherine, 63, 136
Brialy, Jean-Claude, 119

BricoPorno, 142
Broqua, Christophe, 104
Bruni-Tedeschi, Valeria, 84, 90, 116
Burch, Noël, 8, 32
Burdeau, Emmanuel, 63
Butler, Judith, 69–70

Cabiria, 51
Cabral, Camille, 51
Cadinot, Jean-Daniel, 23, 40–1
Cage aux folles, La, 46, 79
Caïd Superstar, 22
Cairns, Lucille, 8, 78, 137
Calle, Sophie, 130
Cam, Brian, 20
Canesi, Michel, 122
Capo d'Istria, Nathalia, 75
Caravaca, Eric, 114
Carax, Léos, 95
Carné, Marcel, 7, 143
Castelnuevo, Nino, 110
Caunes, Antoine de, 45
Caunes, Emma de, 96–100
Cavitch, Max, 9
Cazalé, Nicolas, 29, 30
Ce vieux rêve qui bouge, 129
Ceci est une pipe (journal extime), 130
Cervo, Pascal, 28
Cervulle, Maxime, 22, 92, 142–3
Ceux qui m'aiment prendront le train, 1, 67, 81, 83–7, 89–90, 113, 144
Change-moi ma vie, 24
Chansons d'amour, Les, 8, 110–12
Chapin, Stéphane, 92
Charpentier, Bertrand, 92
Chatte à deux têtes, La, 1, 67, 81, 82–3
Chemins de l'oued, Les, 29, 31
Chéreau, Patrice, 1, 67, 81, 83–7, 90, 112–15, 129, 144
Chibikh, Stéphane, 19, 20, 23
Chiland, Colette, 71–3, 78, 145–6
Chirac, Jacques, 15, 16, 48
Chouchou, 45–8, 148
Choristes, Les, 64
5 x 2 (Cinq fois deux), 10, 116

Citébeur, 13, 14, 19–23, 137
Claire Denis la vagabonde, 35, 63
Clan, Le, 1, 27, 28–31, 55
Clean, 99
Cocteau, Jean, 7, 28, 31
Coleman, Monica, 116
Collard, Cyril, 3, 4, 7, 105
Collin, Edouard, 90
Comme un frère, 113
Confusion des genres, La, 4
Conseil français du culte musulman, 50
Cooper, Dennis, 100–1
Cooper, Sarah, 6
Copi, 131, 147
Copi je t'aime, 131
Corps ouverts, Les, 1, 35–8
Courcet, Richard, 60–1
CPE (*Contrat première embauche*), 50
Cressole, Michel, 67
Cresson, Edith, 108
Crustacés et coquillages, 90–4
Crying Game, The, 54
Cuisine de Cunéo, La, 131
Culture hétéro, vous savez où je la mets?, La, 142

Dalida, 143
Dalle, Béatrice, 95–6
Dancing, 130
Daney, Serge, 7
Dans ma peau, 97
Dans Paris, 110–11
Darke, Chris, 59
De Battre mon cœur s'est arrêté, 95
Debbouze, Jamel, 15
Debray, Régis, 16
Debré, Jean-Louis, 15, 89
Defdaf, Kheireddine, 31
Defert, Daniel, 122
Dekker, Mila, 8
Delaney, Samuel R., 82
Delanoë, Bertrand, 51
Deleuze, Gilles, 55, 124
Delorme, Wendy, 141–2
Deltombe, Thomas, 15
Demoiselles de Rochefort, Les, 109

Demy, Jacques, 7, 31, 90, 94, 109–12, 121
Demy, Mathieu, 107
Deneuve, Catherine, 8, 29, 40, 109–10, 117
Denis, Claire 6, 35, 53, 59–61, 82
Depardieu, Gérard, 40
Depardieu, Julie, 117
Derbyshire, Phillip, 4
Descas, Alex, 60
Despentes, Virginie, 133–8, 143
Desplechin, Arnaud, 89
Dieutre, Vincent, 129–30
Divine, 143
Dix-sept fois Cécile Cassard, 1, 95–6, 110
Doigt de Dieu ou la bite à Lacan, Le, 145–6
Dorléac, Françoise, 109
Douceur, La, 112
Douchet, Jean, 10
Doustaly, Thomas, 115
Douste Blazy, Phillipe, 80–1
Downing, Lisa, 134, 137
Dray, Julien, 48–9
Drôle de Félix, 1, 7, 25–6, 91, 105–6, 112
Du Fresne, Georges, 76
Ducastel, Olivier, 1, 7, 25–6, 90–4, 105–10, 129, 144
Duggan, Lisa, 2
Dumas, Mireille, 73
Dumerchez, Thomas, 29
Duran Cohen, Ilan, 4
Duris, Romain, 95–6, 110
Dustan, Guillaume, 104
Dyer, Richard, 8, 9, 64, 79, 130–1

Echahi, Riyad, 39
Ecoffey, Jean-Philippe, 76
Edelman, Lee, 101
Elkaïm, Jérémie, 35
Elmaleh, Arié, 47
Elmaleh, Gad, 45–8
L'Emploi du temps, 57
Encore, 107

L'Ennemi naturel, 58
Eribon, Didier, 92–3
L'Eternel retour, 31
Eustache, Jean, 110, 111

Fabuleux destin d'Amélie Poulain, Le, 143
Fabuleux destin d'Amélie Putain, Le, 143
Falconer, Colin, 50
Fanik, Patrick, 100
Fassbinder, Rainer Werner, 9, 10, 34, 60, 64
Fassin, Eric, 3, 52–3
Faure, Christian, 1
Ferran, Pascale, 89, 124
FHAR (*Front homosexuel d'action révolutionnaire*), 68
Figgis, Mike, 132
Flamands Roses, Les, 71
Folle de Rachid en transit sur mars, 26
Fontaine, Anne, 89
Forbes, Jill, 120
Foucault, Michel, 85, 121–3, 138
Freud, Lucien, 114
Freud, Sigmund, 72
Friends, 146
Frigo, Le, 147
Frodon, Jean-Michel, 114, 115
Front National, Le, 15, 25
Frot, Catherine, 46

Garçon d'honneur, 110
Garrel, Louis, 96–100, 110–11
GAT (*Groupe activiste transgenre*), 71, 145–6
Gaultier, Jean-Paul, 27
Gay Arab Club, 20
Gazon maudit, 6
Genet, Jean, 7, 26, 63, 64, 144
Ghesquière, Nicolas, 99
Gilbey, Ryan, 116
Giordino, Martine, 119
Girardot, Annie, 98
Giraudeau, Bernard, 9
Girod, Francis, 74–5

Giusti, Stéphane, 107
Godard, Agnès, 54, 57, 58–63
Godard, Jean-Luc, 63, 111
Goldin, Nan, 68, 99
Golubeva, Katherina, 60
Gonzalez, Yann, 40
Gordon, Douglas, 15
Gouttes d'eau sur pierres brûlantes, 9, 34
Graia, Hammou, 57
Grande école, 27, 28
Grandena, Florian, 7
Greenberg, Neil, 113
Griffin, Sean, 6
Grisélidis, 51
Guattari, Félix, 124
Guédiguian, Robert, 89
Guénif-Souilamas, Nacira, 20–1
Guibert, Hervé, 3, 84, 85, 90, 105, 113–14, 130
Guiraudie, Alain, 129
Guyot, Laurent, 121

Haine, La, 36
Halberstam, Judith, 69–70
Hammam, 23, 40–1
Handyside, Fiona, 34
Haneke, Michael, 98
Haraway, Donna, 138
Harem, 23, 40
Hargreaves, Alec G., 14
Harper, Graeme, 132
Hayward, Susan, 48
Hazera, Hélène, 67–8, 71, 79
Hegarty, Antony, 54
Hélène et les garçons, 148
He-say, Vincent, 73
Hesme, Clothilde, 111
Hicham, Mohamed, 57
Hildago, Anne, 51
Hirsch, Julien, 119
Hitchcock, Alfred, 33
Hocquenghem, Guy, 68, 121, 130–1
L'Homme blessé, 7, 84, 114
L'Homme est une femme comme les autres, 45

L'Homme que j'aime, 107
Honoré, Christophe, 1, 7, 8, 9, 28, 29, 64, 89–100, 101–3, 110–12, 113
Hotcast, 20
Hôtel des Amériques, 117–18
How to Ass Ejaculate, 142
How to Female Ejaculate, 142
Huit femmes, 8, 34
Huppert, Isabelle, 96–100, 111

I Live in a Bush World, 131
Ince, Kate, 76, 91
L'Infamille, 112
Innocents, Les, 119, 120
INPES (*Institut national de prévention et d'éducation pour la santé*), 102
Intimacy/Intimité, 97, 114
Intrigues de Sylvia Couski, Les, 79
Irréversible, 97, 116
Ixe, 131

Jacques, Sylvain, 83, 114
J'ai pas sommeil, 6, 59–61, 82
Jamel Comedy Club, 15
Jarman, Derek, 132
Jeancolas, Jean-Pierre, 106
Jeanne et le garçon formidable, 1, 93, 105, 106–9, 112, 145
J'embrasse pas, 117–19, 121
Jeuland, Yves, 92, 114
Joffrin, Laurent, 135
Johnston, Cristina, 3, 12
Jospin, Lionel, 15
Jouvet, Emilie, 133, 138–42
Jubilee, 132
Jules et Jim, 56
Juste une question d'amour, 1

Kaganski, Serge, 143
Kassovitz, Mathieu, 36
Kechiche, Abdellatif, 120
Kechiouche, Salim, 10, 14, 27–35, 146
Kelma, 17
Kipnis, Laura, 135
Kooijman, Japp, 82

Korine, Harmony, 132
Kureishi, Hanif, 114

Labruce, Bruce, 143
Lacan, Jacques, 72, 146
Lagerfeld, Karl, 99
Lagrace Volcano, Del, 68–9
Lalanne, Jean-Marc, 115
Lange, Rémi, 38–9, 130, 133, 142, 147
Lapoirie, Jeanne, 116
Laroque, Michèle, 76
Lauper, Cindy, 98
Lauretis, Teresa de, 138
Lazen, Matthew, 110
Le Pen, Jean-Marie, 15–16, 44
Léaud, Jean-Pierre, 110, 111
Leçon de ténèbres, 129
Ledoyen, Virginie, 107
Lefort, Gérard, 108
Legann, Cyril, 113
Leibowitch, Jacques, 122
Lemaire, Yannick, 61
Leprince Ringuet, Grégoire, 111
Lespert, Yaniss, 101–2
Lestrade, Didier, 2, 3, 4, 80–1, 101, 104, 125–6
Lévi-Strauss, Claude, 142
Libéreau, Johan, 117–24
Lifshitz, Sébastien, 1, 5, 14, 35–8, 53–64, 103, 129, 145, 146
Loin, 39, 41
Lola, 109–10
Lost Highway, 95
Lynch, David, 95

Ma mère, 1, 8, 9, 64, 94, 96–100, 110, 111
Ma vie en rose, 67, 76–9
McCaffrey, Enda, 3, 4,
McGonagle, Joseph, 25
Mackenzie, Scott, 134, 137
McKinney, Mark, 14
Madame H, 142, 147
Mag, le, 71
Magritte, René, 130
Mahawatte, Royce, 23–4

Mahet, Stéphanie, 63
Mamam et la putain, La, 110, 111
Mamère, Noël, 92
Manège, 81
Mangeot, Philippe, 107, 122–3
Manojlovic, Miki, 31
Margot, Lily, 95–6
Marie-France, 79
Maris à tout prix, 92
Marius et Jeanette, 89
Marshall, Bill, 4, 7, 8, 117–24
Martineau, Jacques, 1, 7, 25–6, 90–4,
 105–10, 129, 144
Mastroianni, Chiara, 110, 111
Matoss de blackoss, 20, 21
Mauvais genres, 67, 74–5
Mayne, Judith, 60
Mbembe, Achille, 17
Méhu, Elisabeth, 55
Meier, Pierre-Alain, 75
Melki, Gilbert, 40, 90
Mesbah, Yacine, 47
Metzger, Stéphane, 74
Michelini, Stéphanie, 54, 61
Mignard, Pierre, 101–2
Miller, Claude, 53, 110
Millot, Catherine, 145
Minetto, Valérie, 8
Molière, 95
Mon copain Rachid, 26
Mon voyage d'hiver, 129
Montagut, Jean-Baptiste, 96–100
Moreau, Jeanne, 116
Morel, Gaël, 1, 25, 27, 28–31, 39, 55,
 110, 113
Morrissey, Paul, 53
Mostefa-Châa, Slimane, 146
Mulvey, Laura, 111
Murphy, Kevin P., 2

Nabil, Youssef, 27
Nadeau, Chantal, 4, 78
Nadylam, William, 74
Naissance des pieuvres, 112
Nénette et Boni, 59
Nettoyage à sec, 89

New Punk Cinema, 132–3
New Queer Cinema, 6, 61
Ni Putes Ni Soumises, 50
Nike, 27
Nikitine, Edouard, 58, 61
No Sex Last Night, 130
Noé, Gaspard, 116, 137
Noiret, Philippe, 119
Nolot, Jacques, 1, 67, 81–3, 117–18,
 121, 129
Not-About-AIDS-Dance, 113
Notre trou du cul est révolutionnaire,
 131
N'oublie pas que tu vas mourir, 106,
 112
Nour, Jimmy, 146
Nous deux, 94–5
Nuits Fauves, Les, 3, 4, 7, 105, 112

O., Rachid, 18
Omelette, 130
One Night Stand, 138–42
L'Ordre des mots, 67, 73, 74
Origine contrôlée, 24
Oublier Cheyenne, 8
Ourbih, Pascale, 75–6
Ovidie, 136
Ovidie mène l'enquête, 136
Ozon, François, 1, 8–10, 31–5, 39,
 112, 115–17, 129, 146

PaCS (*Pacte civil de solidarité*), 2, 3, 10
Panik Qulture, 133, 142–3
Parapluies de Cherbourg, Les, 109–10
Paris was a King, 143
Parreno, Philippe, 15
Pas de repos pour les braves, 129
Pasolini, Pier Paolo, 27, 64, 97–8,
 100–1
Pasqua, Charles, 15, 89, 108
PASTT (*Prévention, Action, Santé,
 Travail pour les Transgenres*), 51,
 71
Patachou, 26
Patouillard, Victoire, 107
Paul, Henri, 80

Peau d'âne, 31
Pédale douce, 6, 79
Pédale dure, 6
Pelosi, Guiseppe, 27
Péril jeune, Le, 95
Petit, Aurélia, 8
Petite mort, La, 9, 115
Philippon, Alain, 118
Pialat, Maurice, 53
Pianiste, La, 98
Pichaud, Isabelle, 53, 57
Pidduck, Julianne, 86, 87
Pierre et Gilles, 27, 33, 35
Pinell, Patrice, 104
Pink Flamingos, 143
Placard, Le, 79, 91
Plus belle la vie, 148
Poiret, Jean, 79
Pook, Jocelyn, 62
Pop Porn Party, 142
Porno industriel, 131
Portrait d'une présidente, 67, 79–81
Poupaud, Melvil, 116–17
Poupées russes, Les, 95
Pourquoi pas moi?, 107
Pratt, Murray, 4, 105
Preciado, Beatriz, 5, 138
Preiss, Joana, 96–100, 111
Premiers baisers, 148
Presque rien, 35
Problème de Chirac, Le, 131
Prosser, Jay, 70
Provencher, Denis, 38, 105
Psycho, 33, 148
Pudeur ou l'impudeur, La, 105, 112, 115, 130

Quashie-Vauclin, Guillaume, 146
Quatre cents coups, Les, 111
Queer Factory, 133, 142
Queer Factory Tales – Les Contes de Queer Factory, 142
Querelle, 60

Race d'Ep!, 130
Rachati, Nadem, 40

Raging Stallion, 20
Rajot, Pierre-Loup, 36
Raymond, Gino, 16
Recoing, Aurélien, 57–8
Reed, Lou, 53
Regarde la mer, 8, 9
Régnier, Natacha, 31, 32, 35
Reine Margot, La, 84
Rémès, Eric, 104
Renan, Ernest, 15
René Clair, Jean-Noël, 23–4
Renier, Jérémie, 31, 32, 35
Résistrans, 71
Reucher, Tom, 71, 73
Rêves en France, 91
Rideau, Stéphane, 29, 35, 39
Rigouste, Mathieu, 15
Rimbaud, Arthur, 32
Rita Mitsouko, Les, 121
Rivière, Julien, 77
Rocco Ravishes Prague 4, 136
Rollet, Brigitte, 1
Román, David, 113
Romance, 63, 97
Rombes, Nicholas, 132–3
Rome désolé, 129
Roseaux sauvages, Les, 7, 29, 40
Rosier, Gilles, 27
Roth-Bettoni, Didier, 10, 107, 129, 132
Royal, Ségolène, 43, 44
Royalle, Candida, 136
Ruiz, Jason, 2

Sabaddehine, Karim, 136
Sagat, François, 19–20
Sagnier, Ludivine, 9, 110
Saïd, Edward, 24
Salis, Roberts, 27, 28
Salò o le 120 giornate di Sodoma, 101
Salut cousin!, 45
Salut les musclés, 148
Salvadori, Pierre, 105
Sarkozy, Nicolas, 15, 16, 43–4, 48–53
Sayad, Abdelmalek, 16
Scarborough, 112

Schehr, Lawrence R., 5, 105
Schilling, Laurent, 75
Sciamma, Céline, 112
Scognamiglio, Vittoria, 82
Sedgwick, Eve Kosofsky, 42
Segal, Lynne, 70
Sengewald, Christian, 116
Serlin, David, 2
Serrault, Michel, 79
Seul contre tous, 137
Sex and the City, 146–7
Sex is Comedy, 63
Sex of Madame H, The, 142
Sexe des anges, Le, 131
Sheila, 78
Siffredi, Rocco, 136
Sinapi, Jean-Pierre, 26
Sinfield, Alan, 2, 10, 18, 69, 119
Sirk, Douglas, 43
Sitcom, 9
Sluts, The, 101
Smiths, The, 94
Son frère, 1, 112–15
SOS Racisme, 50
Soukaz, Lionel, 7, 130–2, 144
Sous le sable, 115
Sprinkle, Annie, 136, 143
Stacey, Jackie, 6–7
Stappen, Chris van der, 76
Statross le magnifique, 147
Stévenin, Robinson, 74
Stoller, Robert, 72
Street, Sarah, 6–7
Studio Beurs, 23–4
Sundahl, Deborah, 142
Swamy, Vinay, 25
Swimming Pool, 8

Taboulay, Camille, 108, 109
Taïa, Abdellah, 39
Tarek et ses potes, 20
Tarek, Karim, 38
Tarik el hob, 38–9
Tarr, Carrie, 24, 25–6
Tasca, Catherine, 134
Taubira, Christiane, 15

Tautou, Audrey, 143
Téchiné, André, 1, 7, 8, 29, 39–41,
    113, 115, 117–24, 129, 144, 145
Témoins, Les, 1, 115, 117–24, 144,
    145
Temps qui changent, Les, 1, 39–41
Temps qui reste, Le, 1, 112, 113,
    115–17
Terres froides, Les, 35–8
Texas Political Chainsaw Massacre, 131
Thelma, 75–6
Thelma and Louise, 134, 137
Théry, Irène, 3
13 (Tzameti), 58
37°2 le matin, 95
Thomson, Anna, 9
Thomson, David, 109
Tijou, Brigitte, 80
Tirésia, 146
Titof, 136
Titof and the College Boys, 136
Todeschini, Bruno, 114–15
Todo sobre mi madre, 85
Torres, Romain, 90
Tout contre Léo, 101–2, 112
Trahison des images, La, 130
Trier, Lars von, 132
Trinh Thi, Coralie, 133–7
Trividic, Pierre, 129–30
Trouble Every Day, 59, 95
Truffaut, François, 56, 89, 111

UMP (*Union pour un mouvement
    populaire*), 43
Un amour à taire, 1
Un chant d'amour, 7
Une femme est une femme, 110
Un fils, 53, 57–8
Un moment, 104–5
Un parfum nommé Saïd, 26
Une robe d'été, 9
Un secret, 110
US Go Home, 63

Vallois, Philippe, 26
Vallois, Romain, 27

Vangelo secondo Metteo, Il, 97–8
Vassé, Claire, 108, 109
Veber, Francis, 79
Vecchiali, Paul, 107
Vellay, Cleews, 79–81
Vendredi soir, 59
Vennemani, Jean-Michel, 92
Verdura, Hugo di, 146
Vérité si je mens!, La, 45
Verow, Todd, 143
Viala, Sébastien, 82
Victor, 9
Vie à rebours, La, 29
Vie en face, La, 73
Vie et mort de Pier Paolo Pasolini, 27
Vie normale, La, 45
Villepin, Dominique de, 50
Vincendeau, Ginette, 93, 96, 97, 111, 120, 123
Vincent, Hélène, 76

Vivre me tue, 26
Voleurs, Les, 8

Waldron, Darren, 6, 47, 79
Warhol, Andy, 53
Waters, John, 9, 133, 143
Watney, Simon, 3, 4, 87
Wesh Cousin, 13, 19, 22
Wild Side, 1, 5, 53–64, 145
Wilson, Emma, 7–8

Yeux brouillés, Les, 130

Zap les Superhé(té)ros, 142
Zapatero, José Luis Rodríguez, 43
Zem, Roschdy, 24, 46
Zéraoui, Fouad, 17, 82
Zidane: un portrait du 21e siècle, 15
Zidane, Zinedine, 15
Zidi, Malik, 9, 40
Zingg, Viviane, 121